THI
THE
EXPEI

THE THEATER EXPERIENCE

EDWIN WILSON
Hunter College
The City University of New York

McGRAW-HILL BOOK COMPANY   *New York   St. Louis   San Francisco*
Auckland   Düsseldorf   Johannesburg   Kuala Lumpur   London   Mexico   Montreal
New Delhi   Panama   Paris   São Paulo   Singapore   Sydney   Tokyo   Toronto

This book was set in Palatino by Black Dot, Inc.
The editors were Alison Meersschaert
and Barry Benjamin;
the designer was J. E. O'Connor;
the production supervisor was Judi Frey.
The photo editor was Inge King.
The part-opening illustrations
were done by Cathy Hull;
the drawings were done by Vantage Art, Inc.
R. R. Donnelley & Sons Company was printer and binder.

Cover: "Pippin." Photograph by Martha Swope.

THE THEATER EXPERIENCE

Library of Congress Cataloging in Publication Data

Wilson, Edwin.
     The theater experience.

     Bibliography: p.
     Includes index.
     1. Theater. 2. Drama. I. Title.
PN1657.W5   792   75-11945
ISBN 0-07-070661-1
ISBN 0-07-070662-X pbk.

To my wife, Catherine

CONTENTS

PREFACE   ix

INTRODUCTION   1

PART I   THE AUDIENCE

  1 The Audience's Role   11
  2 The Imagination of the Audience   25
  3 The Perspective of the Audience   39

PART II   PERFORMERS AND THE PARTS THEY PLAY

  4 Acting: Offstage and On   55
  5 Acting for the Stage: Techniques and Styles   67
  6 Dramatic Characters   87

PART III   DRAMATIC STRUCTURE: THE
           ARCHITECTURE OF A PLAY

7   Conventions of Dramatic Structure   105
8   Forms of Dramatic Structure   119

PART IV   POINT OF VIEW

9   Subject Matter: Different Approaches   149
10   Tragedy and Other Serious Drama   167
11   Comedy and Tragicomedy   183

PART V   ENVIRONMENT AND THE VISUAL
         ELEMENTS

12   Stage Spaces   203
13   Scenery and Lighting   231
14   Costumes   259

PART VI   BRINGING THE ELEMENTS TOGETHER

15   The Director   279
16   The Total Experience   295

APPENDIXES

I   Technical Terms   313
II   Major Theatrical Forms and Movements   321
III   Historical Outline   331

SELECT BIBLIOGRAPHY   353

NOTES   355

INDEX   359

PREFACE

Theater is experience, an immediate art whose meaning is grasped through an understanding of the encounter between those who create theater—performers, writers, directors, designers, and technicians—and those who view it—members of the audience. In a departure from the usual historical or genre approaches, this text focuses on the meaning of the theater experience. The aim of the book is to provide an understanding and awareness of the theater event.

Why this approach? Most books begin where theater began—with the Greeks—or where the experience begins for the creators of theater: with the script, or the designer's sketches, or the director's rehearsal procedure. Those texts adopting a historical approach generally devote the first half of the book to a chronological treatment of theater, with subsequent chapters on the actor, designer, and director, among others. In the genre approach, chapters on tragedy, comedy, and farce, for example, are substituted for the history. Some texts attempt to combine the two approaches. In all of these, however, theater tends to be treated as a frozen artifact divided into discreet units: Tragedy, Restoration Drama, the Spanish Golden Age.

In his book *The Empty Space*, Peter Brook speaks of "the immediate theater." In a sense, all theater is immediate—an experience given and received. Treated as a set entity, a remote body of knowledge divorced from the lives of those who view it, theater loses any chance of immediacy. The aim of this text is to analyze and explain what theater is about—what goes on in theater and what it means to the viewer. The experience begins for the audience when it comes into the theater, confronts the environment, and, following that, encounters the performance. The crucial role of the audience— its importance in the dynamic encounter between creators and viewers in theater—is dealt with throughout this text. Students are introduced to a wide range of theater situations, and a great deal of historical and factual information is provided, but it is organized and presented in a different way.

Every effort has been made to relate theater to experiences already familiar to the student. Certain elements in theater have analogues in daily life and, where possible, these provide a key, or bridge, to the theater experience. Acting, for example, is a part of our everyday lives: people imitate those they see around them; they play roles; they alter their behavior to suit given situations. When viewed this way, acting becomes less esoteric. A relatively commonplace experience becomes the basis for understanding the more specialized art of acting for the stage.

The organization of the text reflects the focus on experience, with major parts devoted to the basic elements of theater: the audience; performers and the parts they play; dramatic structure; point of view; and environment. Because the book cuts across traditional lines, there are several appendixes to supplement the main text: one on common technical terms, a second on the chief types and genres, and a third featuring a brief historical survey. These can be used for reference or they can be integrated into a course, where they are applicable as part of an assignment. It is also possible to devote separate class sessions to the appendixes.

The Theater Experience is intended as a text for the introductory theater course offered by most colleges and universities. Generally, the course is aimed at those not intending to major in theater, and this book has been written with that in mind. While it is neither a history nor a "how to" book, there is an abundance of solid information in it. It can serve equally well as the text for a prerequisite course leading to advanced work in theater or for the theater component in a combined arts course. Those students who plan to concentrate on theater can begin in no better way than by examining the actor-audience exchange, by learning the spectator's side of the equation as well as the creator's.

Because the book stresses the encounter between audience and performers, it is assumed that anyone using it will make attendance at performances an integral part of the course. Though the text deals with specific plays, the approach can easily be adapted to a current production readily available to students. Any Shakespearean play, for example, can prove beneficial, as can any Greek play, or work by Ibsen, or more modern piece. As for the plays discussed in the text, it is also assumed that a certain number will be assigned reading for the course. A few plays have been referred to frequently—*Oedipus the King, Hamlet, King Lear, Tartuffe, The School for Scandal, A Doll's House, Death of a Salesman, A Streetcar Named Desire, Waiting for Godot, Raisin in the Sun*—and most of these are available in low-cost anthologies or paperbacks. Again, however, there is considerable flexibility provided by the text, and other plays—preferred by the teacher or more accessible—can easily be substituted. One by-product of the book's approach is that a play read early in the semester can be referred to a number of times as various subjects come up in the text: structure, point of view, design, and so forth. This is only one of several ways in which the text offers possibilities for continued reinforcement throughout a semester's study.

From the beginning—in the approach, the writing style, the organization—the aim has been to provide both teachers and students with a book which is not only informative and incisive but also pleasurable. To that end, the text is replete with examples and illustrations designed to enhance the reader's understanding of the theater event and, most important, to facilitate a grasp of the meaning of the encounter, or transaction, between those who create theater and those who view it. This encounter is the heart of theater.

Much of the material in this book was developed while teaching a course in Introduction to Theater at Hunter College of the City University of New York. To my colleagues and students there, from whom I have learned so much, I express my appreciation. I owe thanks, too, to Inge King for her excellent work on the photographs, to Melissa Moore, who typed the manuscript, and to Barry Benjamin, an exemplary editing supervisor.

Finally, I am especially grateful to Stuart Baker, a friend and colleague who did most of the work on the appendixes, and to Alison Meersschaert, my editor at McGraw-Hill. Editors can be intelligent, patient, helpful, and wise, but rarely all at once. Alison is an exception.

Edwin Wilson

INTRODUCTION

Theater is an experience, not only for those who take part in it, but for those who observe it. Like other experiences—falling in love, attending a football game, or learning to ride a bicycle—it requires our personal presence, and it changes from moment to moment as we encounter a series of shifting impressions and stimuli. It is a kaleidoscopic adventure through which we pass, with each instant a direct, immediate experience. In the theater we live in what critic Suzanne Langer calls the "perpetual present moment," and contained in the present is the fresh remembrance of the past and the anticipation of what is to come. Robert Edmond Jones, an American scene designer and critic, describes it this way:

Theater: a unique experience. *The masks and costumes designed by Patricia Zipprodt are combined with the performances of the actors and actresses, the words of the playwright, and the effects of stage lighting to provide an unusual experience in this scene from Jean Genet's* The Blacks. *(Photo—Martha Swope.)*

All that has ever been is in this moment; all that will be is in this moment. Both are meeting in one living flame, in this unique instant of time. This is drama; this is theater—*to be aware of the Now.*[1]

As Jones suggests, the theater experience has a quality all its own; it is like other experiences—the other arts in particular—but it is also unique. The nature of the theater experience and the ways in which it differs from other experiences will be the subject of this book.

The transitory nature of theater—a quality it shares with all performing arts—sets it apart in a significant way from literature and the visual arts. A painting, a piece of sculpture, a novel, and a book of poems are fixed objects. When they leave the artist's hands (or in the case of a book, when they leave the printer's shop), they are complete. They exist as finished products, and their tangible, unchangeable quality is one reason we value them, in the same way that we value historic buildings or antique automobiles. In a world of change and uncertainty, they remain the same; we can go back to them again and again and, if they have been preserved, they will always be there and always be the same. Michelangelo's statue of David at the Accademia in Florence, Italy, is the same great work of art today that it was the day it was completed in 1504, nearly 500 years ago.

The essence of such art is to catch something at a moment in time and freeze it. With the performing arts, however, this is impossible because they are not objects but events. Music provides a good illustration. Music may have timbre, pitch, and volume, but none of these register except on a time continuum, that is, as they move through time. A note in a melody cannot be held forever as a line in a drawing is forever fixed. Instead, music is created by the perpetual shift of notes, through repetition, variation, and an accumulation of effects. Similarly, theater occurs through time. A cumulative series of sights, sounds, and impressions creates theater.

Objects are a part of theater—costumes, props, scenery, a script—but none of these constitutes the art. Bernard Beckerman explains the difference:

Theater is nothing if not spontaneous. It occurs. It happens. The novel can be put away, taken up, reread. Not theater. It keeps slipping between one's fingers. Stopping, it stops being theater. Its permanent features, facets of activity, such as scenery, script, stage, people, are no more theater than the two poles of a generator are electricity. Theater is what goes on between the parts.[2]

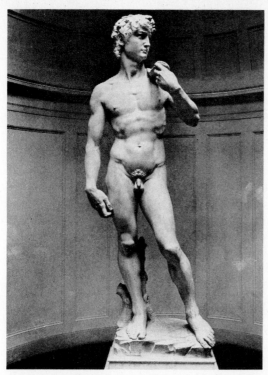

***Michelangelo's* David.** *This masterpiece of sculpture is the same today as when it was created several hundred years ago. Painting and sculpture—unlike theater—are represented by permanent, unchanging works of art. (Photo—Alinari-Scala.)*

The distinction between reading a novel and attending a theatrical performance reminds us that drama is sometimes looked on as a branch of literature. The confusion is understandable: after all, plays are printed in book form like literature, and to compound the confusion, many novels and short stories contain extensive passages of pure dialogue. An example is the following section from Ernest Hemingway's novel *A Farewell to Arms.* It is wartime, and Frederic, the hero, suggests to Catherine, a nurse with whom he is in love, that they should get married. She is afraid, however, that if they marry the authorities will send her home from the front. Catherine speaks:

> "But, darling, they'd send me away."
> "Maybe they wouldn't."
> "They would. They'd send me home and then we would be apart
>   until after the war."

"I'd come on leave."

"You couldn't get to Scotland and back on a leave. Besides, I won't leave you. What good would it do to marry now? We're really married. I couldn't be any more married."

"I only wanted to for you."

"There isn't any me. I'm you. Don't make up a separate me."

"I thought girls always wanted to be married."

"They do. But, darling, I am married. I'm married to you. Don't I make you a good wife?"

"You're a lovely wife."[3]

On the printed page this looks exactly like a play. But there is an important difference; unlike a novel or a poem, a play is written to be performed. In some respects a script is to a stage production what a musical score is to a concert, or what an architectural blueprint is to a building: it is an outline for a performance. Playwrights understand this distinction quite well. They know that the printed form of a play is not the end product of theater, and no less a dramatist than William Shakespeare (1564–1616) offers a good example.

In addition to his plays, Shakespeare wrote poems which he intended for publication. He went to great pains, for instance, to see that his long poem *Venus and Adonis* was published in a handsome edition in 1593. His plays were another matter; during his lifetime they appeared only in random or pirated editions, none of which were supervised by Shakespeare himself. He seems not to have cared at all about their publication, and about half of his plays did not even appear in print while he was alive. The plays were eventually gathered together seven years after his death, when two of his fellow actors published the First Folio, containing thirty-six of this plays. Shakespeare was indifferent and cavalier about the publication of his plays because he knew they would come to life on the stage, not on the printed page. He knew that the *way* performers delivered their lines—their facial expressions, their gestures, their vocal inflections—would play a vital part in a play's ultimate effect upon the audience.

Drama can be studied in a classroom for imagery, character, and theme, just as we study a Hemingway novel or John Milton's *Paradise Lost*, but study of this sort takes place *before* the event. It is a form of preparation for the experience; the experience is the performance itself. Obviously, we have more opportunities to read plays in book form than to see them produced, but when we read a play, we should always attempt to visualize the other aspects of a production in our mind's eye. We should be aware constantly that theater is performance.

Theater is action. *In contrast to sculpture, painting, or literature, theater is a dynamic art, changing from moment to moment as performers interact with one another—and with the audience. Here two characters struggle on a subway in* Dutchman *by LeRoi Jones (Imamu Amiri Baraka). (Photo—Copyright © Alix Jeffry.)*

A performance is the result of many forces coming together—some tangible, some intangible—including the physical presence of the performers, the colors and shapes of the costumes and scenery, and the ideas and emotions expressed in the words of the playwright. Each element of theater is varied and complex, and to understand theater we must study each element separately. Altogether we will examine the following five basic elements of theater:

1 The audience: its function, its general makeup, and the background which each spectator brings to a performance.

2 The performances of actors and actresses, together with the dramatic roles they portray.

3 The structure of the script: the organization of the words, ideas, and actions as they unfold.

4 The point of view adopted by those who create the work. Is it comical or serious? Is it lifelike or fantastic?

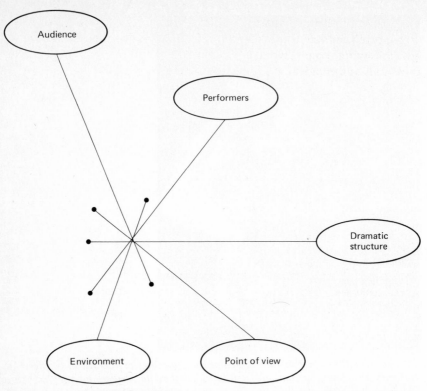

Basic elements of theater. *During a performance, the five elements of theater shown here continually intersect, fuse, and combine to produce the final theater experience.*

5   The environment in which the production occurs—indoors or outdoors, in a small space or a large one—together with the visual effects of costumes, lighting, and scenery.

At every point in time during a performance, two or more of these elements intersect; they fuse and combine to produce theater. In addition to studying the elements separately, we will look at the ways in which they join together to form the whole.

When an audience comes together to witness a performance, an exchange takes place between performers and spectators; the two groups engage in a form of communication or a celebration. At its best, theater affords members of the audience an opportunity to be transported outside themselves or to look deep inside themselves. In the following pages we will attempt to discover what makes this profound and magical experience possible.

POINT OF VIEW

DRAMATIC STRUCTURE

ENVIRONMENT

PERFORMERS   AUDIENCE

1

THE AUDIENCE'S ROLE

In 1959 in a small town in Poland, Jerzy Grotowski (1933–), a young stage director, formed the Polish Laboratory Theater and began a series of experiments to discover the essential elements of theater. He wanted to return to the roots of theater, eliminating everything that was unnecessary no matter how appealing or decorative it might be. In his ruthless pursuit he put each element to the test. Can theater exist without scenery? Yes, a play can be presented on a bare stage without scenery and elaborate lighting effects. Can theater exist without music? Yes, in most straight plays there is no music at all. Can it exist without furniture or props? Again, yes; actors can always

Figure 1-1 **The audience plays a crucial role.** *The audience and the performer are the two key elements of theater. In this picture the two groups come together at a performance of the New York Shakespeare Festival in Central Park. (Photo—George E. Joseph.)*

pantomime drinking a cup of coffee, opening a door, and so forth.

When Grotowski had stripped away all unnecessary elements, he was left with what he called a "Poor Theater," meaning a theater without any embellishments or extraneous features. He described the results of his experiments in his book *Towards a Poor Theatre*:

> By gradually eliminating whatever proved superfluous, we found that theatre can exist without makeup, without autonomic costume, and scenography, without a separate performance area (stage), without lighting and sound effects, etc. It cannot exist without the actor-spectator relationship of perceptual, direct, "live" communion. This is an ancient theoretical truth, of course, but when rigorously tested in practice it undermines most of our usual ideas about theatre.[1]

In other words, Grotowski discovered the two absolutely essential components of theater to be the actor and the audience.

BASIC ELEMENTS: SPECTATOR AND PERFORMER

It is worth noting that Grotowski, beginning with the highly technical, sophisticated theater of the twentieth century and working backward, arrived at precisely the same point as those who study the origins of theater. According to popular legend, Greek theater began in the sixth century B.C. with Thespis, the leader of a Greek chorus. The chorus was a group of men who performed songs, called *dithyrambs*, recounting stories from Greek mythology in a circular, open-air theater. It was Thespis' idea—or the idea of someone like him—to step apart from the chorus as a separate performer. Rather than remain its leader, he stood in opposition to it and exchanged dialogue with its members; in short, he became an actor. It was at this point—when a man impersonated someone else, when he "acted" in front of an audience—that Greek theater began. The process has been the same everywhere, whatever the culture and period: a man or woman stands in front of spectators, begins to impersonate someone else, and theater is born once again.

Following the Greek and Roman periods, theater declined in Europe. Early Christian leaders were strongly opposed to theater, and so for almost a thousand years theatrical performances were confined to acrobats and troupes of traveling actors. Ironically, the same church which so vehemently opposed the theater gave birth to it again in the Middle Ages. Between the sixth and tenth centuries, services of the church—the Mass and Hours—came to include more and more theatrical elements: costumes worn by the clergy, antiphonal music, and even a type of stage setting in the paintings and statuary of large cathedrals. Biblical stories were continuously elaborated in songs called *tropes.* One of these, describing the visit of the three Marys to Christ's tomb after the Resurrection, became a small play. It was called *Quem Quaeritis* after the Latin words in the opening line, which meant "whom seek ye?" Around A.D. 975 the bishop at Winchester, England, wrote stage directions for this tiny drama; from them we learn that the actors playing the angel and the Marys stood apart from one another, as well as the singing choir, to perform their parts. This is the important point: actors stood in front of an audience to play their roles, and once again, theater was established. From this simple beginning the medieval theater grew and spread.

ACTOR-AUDIENCE RELATIONSHIP

Wherever we look for the fundamentals of theater, in Greece in the sixth century B.C., in France and England in the tenth century, or at Jerzy Grotowski's Laboratory Theater in the twentieth century, we discover the primacy of the actor-audience relationship: the immediate, personal exchange whose chemistry and magic give theater its special quality.

People often have difficulty distinguishing between theater and film. After all, the two forms frequently present the same material, and dozens of movies have been adapted from stage productions: *West Side Story, Funny Girl, Sound of Music, A Streetcar Named Desire, Sleuth,* and *Godspell*, for example. In both forms, we see the same characters involved in the same situations. Naturally we recognize certain differences: films can provide outdoor shots made from helicopters or can take us to mountaintops. Films can cut instantaneously from one scene to another, and back again. But these are not the most crucial differences between films and the theater. The experience of being in the presence of the performer is more important to theater than anything else. No matter how closely a film follows the story of a play, no matter how involved we are with the people on the screen, we are always in the presence of an image, never a person.

We all know the difference between an image of someone and the flesh-and-blood reality. How often we rehearse a speech we plan to make to someone we love or fear. We run through the scene in our mind, picturing ourselves in conversation with the other person, but when we meet face to face, it is seldom the same. We freeze or find

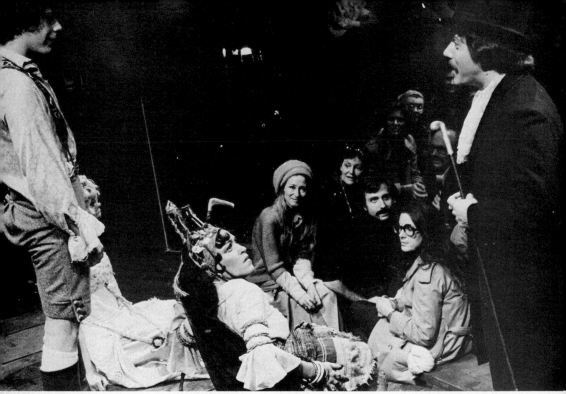

Figure 1-2 Interaction of performers and audience. *For a production of* Candide, *a Broadway theater was transformed to provide stage spaces interspersed among the audience in order to bring the performers and the audience closer together. Such personal contact sets theater apart from films and TV. (Photo—Martha Swope.)*

ourselves unable to speak; sometimes the words gush forth incoherently. Seldom is the encounter the way we planned.

The American playwright Jean-Claude van Itallie (1936–) explained the importance of the actor-audience relationship in the theater, and how theater differs from films and television. In the introduction to one of his plays he wrote:

> Theater is not electronic. Unlike movies and unlike television, it does require the live presence of both audience and actors in a single space. This is the theater's uniquely important advantage and function, its original religious function of bringing people together in a community ceremony where the actors are in some sense priests or celebrants, and the audience is drawn to participate with the actors in a kind of eucharist.[2]

Drama critic Walter Kerr elaborated on the idea of what it means for the audience and actors to be together:

It doesn't just mean that we are in the personal presence of performers. It means that they are in *our* presence, conscious of us, speaking to us, working for and with us until a circuit that is not mechanical becomes established between us, a circuit that is fluid, unpredictable, ever-changing in its impulses, crackling, intimate. *Our* presence, the way we respond, flows back to the performer and alters what he does, to some degree and sometimes astonishingly so, every single night. We are contenders, making the play and the evening and the emotion together. We are playmates, building a structure.

This never happens at a film because the film is already built, finished, sealed, incapable of responding to us in any way. The actors can't hear us or feel our presence; nothing *we* do, in our liveness, counts. We could be dead and the film would purr out its appointed course, flawlessly, indifferently.[3]

Like films, television seems very close to theater, sometimes closer. Television programs often begin with such words as "This program comes to you live from Burbank, California." But the word "live" must be qualified; in one sense, television distorts the meaning we have customarily assigned to the term. Prior to television, "live" in the entertainment or theatrical world meant "in person": not only was the event taking place at that moment, it was taking place before the spectator's eyes. "Live" television means that the event is taking place at that moment, but not in the presence of the viewer. In fact, it is generally far removed from any member of the TV audience, possibly half a world away. With television we see an image on a tube; we are free to look or not look, or even to leave the room. But the effect of a personal encounter, so vital to theater, is missing.

The fascination of being in the presence of a personality is difficult to explain, but not difficult to verify. No matter how often fans have seen their favorite stars on TV or in the movies, they will go to any lengths to see them in person. As another example, at one time or another, each of us has braved bad weather and shoving crowds to see celebrities at a parade or a political rally. The same pull of personal contact draws us to the theater.

A GROUP EXPERIENCE

Theater is a two-way street, involving on the one hand those who create theater—performers, playright, director, designers, and technicians—and on the other hand, the members of the audience. The nature of the theater experience can be examined from either side, and we will consider both viewpoints. Our primary focus, however, will be on the spectator's perspective: what it means to go to the theater and what happens while we are there.

Figure 1-3   Family watches TV. *When audiences see films or television they see images, or pictures, of people on a screen—not the people themselves. The experience, therefore, is once removed from personal contact. (Photo courtesy of Monkmeyer—Freda Leinwand.)*

For the audience, theater is a group experience. Some of the arts—painting, sculpture, literature—provide solitary experiences. The viewer or reader contemplates the work alone, at her or his own pace. This is true even in a museum where people flock to look at a single painting; they are with other people, but they respond as individuals, one at a time. In theater, however, as in the other performing arts, the group experience is indispensable; the performing arts in turn share this with other communal events: religious services, sports, and celebrations. Before the event can take place, a group must assemble—at one time in one place. Gathered together in this way, something mysterious happens to people. Though still individuals, with their own personalities and backgrounds, they take on other qualities as well, qualities which often overshadow their independent responses. Gustav Le Bon, a forerunner of social psychology and one of the first to study the phenomenon of crowds, wrote that a collection of people "presents new characteristics very different from those of the individuals composing it. The sentiments and ideas of all the persons in the gathering take one and the same direction, and their conscious personality vanishes. A collective mind is formed, doubtless transitory, but presenting very clearly defined characteristics."[4] Le Bon went on to say that the most striking peculiarity of a crowd is that although the individuals who compose it are quite different as individuals, once they have been transformed into a crowd, they develop a "collective mind which makes them feel, think, and act in a manner quite different from that in which each individual of them would feel, think, and act were he in a state of isolation. There are certain ideas and feelings which do not come into being or do not transform themselves into acts except in the case of individuals forming a crowd."[5]

Not all crowds are alike. Some are aggressive—groups of people on the street who decide to riot or terrorize a neighborhood. Others are docile—the passengers on an airline flight, for example. The crowd at a football game is different from a gathering at a serious religious observance; and a theater crowd is distinct from all these. In spite of being different, however, the theater audience shares with all such groups the special characteristics of the collective mind.

As an example, one can hardly imagine sitting alone in a theater, clapping and laughing out loud. In a group, however, we feel free to do so. One explanation for this is what behaviorist B. F. Skinner calls *reinforcement*:

> If it is always the individual who behaves, it is nevertheless the group which has the more powerful effect. By joining a group the individual increases his power to achieve reinforcement. . . . The reinforcing consequences generated by the group easily exceed the sums of the consequences which could be achieved by members acting separately. The total reinforcing effect is enormously increased.[6]

This is a complicated subject, of course, and Skinner deals with only one aspect of it. Also this is not the place to try to fathom the mysteries of the group mind or crowd behavior. It is important, however, to note its existence and, beyond that, to emphasize the importance of group behavior to theater. Becoming part of an audience is a crucial element of the theater experience. For a time we share a common undertaking; we are a member of a group focused on one activity—the performance of a play. Not only do we laugh or cry in a way we might not otherwise, we also sense an intangible communion with those around us.

When a collection of individuals responds more or less in unison to what is occurring on stage, their relationship to one another is reaffirmed. If there is a display of cruelty at which we shudder, or sorrow by which we are moved, or pomposity at which we laugh, it is reassuring to have others respond as we do. For a moment we are part

Figure 1-4   Theater is a group experience. *A neighborhood audience shares a laugh at a performance by the traveling unit of the New York Shakespeare Festival. In the theater, the size, attitude, and background of the audience affects the overall experience. (Photo—Friedman-Abeles.)*

of a group sharing a common experience, and our sorrow or joy, which we might have feared was idiosyncratic, is found to be part of a broad human response. If only for a brief time, we transcend our solitary, alienated existence.

AUDIENCE MAKEUP AFFECTS THE EXPERIENCE

Being part of a group is an essential element of theater, but the group itself may vary, and this will alter the occasion. Some audiences are general; the thousands who attend each performance at the Jones Beach musical theater on Long Island every summer would fall into this category, as would the audience at *Unto These Hills*, the play about the Cherokee Indians presented on the Cherokee Reservation in Western North Carolina each summer. These audiences include people of all ages, from all parts of the country, and from all socioeconomic levels. Other audiences are more homogeneous, such as spectators at a high school play, a children's theater production, a Broadway opening night, a political play, or a performance in a prison.

There is a fascinating account of a production at San Quentin prison in 1957.[7] The play, *Waiting for Godot* by Samuel Beckett

(1906–), is of the Theater of the Absurd, existential school, and concerns two tramps who meet on a barren plain each night to wait for an unknown savior named Godot, who never comes. The men are trapped with each other and their boredom. When the play was given at San Quentin, it was the first dramatic performance there in forty-four years. What is more, the play had proved controversial and obscure to audiences throughout America and Europe. As a result, the actors and prison officials were fearful that the performance would be a dismal failure. To everyone's surprise the prison audience not only stayed to watch the entire performance but sat in rapt attention. Later discussion proved that the prisoners understood the play far better than some more learned and sophisticated audiences had. One reason is that they identified so closely with the predicament of the characters, but another reason, no doubt, is that they were an audience united by a strong common bond—that of being prisoners in the same prison.

Still another factor affecting our experience in the theater is our relationship to the other members of the audience. If we are among friends or people of a like mind, we are likely to feel comfortable and relaxed; we readily give in to the group experience. On the other hand, if we feel like an alien—a young person with an older group, a radical with conservatives, a naïve person with sophisticates—we will be estranged from the group as a whole. As we have noted in the account of the performance at San Quentin, the people with whom we attend the theater—their relative homogeneity and our relation to them—strongly influence our response to the total event.

THE SEPARATE ROLES OF PERFORMERS AND SPECTATORS

In recent years numerous attempts have been made to involve members of the audience in the action of the play. Actors have come into the audience to make contact with spectators—shaking hands, touching them, arguing face to face. Spectators, too, have been encouraged to come on stage and join the action. At certain performances of the Living Theater, a group which flourished in the late 1960s, the stage sometimes became so crowded with spectators that a space had to be cleared so the performers could get on with the play.

This attempt to involve audience members directly springs from a worthwhile impulse: the desire to make theater relevant and more in touch with life. But it ignores the manner in which art functions, for art is one thing and life another. On the question of separation between actors and audience, Bernard Beckerman made the following observations:

The performers and spectators must be separated from each other so that the spectators can observe what is happening. But this isolation is not merely utilitarian; it is both physical and psychological. A sacred grove may be selected, a dancing circle may be circumscribed, a platform may be erected. Somehow, an area is defined, which then becomes the servant of the performer. It is manipulable, both as actual and imaginative space; it is the place where presentations can be made. Recently, in drama, we have had instances in productions such as *The Connection* and *The Blacks*, in the work of Jerzy Grotowski, and in novelties such as Happenings, where a breakdown of isolation is sought. Frequently, roles are reversed, and the spectator, instead of being god, becomes scapegoat. Such attempts to erase the line between presenter and presentee only define it more sharply. The auditor becomes acutely aware that he has been cast in the role of a particular kind of spectator. Isolation is not eliminated, merely recharacterized.[8]

PARTICIPATORY AND OBSERVED THEATER

The question of actor-audience separation has been complicated in recent years by the rapid growth of *participatory* theater in which ordinary people play roles and improvise dramatic scenes. In participatory theater, those who take part are not actors and there is no attempt to duplicate a written script. Rather, the emphasis is on education, personal development, and therapy: fields in which theater techniques have opened up new possibilities. In schools, for example, creative dramatics, theater games, and group improvisations have proved invaluable in aiding self-discovery and developing healthy group attitudes. By acting out hypothetical situations or giving free reign to their imaginations, children build confidence, discover creative potential, and overcome inhibitions. In some cases creative dramatics teaches lessons which are difficult to teach by conventional means.

For adults as well as children, sociodrama and psychodrama are coming more and more to the forefront as therapeutic techniques. In sociodrama, attitudes and prejudices are explored between groups: parents and children, students and teachers, legal authorities and ordinary citizens. When young people, for instance, take the parts of the parents, and adults assume the roles of the children, both groups become aware of deep-seated feelings held by the two parties and arrive at a better understanding of one another.

Figure 1-5 Participatory drama: a different form of theater. *A group enacting a sociodrama in Dr. Milton Polsky's class at Hunter College—CUNY: the young man is playing a father chastising his daughter for being a school dropout. Participatory drama is for the benefit of those taking part, not for an audience. Education or personal satisfaction rather than a polished performance is the object. (Photo—Jonathan Ishii.)*

Psychodrama uses some of the same techniques as sociodrama, but is more private and interpersonal; in fact, it can become so intensive that it should be carried out only under the supervision of a carefully trained therapist. In psychodrama individual fears, anxieties, and frustrations are explored. The person might reenact a particularly traumatic scene from childhood, for example.

The various fields of participatory theater are fascinating, and their full potentials have only recently begun to be explored, but our purpose here is to draw the distinctions between participatory drama and observed drama. In participatory drama, theater is a means to another end: education, therapy, group development, and the like. The aim is not public performance, and so there is no emphasis—in fact, quite the reverse—on a carefully prepared, expertly performed presentation before an audience. In observed drama there must always be a separation between the actors and the audience. At times in the contemporary theater, as we have noted, spectators go on stage to be part of the action; at other times actors come into the audience to engage in repartee with a spectator. If the spectator takes part, though, he or she is no longer an observer, but a participant. For those moments the observer has changed roles and becomes what Bernard Beckerman calls the "presenter" rather than the "presentee." Our concern here is with those who observe theater, and it is from their perspective that we are examining theater. By definition, the experience of the observer is not one of direct, physical contact but rather of the imagination, a subject to be explored in the next chapter.

SUMMARY

1 The actor and the audience form the two basic elements of theater. The encounter between the two is the foundation of theater—the one ingredient essential to its existence.

2 The actor-audience relationship is a "live" relationship: each is in the other's presence, in the same place at the same time. It is the exchange between the two which gives theater its unique quality.

3 Theater—like other performing arts—is a group experience; also, the makeup of the audience has a direct bearing on the effect of the experience.

4 Participants and spectators play different roles in the theater experience, the latter's role being to observe and respond.

5 There is a difference between participatory and observed theater. In the former, nonactors take part, usually for the purpose of personal growth and self-development. In the latter, a presentation is made by one group to another, and the spectators do not participate physically in the experience.

By observing and responding, the audience plays a vital part in every theater event. The exact nature of the audience experience will be better understood when examined in detail in Chapter 2.

2

THE IMAGINATION OF THE AUDIENCE

For those who take part in it, theater is a direct experience: a stage carpenter builds scenery, a scene designer paints it, an actress wears a costume and stands on stage in a spotlight. Theirs is the experience of someone who cuts a finger or is held in an embrace: the pain or the warmth is felt directly and physically.

As members of the audience, we feel a different kind of pain or warmth: a no less immediate, but separate sensation. As spectators in the theater we are presented with a number of stimuli—we sense the presence of other audience members, we observe the movements

Figure 2-1 **Fantasy in the theater.** *In* The Birds *by the Greek playwright Aristophanes performers play the part of birds who go to an imaginary land called Cloudcuckoo Land. Theater audiences accept many kinds of unreality and make-believe, and make amazing leaps of the imagination. (Actors Workshop of San Francisco. Photo—Hank Kranzler.)*

and gestures of performers and hear the words they speak, and we see costumes, scenery, and lighting. From these we form mental images or make imaginative connections which provoke joy, laughter, anger, sorrow, or pain. All this occurs, however, without our moving from our seats.

THE DRAMATIC IMAGINATION OF SPECTATORS

We naturally assume that those who create theater are highly imaginative people and that their minds are full of vivid, exciting ideas which never occur to the rest of us. If we carry this idea too far, however, and conclude that we in the audience have limited or nonexistent theatrical imaginations, we are doing ourselves a great injustice. As we have noted earlier, theater is a two-way street—an exchange between actors and audience—and this is nowhere more evident than in the creation of illusion. Illusion may be initiated by the creators of theater, but it is completed by the audience.

A group of tough gamblers, ready to shoot crap, stand around singing "The Oldest, Established, Permanent, Floating Crap Game in New York"; then their leader, Sky Masterson, breaks into song, "Luck Be a Lady," while he takes the dice. We in the audience know this is not real: gamblers in the back alley do not sing; they get down on their knees and get on with the game. But this is what we accept in the musical comedy *Guys and Dolls*. In the eerie world of Shakespeare's *Macbeth*, when three witches appear out of the mist, or Banquo's ghost interrupts Macbeth's banquet, we know it is fantasy; witches and ghosts, at least the kind from *Macbeth*, do not appear in everyday life. Again we take such fantasy at face value.

The main character of the expressionistic play *The Adding Machine* by Elmer Rice (1892–1967) is called Mr. Zero. The play, written in 1923 and depicting man's loss of identity and individuality in the machine age, continues to be prophetic even now. Mr. Zero, however, is not a name from a telephone book—it is not meant to be. Rather, it is symbolic of the character: he is nothing—a cipher, zero. His friends do not have ordinary names either. They are Mr. One, Mr. Two, Mr. Three, etc. Another symbolic character in the play, Mr. Shrdlu, has been a proofreader and gets his name from the jumbled letters of a typesetting machine.

An example in *The Adding Machine* of our acceptance of the fantastic in theater occurs when Mr. Zero dies and goes to heaven; he is shown in afterlife carrying on conversations with Mr. Shrdlu and Daisy, a girl who had worked with him in his office for many years.

Figure 2-2 *Back-alley gamblers sing a song. In the musical,* Guys and Dolls, *the hero sings "Luck, Be a Lady Tonight" as he rolls dice in a crap game. This could never happen on a real street corner, but is completely believable in the theater. (Original Broadway production. Photo—Graphic House, Inc.)*

Other plays have also shown a form of heaven on stage. The third act of *Our Town* by Thornton Wilder (1897–) shows the cemetery where the young girl, Emily, joins others who have died. The dead sit on straight chairs, representing tombstones, and talk to one another as if they were alive. The musical *Carousel,* based on the play *Liliom,* shows the hero in heaven, where he asks a chance to go back for one day on earth to see his young daughter.

We know that if there is a life after death it is not as immediately visible as in these plays, but we gladly accept the reality of it in the theater.

As spectators we make other drastic adjustments in the theater. Shifts in time and place have always been accepted by audiences. Someone on stage dressed in a Revolutionary uniform says, "It is the winter of 1778, at Valley Forge," and we do not question it. What is more, we accept rapid movements back and forth in time. *Flash-*

backs—abrupt movements from the present to the past and back again—are commonplace in modern drama. Similar devices were used in medieval mystery and morality plays. The medieval play *Abraham and Isaac*, for instance, is set in Old Testament days, but it contains several references to the Christian Trinity, obviously a religious concept introduced centuries later. The medieval audience accepted the shift in time as a matter of course, just as we do in theater today.

Eugene Ionesco (1912–), a Rumanian-born French dramatist, fills his plays with bizarre and fantastic concepts. In his play *Rhinoceros*, a man turns into a rhinoceros. Another play, *A Stroll in the Air*, features a man who rises from the stage floor each time he speaks; at times he walks several feet off the ground. In Ionesco's *Amédée*, a corpse, dead many years, continues to grow; it is in the next room, and during the play pushes through the wall of the apartment on stage.

One definition of farce is a "type of comedy based on an absurd premise and marked by wild improbabilities of plot." Many plays of Aristophanes (445–380 B.C.), a Greek comic writer, fit the definition perfectly. There are times when he seems to know no bounds in creating ridiculous situations. In *The Clouds*, Aristophanes pictures Socrates as a man who can think only when perched in a basket suspended in the air. In *The Birds*, two ordinary men convince a chorus of birds to build a city between heaven and earth. The birds comply, calling the place Cloudcuckoo Land, and the two men sprout wings to join them.

In theater, people become animals, animals become people, and at times characters are even invisible like the 6-foot rabbit in *Harvey*. The improbabilities of farce have continued from Aristophanes right up to the present. A perennial farce is *Charley's Aunt* (as a Broadway musical, it was called *Where's Charley?*) in which a man dresses up like his elderly aunt. In real life his ludicrous disguise would fool no one, but in the theater we never doubt for a second that it fools the other characters on stage.

Philadelphia, Here I Come is a play about a young Irishman on the night before his departure for America. The leading character is played by two actors, one representing the public man, the other, the private man. Both actors are on stage together, but the other characters can see only the public man. When the latter hesitates to declare his love to his girl or express his deeper emotions to his father, the private man urges him on. The two halves of the one man are personified, in other words, by two separate actors, a convention we in the audience accept without question.

In the theater, our imagination allows us to conceive people and events we have never seen or experienced and to transcend our physical circumstance to the point where we forget who we are, where we are, or what time it is. How is this possible? It works in the same way that our imagination works for us in everyday life. Perhaps we can understand this process better if we look closely at two tools of our imagination, usually considered poetic devices, but actually potent forces in real life: symbol and metaphor.

FUNCTIONS OF SYMBOL AND METAPHOR

Symbol

A symbol is a sign, token, or emblem that signifies something else, something far more complex and profound than the symbol itself. The cross, for example, is a symbol of Christ and, beyond that, of Christianity as a whole. The peace symbol, a V formed by two fingers, and the black power salute of the raised clenched fist are both powerful symbols. Some signs stand for a single, uncomplicated idea or action. In everyday life we are surrounded by them: road signs, such as an S curve, audible signals, like sirens or fog horns, and a host of mathematical and typographical symbols: $-$, $+$, \$, 1/4. We sometimes forget that language itself is symbolic. The letters of the alphabet are only lines and curves on a page. And words are an arrangement of letters which by common agreement represent something else. The same four letters mean different things depending on the order in which they are placed: pear, reap, rape. They set three different imaginative wheels in motion and signal a response which varies greatly from word to word.

Flags are symbols: lines, shapes, and colors which in given combinations become immediately recognizable. At times, symbols exhibit an incredible emotional power, and flags are a good example, embodying a nation's passions, fears, and ambitions. The symbolic force of the American flag was illustrated very clearly during the Vietnam war. At the height of the conflict, some citizens displayed it more prominently than usual on lapel pins, window decals, and bumper stickers with slogans like "These colors don't run." In answer to this, members of the counterculture used the flag to make shirts and hats and painted it on motorcycles. In this case a powerful symbol became invested with two meanings: on the one hand, it meant strong approval of United States involvement, on the other, vehement disapproval.

In the commercial world, the power of the symbol is acknowledged in the value placed on a trademark. As an example, in 1972 Standard Oil Company of New Jersey changed its name, but before doing so it spent five years of computer research to find what it considered the best one and finally came up with "Exxon." The company then spent $125 million changing its stationery, service station signs, etc., to the new name. The term *status symbol* is a frank recognition of the importance of personal possessions in conferring status on the owner. The kinds of cars people drive, the way they dress, the furnishings of their homes: these indicate the kinds of people they are—at least that is the theory. Whatever form it takes—language, trademark, or flags—a symbol embodies the total meaning of an idea, nation, religion, or product.

Metaphor

A similar transformation takes place with metaphor, another form of imaginative substitution. With metaphor we announce that one thing *is* another, in order to describe it or point up its meaning more clearly. (In poetry, you will remember, a simile says that one thing is *like* another; metaphor simply states that one thing is another.) Calling the government "the ship of state" or a religious leader a "shepherd" involves the use of a metaphor. As with symbol, metaphor is part of the fabric of life, as the following expressions suggest:

> "A real drag."
> "War is hell."
> "It's raining cats and dogs."
> "Everything's coming up roses."
> "Time flies."
> "It was a heavy scene."
> "Out of sight."
> "Do you dig?"
> "Cool, man, cool."

These are metaphors; we are saying one thing but describing another. Everyone knows, for instance, that the statement "everything's coming up roses" does not mean a field of flowers is suddenly springing up. The person saying it might be standing on a city street in the dead of winter. Still, the meaning is unmistakably clear. We can see from the above examples that metaphor, like symbol, is part of everyday life.

"REALITY" OF THE IMAGINATION

Some people believe—or think they believe—only the tangible and objective. They want an object they can see, touch, and measure; for them, anything which defies this test has an air of fakery about it. In modern society, this has been a widely held attitude.

Our reliance on symbol and metaphor, however, shows how large a part imagination plays in our lives. Men go to battle and die for a flag or slogan, and the more than 100 million automobiles in the United States can be brought to a halt, not by concrete walls or battalions of armored tanks, but by a small colored light changing from green to red. Imagine attempting to control traffic, or virtually any type of human activity, without symbols. Beyond being a matter of convenience, symbols are necessary to our survival.

The same holds true for metaphor: we cannot express fear, anxiety, hope, or joy—any of the deep human feelings—except indirectly. Even scientists, the men and women we presume to be superrealists, turn to metaphor at crucial times. They discuss the "big bang" theory of creation, and talk of "black holes" in outer space. Neither description is scientifically accurate, but it communicates what scientists have in mind, in a way that equations and logical language never can.

Dreams provide another example of the power of the imagination. You dream you are falling off a cliff when suddenly you wake up and find you are not flying through the air but lying in bed. Significantly, however, the dream means more to you than the objective fact of your lying in bed. We have recognized this ever since Sigmund Freud presented his monumental work on the subconscious. Despite variations and corrections of his theories, no one today disputes Freud's notion of the importance and "reality" of dreams, nightmares, or symbols in the minds of men and women. Even when a product of the imagination cannot be verified by outside observation, or proved scientifically, it nevertheless exists in the mind, and in those terms is entirely real. A young woman feeling alienated and alone is told she cannot feel lonely because she is not alone: she is sitting elbow-to-elbow in a football stadium or on a crowded bus. But in her mind she knows she is alone. And she is.

Theater functions in precisely the same way. Though not real in a literal sense, it can be painfully real in an emotional or intellectual sense. Harold Clurman named one of his books on the theater *Lies Like Truth*, and theater—like dreams or fantasies—can sometimes be more truthful about life than a mundane, objective description. This is a paradox of dreams, fantasies, or art, including theater: by probing deep into our psyches to reveal inner truths, they can be more real than outward reality.

SEPARATING STAGE REALITY FROM FACT

No matter how strong the "reality" of the theater is, it is different from the physical reality of everyday life. In recent years there have been attempts to make theater less remote from our daily lives. Partly as a result of this trend theater and life have become deeply intertwined. There are "staged" political demonstrations, for instance, and we hear of "staged news." This confusion and interaction has been heightened, of course, by the emergence of TV and film documentaries which cover real events, but have also been edited. How real, we may ask, are the news films we see? In the last few years, plays have been presented which were largely transcripts of court trials, such as *The Trial of the Catonsville Nine* and *The Matter of J. Robert Oppenheimer.* These were part of a new movement called the Theater of Fact, with reenactments of material gathered from actual events. When the news becomes "staged" and theater becomes "fact," it is difficult to separate the two.

While this points up rather vividly the close relationship between theater and life, nevertheless when we see a performance, even of events which have actually occurred, we are always aware on some level that we are in the theater. No matter how authentic the reenactment, we know it is a replay and not the original. Most of us have seen plays with a stage setting so real we marvel at its authenticity: a kitchen, for instance, in which the appliances actually work, with running water in the faucets, ice in the refrigerator, and a stove on which an actor can cook. What we stand in awe of, though, is that the room *appears* so real when we know, in truth, it is not. We admire the fact that, not being a real kitchen, it looks as if it were.

We are reminded quite abruptly of the distinction between stage reality and physical reality when the two lines cross. If an actor unintentionally trips and falls on stage, we suddenly shift our attention from the character to the person playing the part. Has he hurt himself? Will he be able to continue? Will someone rush in from offstage? A similar thing happens when an actor forgets lines, or a sword falls accidentally in a duel, or a dancer slips in a musical number.

We remember the distinction, also, at the moment when someone else *fails* to remember it. Children frequently mistake actions on stage for the real thing, warning the heroine of the villain's plan, or assuming that the blows on the head of a puppet are actually hurting him. There is a famous story of a production of *Othello* in which a spectator ran on stage to prevent the actor playing Othello from strangling Desdemona. As another instance, in the summer of 1972, the Street Theater of Ossining, New York, was presenting *Street Sounds* by the black playwright Ed Bullins (1935–). The play opens with two black policemen coming through the audience, going on stage, and beating a fifteen-year-old black youth. At one performance a spectator ran on stage in the midst of the beating to stop the actors playing the policemen. In each of these cases, the distinction between fantasy and reality disappeared for the spectator, who mistook the imagined event for the the real one.

There have been instances where people considered a symbol or a fantasy as the fact itself. J. A. Hadfield reports this was frequently the

Figure 2-3 *Theater of fact: a departure from traditional theater. Gaining importance in recent years has been the re-creation or interpretation on stage of an actual event such as a court trial or government inquiry. In the play* In the Matter of J. Robert Oppenheimer *we see a hearing before the Board of the Atomic Energy Commission investigating the loyalty of the well-known atomic physicist, Dr. Oppenheimer, played by Joseph Wiseman, the actor with the pipe. (Photo courtesy of Center Theatre Group, Mark Taper Forum, Los Angeles.)*

case with the dreams of primitive man: "He considered that if in his dream he saw himself in a neighboring hostile village, he had actually been in that village, and if he saw the villagers in his dream preparing for battle, this would be quite enough for him to report the fact, and his tribe would immediately prepare to meet the onslaught."[1]

One manifestation of insanity occurs when a person cannot separate the real from the imagined. Most people, however, are always aware of the difference. The result is that our minds manage two seemingly contradictory feats simultaneously: we know on the one hand that an imagined event is not objectively real, but at the same time we go along with it completely as fantasy.

In *King Lear*, Cornwall, one of Lear's evil sons-in-law, stands over the elderly, helpless nobleman, Gloucester. He puts his thumbs in the old man's eyes, and, with the words, "Out vile jelly! Where is thy lustre now?" pushes his thumbs into the sockets, and blinds him, while we sit still in our seats. We are struck dumb; we identify with the pain and agony of the old man, and we watch horrified at the level to which his enemies have sunk. And yet we do nothing—we sit in our seats, and the reason is that we know this is not actually happening to the actor playing Gloucester. We could not stand to watch one man treat another so cruelly if it were.

We accept all kinds of theater, the most realistic as well as the most fantastic, because of a "willing suspension of disbelief." This is the term the poet and critic Samuel Taylor Coleridge used to explain the phenomenon of our accepting so completely the products of our imaginations, particularly as they occur in art. Having separated at the outset the reality of art from the reality of everyday life, the mind is prepared to go along with the former without reservation.

THEATER IS A METAPHOR

Theater operates on the level of symbol, metaphor, and dreams. Mr. Zero, for example, is a symbol. So are virtually all dramatic characters, as well as much scene and costume design. In later chapters we will study in detail the ways in which theater makes use of these elements of the imagination. Beyond using symbols and metaphors, however,

Figure 2-4 King Lear comforts the blinded Gloucester. Because theater is a product of the imagination and is not actually happening, audiences are able to accept fantasy, and also able to endure such horrible sights as the blinding of Gloucester in Shakespeare's King Lear. *(Photo—The Tyrone Guthrie Theater, Minneapolis, Minn.)*

one could say that theater itself is a metaphor. When an actress stands on stage dressed as Joan of Arc, she does not say, "I am going to act *like* Joan of Arc," as in a simile; rather, by her presence she proclaims, "I am Joan of Arc." In the same way, the theater program does not say, "A room designed to look like the Dauphin's palace." It says simply, "The Dauphin's palace." Everything we see in theater—an entire performance, including the action and the scenery—can be viewed as a giant metaphor.

When the metaphor succeeds, we see before us a complex creation which mirrors life. It takes us inside our subconscious and lets us either laugh at ourselves or learn to look at our deepest fears. At such moments we suspend disbelief; theater is undeniably real even though we are not in the action at all, but sitting still. Such is the power of the imagination.

SUMMARY

1 For the observer, theater is an experience of the imagination and the mind, which seems capable of accepting almost any illusion as to what is taking place, who the characters are, and when and where the action occurs.

2 Our minds are capable of leaps of the imagination not just in the theater, but in our everyday lives where we employ symbol and metaphor to communicate with one another and to explain the world around us.

3 The world of the imagination—symbols, metaphors, dreams, fantasies, and various expressions of art—is "real" even though it is intangible and has no objective reality. Frequently it tells us more about our true feelings than any form of logical discourse.

4 In order to take part in theater as an observer, it is important to keep the "reality" of fantasies and dreams separate from the real world. By making this separation, we open our imaginations to the full range of possibilities in the theater.

5 Theater makes frequent use of symbols and metaphors—in writing, acting, design, etc.—and theater itself can be viewed as a metaphor.

For spectators, the experience of theater is conditioned not only by the event itself—by the performers, the script, the scenery and costumes—but by their own knowledge and experience acquired *before* the event begins. Members of the audience do not arrive at the theater empty-handed; and what they arrive with is the subject we turn to next.

3

THE PERSPECTIVE OF THE AUDIENCE

Audience members bring more to a performance than their mere presence; they bring a background of personal knowledge and experience which helps form the impressions they receive from a production. This background or perspective can be considered from three points of view: (1) an awareness of the social, political, and philosophical world in which the play was written or produced; (2) specific information about a play or playwright; (3) memories or experiences of the individual spectator.

Figure 3-1 Contemporary theater reflects a changing society. The figure leaping high in the air in the Broadway production of Hair is symbolic of the way theater has broken traditional bounds in recent years. This rock musical featuring young people with long hair brought a new experience to Broadway and reflected new experiences in the society. Theater frequently mirrors such cultural shifts in society. (Photo—Martha Swope.)

LINK BETWEEN THEATER AND SOCIETY

All art, including theater, is related to the society in which it is produced. Charges are sometimes made against artists that they are "antisocial," "subversive," or "enemies of the state," with the strong suggestion that artists are outsiders or invaders of a culture. To be sure, art frequently challenges society and is sometimes on the leading edge of history, appearing to forecast the future. But more often than not such art simply recognizes what is already present in society but has not yet surfaced. A good example is the abstract art which emerged in Europe in the early part of the twentieth century. At first it was considered an aberration or freak: an unattractive series of jagged lines and patches of color with no relation to nature, truth, or anything human. In time, however, abstract art came to be recognized as a genuine movement whose disjointed and fragmentary lines reflect the quality of much of modern life.

Art grows in the soil of a specific society. It must in order to take root. With very few exceptions—and those soon forgotten—art is a mirror of its age, revealing the prevailing attitudes, underlying assumptions, and deep-seated beliefs of a particular group of people. Art may question society's views or reaffirm them, but it cannot escape them; the two are indissolubly linked like a man and his shadow. When we speak of art as being "universal," we mean that the art of one age has so defined the characteristics of human beings that it can speak eloquently to another age, but it should never be forgotten that every work of art first emerges at a given time and place and can never be adequately understood unless the conditions surrounding its birth are also understood.

Greek Theater and Culture

A study of theater at significant periods of history confirms this close link between art and society. In ancient Greece, for example, civilization reached a high point during the rule of Pericles in the latter part of the fifth century B.C. This was the Golden Age of Greece, when politics, art, architecture, and theater thrived as they never had before, and rarely have since. As the Greeks of that period gained control over the world around them and took new pride in human achievements, they developed ideals of beauty, order, symmetry, and moderation which permeated their entire culture, including theater.

By the fifth century B.C., standard forms of drama had emerged in Greece for both tragedy and comedy. Playwrights introduced innovations—but essentially they adhered to prescribed conventions. One of

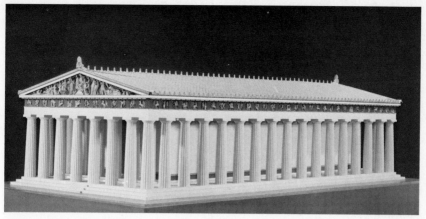

Figure 3-2 The symmetry of the Parthenon. *The formalism and sense of order of Greece in the 5th Century* B.C. *is reflected in the Parthenon, located atop the Acropolis in Athens, recreated here in a model. All art, including theater, reflects the attitudes and values of the society in which it is created. (Photo courtesy of the Metropolitan Museum of Art Purchase, 1890, Levi Hale Willard Bequest.)*

these conventions required a limited number of scenes in each play. A second convention reflected the society's sense of propriety—although bloody deeds occurred in the myths on which most Greek plays were based, these deeds never took place in sight of the audience: all murders, suicides, and other acts of violence took place offstage. To reinforce the Greek notion of moderation, a third feature of most Greek tragedies was that any character in a play who acted in an excess of passion was punished or pursued by avenging furies. At the conclusion of the plays, gods frequently appeared to reestablish order in the world.

Elizabethan Theater and Culture

Another example of the strong link between theater and society—one which stands in sharp contrast to the classic Greek period—is the Elizabethan age in England. Named after Queen Elizabeth, who reigned from 1558 to 1603, this period saw England become a dominant force in the world. Under Elizabeth's rule England was forged into a unified country; trade and commerce flourished, and with the defeat of the Spanish Armada in 1588, an age of exploration for England was in full bloom. England was expanding on all fronts and feeling self-confident in the process, and these characteristics were reflected in the drama of the period. The plays of Shakespeare, Christopher Marolwe (1564–1593), and their contemporaries are quite different from the restrained, formal drama of the Greeks. A single play might move from place to place and cover a period of many years. The plays have an expansiveness of characters and action, and there is no hesitancy whatsoever about showing murder and bloodshed on stage. At the end of an Elizabethan play corpses frequently cover the stage in full view of the audience.

Radical Theater and Today's Culture

Moving to a more contemporary period, we find once again a tie between theater and society. The group formed by Jerzy Grotowski, the Polish director discussed in Chapter 1, was only one of many groups at the mid-twentieth century seeking to challenge traditional concepts in theater. This occurred at the same time that society in general was challenging traditional concepts.

For these theater groups, there was a double impulse at work. On the one hand, they felt that the theater of the past was no longer relevant to the problems of the present and that new forms must be found to match the challenges and aspirations unique to the latter part of the twentieth century. On the other hand, they had an impulse to look back past the traditions of the last twenty-five hundred years to the beginning of theater, to scrape off the many layers of formality and convention accumulated through the centuries and rediscover the roots of theater. In many cases these two impulses led to similar results, and from the experiments of the radical theater movement, sometimes called the *New Theater*, several significant departures from traditional theater practice were developed. Among them were the following: (1) emphasis on nonverbal theater, that is, theater where gestures, body movements, and sounds without words are stressed rather than logical or intelligible language; (2) reliance on improvisation or a scenario developed by actors and a director to tell the story rather than a written text; (3) interest in ritual and ceremony; (4) stress on the importance of the physical environment of theater, including the spatial relationship of the actors to the audience.

The New Theater movement was at its height in the decade of the 1960s, a decade that saw an emphasis on political confrontations, black power, and women's liberation. The "revolution" in theater was intimately connected to revolutions taking place in society at large.

The three periods we have noted are only examples, illustrating the close relationship between a given society and the art and theater it produces. One could find comparable links in virtually every culture.

Figure 3-3 **Ritualistic Theater.** *Among new forms emerging in the contemporary theater is ritual—also an ancient form of theater. In its modern form it emphasizes the commununal, nonverbal aspects of theater with a premium on the physical movements of the performers and on the group development of the ceremony or story. Here we see a ritualistic scene by performers from the Living Theatre. (Photo courtesy of Magnum—Max Waldman.)*

Figure 3-4 Theater of Protest. *Typical of the diversity of theater in recent years are theatrical events taking a strong political stand or making a political statement. These giant figures protest the violence and bloodshed of the Vietnam war. (Photo courtesy of Magnum—Burk Uzzle.)*

Whatever the period in which it was first produced, drama is woven into the fabric of the time.

The Audience and the Cultural Background

When we as spectators see a play that has been written in our own day, we automatically bring with us a deep awareness of the world from which the play comes because we come from the same world. Through the books we read, through newspapers and television, through discussions with friends, we have a background of common information and beliefs. Our shared knowledge and experience is much larger than most of us realize, and this forms a crucial ingredient in our theater experience.

In the case of plays from the past, however, we have to compensate for a lack of this kind of knowledge. To understand fully a play written many years before, we have to become acquainted with the history, the culture, the psychology, and the philosophy of the period in which it was produced. We can appreciate a classic without such knowledge, but this kind of background information makes our experience that much richer.

BACKGROUND INFORMATION ON A PLAY OR PLAYWRIGHT

In some cases it is not the period surrounding the play about which we need additional knowledge, but the play itself. In plays from the past as well as contemporary plays, there are sometimes difficult passages or obscure references which it is helpful to know before we see a performance of the play. As an example, we can take a segment from Shakespeare's *King Lear*: the scene in the third act when Lear appears on the heath in the midst of a terrible storm. Earlier in the play Lear had divided his kingdom between two daughters, Goneril and Regan, who he thought loved him, but who he discovered had deceived him. Gradually they stripped him of everything: his possessions, his soldiers, even his dignity. Finally they send him out from their homes to face the wind and rain in open country. As the storm begins, Lear speaks the following lines:

> Blow, winds, and crack your cheeks! Rage! Blow!
> You cataracts and hurricanoes, spout
> Till you have drenched our steeples, drowned the cocks!
> You sulphurous and thought-executing fires,
> Vaunt-curriers of oak-cleaving thunderbolts,
> Singe my white head! And thou all-shaking thunder,
> Strike flat the thick rotundity o' the world. . . .

Even if we do not understand every reference, we realize that Lear is invoking the heavens to bring on a terrifying storm. The sounds of the words alone—the music of the language in its combinations of vowels, rhythm, and inflections—convey the sense of a raging storm. But how much more the passage will mean if in addition we understand the meanings of key words and phrases. Let us examine the passage more closely: In the first line the expression "crack your cheeks" refers to pictures in the corners of old maps showing a face puffed out at the cheeks, blowing the wind.[1] Shakespeare is saying that the face of the wind should blow so hard that its cheeks will crack. In the second line, "cataracts and hurricanoes" refer to water from both the heavens and the seas. In line three, the word "cocks" refers to weathercocks on the tops of steeples; Lear wants there to be so much rain that even the weathercocks on the steepletops will be covered with water. In line four, "thought-executing" means as quick as thought; in other words, fires should ignite instantaneously. "Vaunt-curriers" of line five suggests that lightning is followed by thunder bolt; first the fire comes and then a bolt which can split an oak tree. Line seven, "strike flat the thick rotundity o' the world," conveys the image of a storm so powerful that the round earth will be flattened. If we are aware of these meanings, we can join them with the sounds of the words and the rage which the actor expresses in his voice and gesture to get the full impact of the scene.

Turning to the contemporary theater, playwrights today frequently employ special techniques which will confuse us if we do not understand them. The German playwright Bertolt Brecht (1898–1956), who lived and wrote in the United States during the 1940s, wished to provoke his audience into thinking about what it was seeing. To do this, he interrupted the story with a song or a speech by a narrator. The theory is that when a story is stopped in this manner, the audience has an opportunity to consider more carefully what it has seen and to relate the drama on stage to other aspects of life. If one is not aware that this is Brecht's purpose in interrupting the action, one might naturally conclude that he was simply a careless or inferior playwright. In this, as in similar cases, knowledge of the play or playwright is indispensable to a complete theater experience.

BACKGROUND OF INDIVIDUAL SPECTATORS

One background element which every member of the audience brings to a theater experience without additional study is that person's individual memories and experiences. Each one of us has a personal catalog of emotional scars, childhood memories, and private fantasies, and anything we see on stage which reminds us of them has a strong impact on us. *What the Wine Sellers Buy*, a play by the black playwright Ron Milner (1938–), depicts the struggle of a young black man torn between achieving material wealth and prestige by following in the footsteps of an affluent drug seller and remaining relatively poor by adhering to the precepts of honor and decency taught him by his mother. As a spectator, a young black man or for that matter any young man who has faced a choice between two such conflicting goals, will be strongly involved in the action on stage. He will see himself up there with the hero and will say silently: "That's the way it is; I know how it feels; I know what he's going through."

In the story of Antigone, treated in a play by Sophocles (497–406 B.C.) in Greece in the fifth century B.C., and more recently by the French playwright Jean Anouilh (1910–) during World War II, the young woman Antigone adamantly opposes her uncle Creon, the ruler of the state, because he is a political pragmatist making compromises and she is an idealist who believes in higher principles. Once again, any young woman who has ever tried to oppose corruption or complacency in an entrenched political regime will recognize herself in Antigone. She will feel a special affinity for the character, and the performance will mean more to her in personal terms than to someone who has no direct relationship to the situation. Any activity on stage which reminds us of something in our own lives will trigger deep, personal responses which become part of the equation of our theater experience.

VARIETY OF EXPERIENCES IN MODERN THEATER

For the audience, the attitude or frame of mind with which a person approaches a theater event plays an important part in how the person responds to it. If someone goes to the theater expecting very little and the production turns out to be exciting, the pleasure will be greatly increased. At the same time, if a production has been praised too highly by newspapers or friends, a person will be keenly disappointed if the production does not measure up to expectations.

One preconception frequently held by spectators which can lead to confusion or disappointment in the contemporary theater is the

Figure 3-5 The formality of the traditional Broadway theater. All Broadway theaters have the same style and shape, except for one or two altered in recent years. The Majestic Theater, shown here, typifies the elaborate, formal architecture of the picture-frame stage. This type of theater prevailed throughout the United States for most of the late 19th and early 20th centuries. (Photo, Museum of the City of New York, Theatre and Music Collection.)

expectation that all theater experiences are alike. In the past a single experience of theater was often the case. In Greece during the classical period, and in Elizabethan England, the types of plays presented and the way they were produced were reasonably uniform. The same is true for other societies in which theater flourished: Spain in the sixteenth and seventeenth centuries, for instance, or France in the seventeenth century. The cultures of these countries were homogeneous and self-contained, with the result that their theater sprang from a single vision. The tendency to see theater in this way has run strong even in our own time. For example, as recently as the middle of the twentieth century theater for many people in America was synonymous with Broadway.

The Broadway Theater

Broadway, a street in Manhattan, is the name given to the professional theater in New York City. From 1920 until the early 1950s most new plays written in the United States originated there, and productions in other areas were usually copies of Broadway productions. Broadway itself was confined and standardized; it consisted of an area in Manhattan roughly six blocks long and a block and a half wide. The thirty or more theaters located in these few blocks were the same size, seating between 700 and 1,400 people, and had the same style of architecture, as well as the same type of stage: a picture-frame stage.

Productions sent on tour from Broadway to the rest of the country were exact replicas of the original. Scenery was duplicated down to the last detail, and New York actors often played roles they had on Broadway. Nonprofessional theaters copied Broadway as well; acting versions of successful plays were published for colleges, schools, and community theaters, providing precise instructions for the movements of the actors and the placement of scenery on stage.

The Broadway concept gave the theater a yardstick of excellence and produced outstanding work, but in the period just after World War II the realization grew that there were large numbers of people in the United States for whom Broadway was remote—not just geographically, but spiritually.

Diversity of Contemporary Theater

Unlike ancient Greece and other cultures of the past, our society is diverse and complex, with people of widely different ethnic and social backgrounds caught up in crosscurrents of opinion. Since theater reflects society, it is difficult to see how any one form of theater today—however profound—can speak equally to all of us. As if in

Figure 3-6 Street Theater. *Among the many new kinds of theater experience to emerge recently is street theater—performances held in a park or a city street rather than in a theater building. Crowds stand around an improvised stage and the atmosphere is usually less formal than traditional theater. (Photo—Peter Arnold.)*

response to the complexity of the modern world, in the years immediately after World War II people began searching for new forms in theater and for alternative locations in which to present drama.

The New Theater movement, described earlier, was part of this search, but there were other explorations as well: some along traditional lines, some unconventional. As a result of these endeavors we have a multiplicity of theater experiences open to us today. In New York, in addition to Broadway, there is off-Broadway and off-off-Broadway theater, the latter taking place in church basements, lofts, and empty warehouses—almost any place where people can gather together to see a performance. More significantly, the professional theater outside New York City has grown rapidly. Today there are active professional theaters in cities throughout the United States: Los Angeles, San Francisco, Seattle, Minneapolis, St. Louis, Houston, Dallas, Atlanta, Chicago, Cincinnati, New Haven, and Washington, D.C.

There is a strong black theater movement with members of the black community attending plays written and performed by blacks whose subject matter directly relates to the black experience. There are theaters devoted primarily to political satire: a good example being the Second City troupe in Chicago, which improvises skits on political themes suggested by the audience. There are cabaret and dinner theaters in which the atmosphere of a nightclub or restaurant is combined with that of a theater; in an informal setting guests eat and drink before watching a performance.

Today there is theater for almost everyone, in many kinds of places, under widely varying conditions, and for very different purposes. With theater taking so many forms, it is important in approaching the subject not to have a preconceived or too fixed notion of what it is.

SUMMARY

1 Theater—like other arts—is closely linked to the society in which it is produced; it mirrors and reflects the attitudes, philosophy, and basic assumptions of its time.

2 A spectator attending a play written in his or her own day brings to it an awareness of the society's values and beliefs, and this background information forms an important part of the overall experience.

3 A play from the past can be understood better if the spectator is aware of the culture from which it came.

4 For any play which presents difficulties in language, style, or meaning, familiarity with the work itself can add immeasurably to a spectator's understanding and appreciation of the play in performance.

5 Each individual attending a theater event brings to it a personal background of experience which becomes a vital ingredient in his or her response to the event.

6 In the past, theater experiences were relatively uniform within a given society, but in contemporary society they are far more varied as to time, place, content, and purpose.

7 Members of the audience should approach theater with as few preconceptions about its form as possible.

We have observed the part the audience plays in the theater experience and studied how it should approach a theater experience. In the following section we will turn to the other half of the actor-audience equation, as we take up the work of the performer.

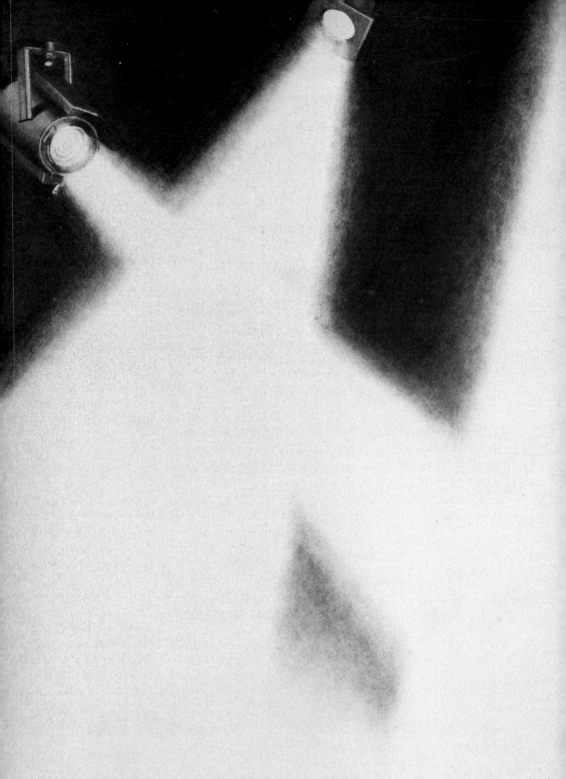

POINT OF VIEW

DRAMATIC STRUCTURE

PART TWO

PERFORMERS AND THE PARTS THEY PLAY

ENVIRONMENT

PERFORMERS   AUDIENCE

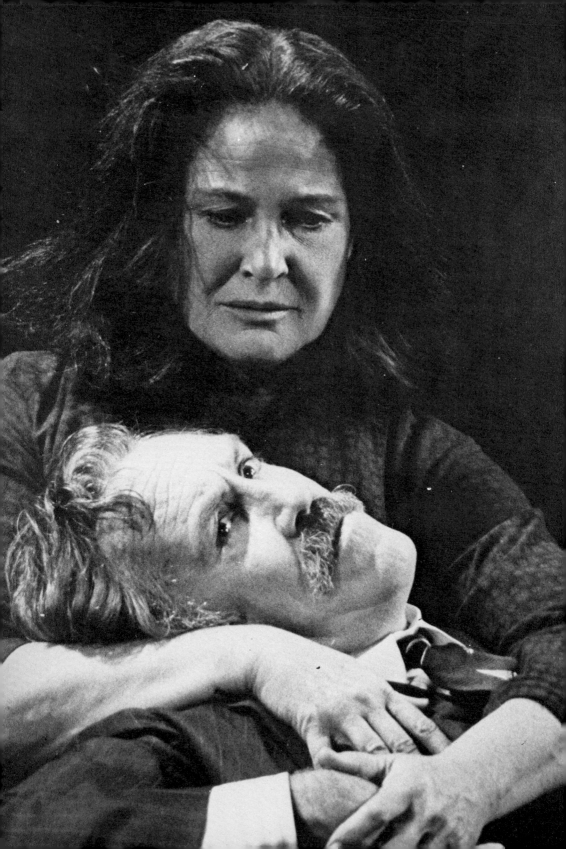

4

ACTING:
OFFSTAGE AND ON

Performers bear a heavy responsibility in making the theater experience meaningful and enjoyable. By their presence they set theater apart from films, television, and the visual arts, but more than that, they serve as the direct, immediate contact which members of the audience have with theater. They embody the heart and soul of theater. The words of the script, the characters created by the dramatist, and the scenery and costumes only come to life when an actor or actress steps on a stage. More than anything else, the theater experience is a response to performers and the characters they portray.

Figure 4-1 Playing a part: in the theater and in life. Colleen Dewhurst plays *a mother figure to the guilt-ridden character played by Jason Robards in Eugene O'Neill's* A Moon for the Misbegotten. *Such roles are not confined to the stage; in everyday life people play parts as well. (Photo—Martha Swope.)*

ACTING IN EVERYDAY LIFE

A good place to begin a study of acting is with the popularly held misconception that acting is only for actors and quite removed from the lives of ordinary people. Many people feel that acting is an exotic occupation in a world of unreality and make-believe. Actors and actresses are regarded alternately as glamorous and superficial, and it is presumed that anyone who steps on stage is an exhibitionist. Before examining stage acting, it might be helpful to consider acting in everyday life, for as many psychologists and sociologists know, there are significant similarities between the two.

Erving Goffman states in his book *The Presentation of Self in Everyday Life,* "Life itself is a dramatically enacted thing. All the world is not, of course, a stage, but the crucial ways in which it isn't are not easy to specify."[1] Goffman is saying, in effect, that acting is so much a part of the real world that it is often difficult to identify it.

Imitation

It may surprise some of us to realize to what degree acting is a part of our lives, beginning almost the day we are born. Acting takes several forms, one of the most common being imitation, where one person mimics or copies another's vocal patterns, gestures, facial expressions, posture, and the like. Children are among the best imitators in the world, and we are frequently amused at a child who imitates a parent or some other grownup: the five-year-old-girl, for instance, who puts on a long dress, makeup, and high heels.

For children, imitation is more than just a matter of show; it is also a way of learning: it is a question, in other words, of education and survival. The child watches a parent open a door or walk up stairs and learns by imitation how to complete the same maneuvers. Speech patterns, too, are a matter of imitation on the part of children.

As we grow older, imitation continues to be a part of our experience: in every class in school, from elementary through college, there is usually one person—a clever mimic—who imitates the teacher or the principal with great humor, and sometimes cruelty. A familiar type of imitation is the attempt to emulate the life-style of a hero: a singer, film actor, or other well-known personality. In the fifties it was Elvis Presley or James Dean; in the sixties, the Beatles; and in the early seventies, Isaac Hayes or Mick Jagger. The imitator adopts the same wardrobe, the same stance, the same physical movements, the same hairstyles as the hero or heroine.

Role Playing

A second type of acting prevalent in our daily lives is role playing, about which much has been written in recent years. Broadly speaking, roles can be divided into social and personal. Social roles are general roles recognized by society: father, mother, child, police officer, store clerk, teacher, student, business executive, physician, and so on. Every culture expects definite types of behavior from people in these roles. For many years in Western culture, for example, the roles of women as secretaries or housewives were considered subordinate to the roles of men. Even when women held similar positions to those of men in business and the professions, they frequently received smaller salaries for the same job. In recent years, women's liberation has challenged the notion of subservient roles for women. So entrenched was the idea, however, that it took an entire movement to call it into question. ("Consciousness raising" was one aspect of the movement making people aware of social attitudes to women.) Before changes could be made in the subordinate roles some women played, everyone had to understand that they *were* roles. The same challenge has been hurled at other roles. Positions of authority, for instance, such as those held by teachers, parents, priests, rabbis, who for generations were treated with respect by society, have been questioned in recent years.

In role playing, anyone occupying a given position is expected to adopt a predetermined attitude: a store clerk, for instance, is expected to take care of customers with patience and courtesy, and not bring individual frustrations to the job. It is important to remember, too, that each of us fills not one but many social roles. A young woman in college, working part time, might have the following roles: student, employee, daughter, sister, and friend, not to mention female, young person, and citizen.

Aside from social roles, we develop personal roles with our family and friends. For example, some of us become braggarts, boasting of our feats and accomplishments, some of them imaginary, and we embellish the truth to appear more impressive than we are. Others become martyrs, constantly sacrificing for others, and letting the world know about it. A third type consists of conspirators, people who pull their friends aside to establish an air of secrecy whenever they talk. Frequently, two people, of the same or a different sex, fall into complementary roles, one dominant and the other submissive, one active and the other passive. In some cases this takes the form of a sadomasochistic relationship.

Recent Studies

We have quoted from Erving Goffman's work on acting in daily life. Studies by others—scholars and popular writers alike—attest to the importance of various kinds of acting in real life. Among recent studies on this subject are *Games People Play*, a successful book of a few years ago concerned with role playing in interpersonal relationships, and *Body Language*, dealing with the gestures and movements we make to signal feelings, emotions, and responses to one another.

In a more scholarly vein, writers have argued that only in our various roles do we have any personality at all. Robert Ezra Park in an important book, *Race and Culture*, noted a relationship between the words "person" and "mask"—the latter being closely associated with theater. He writes:

> It is probably no mere historical accident that the word person, in its first meaning, is a mask. It is rather a recognition of the fact that everyone is always, and everywhere, more or less consciously, playing a role. . . . It is in these roles that we know each other. It is in these roles that we know ourselves.[2]

Role Playing Illustrated in Drama

Interestingly enough, drama contains many illustrations of the kind of acting we do in our everyday lives. A good example is a scene from *Death of a Salesman* by Arthur Miller (1916–), in which Happy, the salesman's son, tries to be a "big shot" in a restaurant where he is scheduled to meet his father and his brother, Biff. Happy's father, the salesman, has just lost his job and is on the verge of losing his sanity as well. Happy should be thinking only of his father, but he cannot resist trying to impress a woman who enters the restaurant. (Biff, Happy's brother, enters in the middle of the scene. As the scene begins, Stanley, the waiter speaks to Happy about the woman.):

Stanley	I think that's for you, Mr. Loman.
Happy	Look at that mouth. Oh, God, and the binoculars.
Stanley	Geez, you got a life, Mr. Loman.
Happy	Wait on her.
Stanley	[*Going to the Girl's table*] Would you like a menu, ma'am?
Girl	I'm expecting someone, but I'd like a—
Happy	Why don't you bring her—excuse me miss, do you mind? I sell champagne, and I'd like you to try my brand. Bring her a champagne, Stanley.
Girl	That's awfully nice of you.

*Figure 4-2 **Playing the "big shot."*** *A scene from the Broadway production of Arthur Miller's* Death of a Salesman *in which Happy tries to impress a woman with how important he is. He overstates his accomplishments just as people in life sometimes do. (Photo—Graphic House, Inc.)*

Happy	Don't mention it. It's all company money. [*He laughs*]
Girl	That's a charming product to be selling, isn't it?
Happy	Oh, gets to be like everything else, selling is selling, y'know.
Girl	I suppose.
Happy	You don't happen to sell, do you?
Girl	No, I don't sell.
Happy	Would you object to a compliment from a stranger? You ought to be on a magazine cover.
Girl	[*Looking at him a little archly*] I have been. [*Stanley comes in with a glass of champagne*]
Happy	What'd I say before, Stanley? You see? She's a cover girl.
Stanley	Oh, I could see, I could see.
Happy	[*To the Girl*] What magazine?
Girl	Oh, a lot of them. [*She takes the drink*] Thank you.

Happy	You know what they say in France, don't you? "Champagne is the drink of the complexion" - Hya, Biff! *[Biff has entered and sits with Happy]*
Biff	Hello, kid. Sorry I'm late.
Happy	I just got here. Uh, Miss - ?
Girl	Forsythe.
Happy	Miss Forsythe, this is my brother.
Biff	Is Dad here?
Happy	His name is Biff. You might've heard of him. Great football player.
Girl	Really? What team?
Happy	Are you familiar with football?
Girl	No, I'm afraid not.
Happy	Biff is quarterback with the New York Giants.
Girl	Well, that is nice, isn't it? *[She drinks]*
Happy	Good health.
Girl	I'm happy to meet you.
Happy	That's my name. Hap. It's really Harold but at West Point they called me Happy.
Girl	*[Now really impressed]* Oh, I see. How do you do? *[She turns her profile]*
Biff	Isn't Dad coming?
Happy	You want her?
Biff	Oh, I could never make that.
Happy	I remember the time that idea would never come into your head. Where's the old confidence, Biff?
Biff	I just saw Oliver—
Happy	Wait a minute. I've got to see that old confidence again. Do you want her? She's on call.
Biff	On, no. *[He turns to look at the Girl]*
Happy	I'm telling you. Watch this. *[Turning to the Girl]* Honey? *[She turns to him]* Are you busy?
Girl	Well, I am . . . but I could make a phone call.
Happy	Do that, will you, honey? And see if you can get a friend. We'll be here for a while. Biff is one of the greatest football players in the country.
Girl	*[Standing up]* Well, I'm certainly happy to meet you.
Happy	Come back soon.
Girl	I'll try.
Happy	Don't try, honey, try hard.[3]

In this scene, Happy is pretending to be something he is not. He is "playing the role" of the successful operator—the man with numerous accomplishments and abilities, which, of course, he does not actually possess. Like imitation and similar activities, this kind of "acting" is encountered frequently in daily life.

ACTING ON STAGE

Earlier we said that acting is fundamental to theater, but clearly it is also fundamental to human behavior. It is part of the fabric of our lives. When we understand this fully, we no longer look on acting as mysterious or frivolous. Also, the better we understand acting in daily life, the better we understand acting for the stage. There are similarities between the two: the processes and techniques which ordinary people employ to convey an image of themselves—words, gestures, "body language," tone of voice, subtle suggestions of intent—are the same tools actors use to create a stage character. Further, an actor or actress plays both a social and a personal role. An actress playing the part of a matronly woman dominating her household adopts the mannerisms and attitudes of a strong mother figure as understood in a given society.

For all the similarities between the two kinds of acting, however, the differences are crucial and reveal a great deal about the nature of stage acting. Some of the differences are obvious. For one thing, actors on stage are always being observed. In real life there may be observers, but their presence is not essential to the event. Bystanders on a street corner where an accident has occurred form a kind of audience, but their presence is incidental and unrelated to the accident itself. On stage, however, the actor is always on display and always in the spotlight.

The stage actor, too, is called on to play roles he or she does not play in life. A scene between a father and his son arguing about money, or between a young husband and wife discussing whether they will have children or not, is one thing when it actually occurs, but something quite different on stage. Generally, the roles we play in life are genuine. A man with children, if he accepts his responsibilities toward his children, does not just play a father, he *is* a father. A woman who writes for a magazine does not just play a magazine writer, she *is* one. In real life, a lawyer knows the law, but on stage, an actor playing the role of a lawyer may not know the difference between jurisprudence and habeas corpus, and probably has never been inside a law school. To play widely divergent parts or parts outside the personal experience of the actor requires a stretch in imagination and ability. A young actress at one time or another might be called on to play parts as dissimilar as the fiery, independent Antigone in Sophocle's play, the vulnerable, lovestruck Juliet in *Romeo and Juliet,* or the neurotic, obsessed heroine in Strindberg's *Miss Julie.*

At times actors even have to *double*, that is, play several parts in one play. In the Greek theater it was customay to have only three principal actors, and they had to play several parts, putting on masks and different costumes to assume the various roles. Bertolt Brecht, a German dramatist, wrote many large-cast plays which call for doubling. His play *The Caucasian Chalk Circle* has forty-seven speaking parts, but it can be produced with no more than twenty-five actors. *The Screens*, a play by the French playwright Jean Genet (1910–) has ninety-eight characters, but as Genet himself has written, "each actor will be required to play five or six roles."

Another important difference between acting on stage and in real life is that a theatrical performance is always conscious. There is an

Figures 4-3a and 4-3b Performers play different parts. In the theater performers must play diverse parts as well as people unlike themselves. Ms. Julie Harris, one of the most versatile actresses in the modern theater, has played historical figures and contemporary ones, young people and old people. On the right she plays the volatile, modern, romantic heroine in A Shot in the Dark, which contrasts sharply with her portrayal of Joan of Arc in The Lark on the left. (Photo on right—UPI; photo on left—The New York Public Library at Lincoln Center, Theatre Collection. Astor, Lenox and Tilden Foundations. Photo by George Karger.)

a

awareness by actors and audience that the presentation has been planned ahead of time. Paradoxically, this consciousness of a performance sometimes leads to a more truthful reenactment than we encounter in real life. The facade or false face people sometimes present can never occur in stage acting because there is no attempt to deceive anyone in that way. As Theodore Shank explains it: "Acting is not pretense. An actor does not pretend to be Macbeth as an imposter pretends to be what he is not; instead he creates an appearance which is intended for perception as an illusion."[4]

Shank's statement that an actor "creates an appearance which is intended for perception as an illusion" underscores a significant difference between acting for the stage and acting in life, namely, that dramatic characters are not real people. In discussing symbol and metaphor earlier, we said that an actress standing on stage in the role of Joan of Arc was a metaphor for Joan. Any stage character—Joan of Arc, Antigone, Oedipus, Hamlet—is a symbol or an image of a person. Stage characters are fictions created by dramatists and actors

b

Figures 4-4a and 4-4b Doubling: playing two parts in one play. *Sometimes performers must play two or more roles in one play. They must have the ability to transform themselves quickly—and completely—from one part to another. In the New York Shakespeare Festival's* Pericles, *actor Lex Monson plays the autocratic King of Antioch in one scene and a lowly fisherman in a later scene. (Photos—George E. Joseph.)*

to represent people. They remind us of people—in many cases they seem to *be* the people—but they are not. They have no corporal reality as you and I do, but rather exist in our imaginations.

Dramatic characters vary enormously: some are fully rounded individuals; others are merely sketched in; some appear only briefly; some are recognizable human types; others are more symbolic, standing for some theme or idea. To interpret these characters and bring them to life on the stage, actors must acquire a number of special skills. Acquiring such skills is a task that those of us who merely play our own roles in life never face.

SUMMARY

1   Acting is not as mysterious or removed as it is sometimes thought to be; all human beings engage in certain forms of acting.

2   Imitation and role playing are excellent examples of acting in everyday life.

3   Acting on the stage differs from acting in everyday life, in the first place, because the stage actor or actress is always being observed by an audience.

4   Acting for the stage involves playing roles for which the performer has no direct experience in life.

5   Stage performers must play roles which are symbolic and which make special demands on their skills and imagination.

Having discussed in general terms the requirements for stage acting, we turn in the next chapter to a more detailed examination of the art of acting.

5

ACTING FOR THE STAGE: TECHNIQUES AND STYLES

Broadly speaking, we can point to two major ways in which performers master their art. The first is to develop the insights and to learn the techniques necessary to make characters truthful and lifelike. The second is to acquire those special skills demanded by theater, including the development of the voice and body through training and discipline.

MAKING DRAMATIC CHARACTERS BELIEVABLE

In order for the audience to believe the characters on stage, performers must be credible and convincing in their roles. Actors and actresses must study human behavior carefully so that they can

Figure 5-1 The challenge of acting for the stage. An actress must learn to develop both outward techniques and inner emotional resources to play convincingly a character like Laura, the crippled heroine of Tennessee Williams's The Glass Menagerie. *(Photo—Copyright © Alix Jeffry.)*

present the outward appearance of the character accurately. They must also understand and transmit the inner feelings of the character they portray. One enemy of credibility on the stage is exaggeration. The stage is a show place: a performer stands on a platform in the spotlight—the focus of the audience's attentions. The natural temptation under these circumstances is to "show off." By this we mean using broad, grandiose gestures, speaking in a loud, rhetorical voice, or otherwise calling attention to oneself. Some exaggeration is necessary in stage acting, and certain roles call for eloquent speech and the grand gesture, particularly in traditional theater, but never to the point of overacting, or doing too much. When the audience focuses on the actor's behavior, the character is forgotten; in its most extreme form overacting becomes laughable.

In view of this it is not surprising that throughout the history of theater we find commentators cautioning performers against excessive, unnatural acting. In Shakespeare, Hamlet's advice to the Players is an example:

> Speak the speech, I pray you, as I pronounced it to you, trippingly on the tongue: but if you mouth it, as many of your players do, I had as lief the town-crier spoke my lines. Nor do not saw the air too much with your hand, thus, but use all gently; for in the very torrent, tempest, and, as I may say, the whirlwind of your passion, you must acquire and beget a temperance that may give it smoothness. O, it offends me to the soul to hear a robustious periwig-pated fellow tear a passion to tatters, to very rags. . . .
> Be not too tame neither, but let your discretion be your tutor: suit the action to the word, the word to the action; with this special observance that you o'erstep not the modesty of nature: for anything so overdone is from the purpose of playing, whose end, both at the first and now, was and is, to hold as 't were, the mirror up to nature. . . .

Shakespeare himself was an actor, and no doubt he had seen performers "saw the air" with their hands and "tear a passion to tatters."

In France in the seventeenth century, Molière (1622–1673) spoke out for honest acting in his short play *The Impromptu of Versailles*. He mocked actors in a rival company who ended each phrase with a flourish in order to get applause. (The term *claptrap*, incidentally, comes from the habit of actors of that period punctuating a speech or an action with some final inflection or gesture, thereby setting a "clap trap" and provoking applause.) Molière criticized actresses who preserved a silly smile even in a tragic scene; he pointed to the ridiculous

Figure 5-2 *Exaggerated acting. Acting is "larger than life," but most theater practitioners warn against overacting. This 19th century interpretation of* Hamlet *would seem unnatural and perhaps even laughable to us today. (Photo—N. Y. Public Library at Lincoln Center, Theatre Collection. Astor, Lenox, and Tilden Foundations. Photo by Peter North.)*

practice of two performers in an intimate scene—two young lovers together or a king alone with his captain—declaiming as if they were addressing the multitudes.

In England, throughout the eighteenth and nineteenth centuries, acting alternated between exaggerated and natural styles. Most actors tended toward the former approach, but every generation or so a performer came along to bring acting back to a more natural, down-to-earth style. A good example was the actor David Garrick (1717–1779), who in the eighteenth century gained fame for his reasonable approach to acting. A commentator described the contrast between Garrick and his predecessors in playing Richard III:

> Instead of declaiming the verse in a thunderous, measured chant, this actor [Garrick] *spoke* it with swift and "natural" changes of tone and emphasis. Instead of patrolling the boards with solemn pomp, treading heavily from pose to traditional pose, he moved quickly and gracefully. Instead of standing on his dignity and marbling his face into a tragedian's mask, his mobile features illustrated Richard's whole range of turbulent feelings. He seemed, indeed, to identify himself with the part. It was all so *real.*[1]

REALISM IN ACTING

Believability in acting is as old as the profession, but it became even more crucial toward the end of the nineteenth century. In the wake of Darwin, Marx, and Freud, traditional values of society were being challenged. There was an inexorable movement away from long-held beliefs and a formal, absolutist approach to life. Following the new ideas, life was to be looked at squarely and uncompromisingly; we would see people as they were, without the embellishments of "art."

In the theater this trend toward *realism* led to an attempt to avoid any kind of formal, exaggerated theater and to depict people and events as "real." The emphasis was not to be on fairy tales or make-believe, on kings or knights in armor in faraway places, but on what was happening to ordinary people in familiar surroundings. In realism, dialogue would not be in the form of poetry or elevated prose, but normal conversation, and the actors would behave like people we know and recognize from life around us. The extreme form of this movement was *naturalism*, whose adherents endeavored to reproduce life in the theater exactly as it appeared in the home or on the street. Events on the stage were to have the same look of authenticity that a documentary film has on the screen.

There had been forerunners of realism in the theater among playwrights, but stage realism really took hold in drama in the late nineteenth century. Three playwrights—Henrik Ibsen (1828–1906) of Norway, August Strindberg (1848–1912) of Sweden, and Anton Chekhov (1860–1904) of Russia—each produced a series of strongly realistic plays. Together they set the pattern for the next century in this type of theater. Their dramas presented characters with life histories, with motives and anxieties, which audiences could immediately identify as truthful from their own experiences or observations. Because audiences could verify the behavior and the appearance of characters, performers were required to be more truthful and more lifelike than ever before. Not only the spirit of the part, but all the details had to conform to what people saw of life on their own. This placed great demands on actors and actresses to avoid any hint of fakery or superficiality.

Stanislavski

The man most responsible for developing a technique for realistic acting was Constantin Stanislavski (1863–1938). A cofounder of the Moscow Art Theater in Russia and director of Chekhov's most important plays, Stanislavski was an actor as well as a director. During

Figure 5-3 **Realistic acting.** *In contrast to some of the classics, which invite full-blown acting, many modern plays require more natural and believable performances—closer to what we see in everyday life. A good example is the scene at a kitchen table from Clifford Odets'* Awake and Sing. *(Photo—N. Y. Public Library at Lincoln Center, Theatre Collection. Astor, Lenox and Tilden Foundations. Photo by Vandamm.)*

his lifetime he evolved a system which has been the model, or starting point, for virtually every approach to realistic acting since.

At first glance, it would seem to be the easiest thing in the world for an actor to stand on stage and be himself: to wear his own clothes and to speak normally. All we have to remember, however, is what it is like to stand up in front of a classroom to make a statement or give a report. Even if we only have to "say a few words," our mouth goes dry, our legs tremble, and the most difficult task in the world is to "be natural." You can multiply this feeling—"stage fright" it is sometimes called—many times over for an actress who stands on stage, bright lights in her eyes, trying to remember lines and movements, knowing that hundreds of eyes are focused on her. Fine actors and actresses learn to deal with the feeling—and even turn it to advantage—but many will admit that they never completely lose the terror any human being feels when being observed and judged by others.

Stanislavski, keenly aware of this problem, wrote:

All of our acts, even the simplest, which are so familiar to us in everyday life, become strained when we appear behind the footlights before a public of a thousand people. That is why it is necessary to correct ourselves and learn again how to walk, sit, or lie down. It is essential to re-educate ourselves to look and see, on the stage, to listen and to hear.[2]

Stanislavski went about that "re-education" to get rid of mechanical, external acting and to put in its place naturalness and truth. In his words: "The actor must first of all believe in everything that takes place onstage, and most of all, he must believe what he himself is doing. And one can only believe in the truth."[3]

To give substance to his ideas, Stanislavski studied how people acted in everyday life and how they communicated feelings and emotions, and then he found ways to accomplish the same things on stage. He developed a series of exercises and techniques for the actor which had the following broad aims:

1 To make the outward activities of the performer—the gestures, the voice, the rhythm of movements—natural and convincing.

2 To have the actor or actress convey the inner truth of a part. Even if all the visible manifestations of a character are mastered, a performance will appear superficial and mechanical without a deep sense of conviction and belief.

3 To make the life of the character on stage not only dynamic but continuous. Some actors tend to emphasize only the high points of their part; in between, the life of the character stops. In real life people do not stop living, however.

Importance of Specifics in Acting

One of Stanislavski's techniques was an emphasis on concrete details. A performer should never try to act "in general," that is, try to convey the idea of a feeling such as fear or love in some vague, amorphous way. In life, Stanislavski said, we express emotions in terms of specifics: an anxious woman twists a handkerchief, an angry young boy throws a rock at a trash can, a nervous businessman jangles his keys. Actors and actresses must find the same concrete activities. Stanislavski points out how Shakespeare has Lady Macbeth in her sleepwalking scene—at the height of her guilt and emotional upheaval—try to rub blood off her hands.

Many times playwrights provide actors with such specifics: King Lear wants his coat unbuttoned in his final moments; Laura in *The Glass Menagerie* by Tennessee Williams (1912–) has her glass animals; the mute girl, Catherine, in Bertolt Brecht's *Mother Courage* beats a drum to warn a nearby town of imminent danger.

The English playwright Harold Pinter (1930–) has a scene in *The Homecoming* which makes effective use of a glass of water. In the scene, Ruth and her husband, both English, have just come back from America to visit his family. Shortly after they arrive, in the middle of the night, Ruth is alone in the living room when Lennie, one of her husband's brothers, enters. Ruth and Lennie, both equally mysterious, confront one another, each battling for dominance over the other. There is a strong undertone of violence and sexuality in the scene. Lennie, having attempted to intimidate Ruth with a barrage of words, tries to take a glass of water from her and the struggle continues:

Lenny And now perhaps I'll relieve you of your glass.
  Ruth I haven't quite finished.
Lenny You've consumed quite enough, in my opinion.
  Ruth No, I haven't.
Lenny Quite sufficient, in my opinion.
  Ruth Not in mine, Leonard.
                    [*Pause*]
Lenny Don't call me that, please.
  Ruth Why not?
Lenny That's the name my mother gave me.
                    [*Pause*]
       Just give me the glass.
  Ruth No.
                    [*Pause*]
Lenny I'll take it, then.
  Ruth If you take the glass . . . I'll take you.
                    [*Pause*]
Lenny How about me taking the glass without you taking me?
  Ruth Why don't I just take you?
                    [*Pause*]
Lenny You're joking.
                    [*Pause*]
       You're in love, anyway, with another man. You've had a secret liaison with another man. His family didn't even know. Then you come here without a word of warning and start to make trouble.
       [*She picks up the glass and lifts it toward him.*]
  Ruth Have a sip. Go on. Have a sip from my glass.
                    [*He is still.*]
       Sit on my lap. Take a long cool sip.
       [*She pats her lap. Pause.*]
       [*She stands, moves to him with the glass.*]

Figure 5-4 Techniques of acting. *In keeping with Stanislavski's notion that performers should concentrate on specific objects, playwright Harold Pinter has given the performers in* The Homecoming *a glass of water as a symbol of the power struggle between Ruth and Lennie. (Photo—N. Y. Public Library at Lincoln Center, Theatre Collection. Astor, Lenox and Tilden Foundations.)*

	Put your head back and open your mouth.
Lenny	Take that glass away from me.
Ruth	Lie on the floor. Go on. I'll pour it down your throat.
Lenny	What are you doing, making me some kind of proposal?

[*She laughs shortly, drains the glass.*]

Ruth Oh, I was thirsty.

[*She smiles at him, puts the glass down, goes into the hall and up the stairs.*]

[*He follows into the hall and shouts up the stairs.*]

Lenny What was that supposed to be? Some kind of proposal?

When a script does not indicate such tangible actions, the actor or actress must find them. Michael Chekhov, nephew of the playwright and a follower of Stanislavski, coined the term "psychological gesture" for a typical, characteristic movement or activity which would sum up a character's motives and preoccupations. A man who is confused, or has trouble "seeing clearly," for example, might continually try to clean his glasses.

Along with the use of concrete objects and gestures, Stanislavski urged actors to concentrate their attention on people or items in their immediate area, a "circle of attention" he called it. When the actor has established a small circle of attention, he can then enlarge his concentration outward from this point. In this way he will stop worrying about the audience and lose his self-consciousness.

Inner Truth

To achieve a sense of inner truth, Stanislavski had several ideas, one being the "magic if." "If" is a word which can transform our thoughts. Through it we can imagine ourselves in virtually any situation. "If I suddenly became rich. . . ." "If I were in Europe. . . ." "If I had great talent. . . ." "If that person who insulted me comes near me again. . . ." "If" is a powerful lever of the mind which can lift us out of ourselves and give us a sense of absolute certainty about imaginary circumstances. In this sense, it is similar to the reality of dreams and fantasies discussed earlier. To take an example: if we spend a night alone in a strange room—in a cabin in the woods or a house far from home—and we hear a noise in the night, such as a floorboard creaking or a door opening, we become frightened, particularly if there have been stories of burglaries or break-ins in the area. If the noise comes again, our anxiety increases. We lie absolutely still, our breath shortens and our heartbeat quickens. Finally, after a time, if nothing has happened, we find the courage to get out of bed and turn on a light. It turns out to be nothing—a rusty hinge on a door, or a tree limb brushing the side of the house—but before we discovered the truth, the power of the "magic if" had worked its magic: we were convinced we were in great danger.

Stanislavski urges actors to use this same power of fantasy and imagination as a tool to induce reality on the stage. A performer can never actually *be* a dramatic character, but the performer can use "if." "If *I* were a frightened, crippled young woman, how would *I* feel about meeting a young man I once admired?" This is the question an actress playing Laura in *The Glass Menagerie* can ask herself. Through the power of imagination she can put herself in Laura's place.

Emotional Recall

Another means Stanislavski suggests to achieve believability is the actor's recollection of a past moment in his or her own life similar to the one in the play: perhaps a scene of farewell, such as Emily saying goodbye to her family in Thornton Wilder's *Our Town*. Though dead, Emily is allowed to go back to earth for one day, after which she must leave forever. The actress playing Emily might recall a time in her own life when she had to say goodbye and was reluctant to do so, the first time she left home or the time she said goodbye to a young man she loved. Again, Stanislavski emphasizes details; the important thing for the actress to remember is where she was, what she wore, who she was with—not how she felt. From these concrete facts and images the feeling will follow. In Stanislavski's words:

> On the stage there cannot be, under any circumstances, action which is directed immediately at the arousing of a feeling for its own sake. . . . All such feelings are the result of something that has gone on before. Of the thing that goes before, you should think as hard as you can. As for the result, it will produce itself.[5]

Through Line of a Role

Finally, in order to develop continuity in a part, the actor or actress should find the *superobjective* of the character. What is it, above all else, that the character wants from life? What is the character's driving force? If a goal can be established toward which the character strives, it will give the performer a core or *through line* which can be grasped, as a skier on a ski lift grabs a towline and is carried to the top.

Harold Clurman (1901–), a well-known critic and director, refers to the through line as the *spine*, and when directing a play, he assigns a spine or superobjective to characters as a group and to each character individually. For Chekhov's *Uncle Vanya*, Clurman says that all the characters are dissatisfied with their lives, and grumble a great deal; their spine therefore, is "to make life better, find a way to be happy."[6] The title character, Vanya, hopes to escape from his dull, frustrating existence, but he fails. Other characters follow equally futile courses in pursuit of happiness—their spine or superobjective in the play.

Since Stanislavski's time, some actors and directors, like Harold Clurman, have adapted his system while others have developed their own, but all have been influenced by his approach. Whatever technique an actor employs, it should be obvious that a great deal of work goes into the creation of a realistic character on stage. Externally, the actor or actress must observe and reproduce in minute detail the way people behave; internally he or she must develop an identity with the character's deepest feelings and emotions.

ACTING: SPECIAL DEMANDS OF THE STAGE

If one important task of a performer is to achieve credibility and truthfulness, a second major task is to meet the special demands of the stage and of individual roles.

Vocal Projection

One of the primary requirements for an actor or actress is to be seen and heard by the audience. In a modern, realistic play this requirement is made more difficult by the necessity of maintaining believability. The words of a man and a woman in an intimate love scene in real life would be barely audible even to people a few feet away. In the theater, however, every word must be heard by the entire audience; and to be heard throughout a theater seating a thousand people, a performer must *project*, that is, throw the voice into the audience so that it penetrates to the uttermost reaches of the theater. The performers must strike a balance, therefore, between credibility—in the case of a love scene this means confidential, quiet tones—and the necessity of projection. In order to develop projection, and to achieve the kind of balance just described, the performer must train and rehearse extensively.

In traditional theater—the theater from the fifth century B.C. in Greece to the middle of the nineteenth century—vocal demands on actors and actresses were even greater. The language of the plays was most often poetry, and this required intensive training in order for the performer to speak it distinctly. There were added problems of projection, too. Greek amphitheaters, while marvels of acoustics, seated 15,000 spectators in the open air, and to throw the voice to every corner of the theater without strain was no small task.

In the Elizabethan period in England, Christopher Marlowe, a contemporary of Shakespeare's, wrote superb blank verse which makes severe demands on a performer's vocal abilities. An example is a speech in Marlowe's *Doctor Faustus*, addressed by Faustus to Helen of Troy, who has been called back from the dead to be with Faustus. In the speech Faustus says to Helen:

> O' thou art fairer than the evening's air
> Clad in the beauty of a thousand stars;
> Brighter art thou than flaming Jupiter
> When he appear'd to hapless Semele;
> More lovely than the monarch of the sky
> In wanton Arethusa's azured arms;
> And none but thou shalt be my paramour!

These seven lines of verse are part of a single sentence, and when spoken properly, should be delivered, if not in one breath, at least at one time, carrying the meaning from one line to the next. How many of us could manage that? A fine classical actor can speak the entire section at one time, giving it the necessary resonance and inflection as well. Beyond that, he can stand on the stage for two or three hours delivering such lines.

With the use of microphones and sound amplification so widespread today, we have increasingly lost our appreciation of the power of the spoken word. In the past, public speakers from Cicero to Abraham Lincoln stirred men and women with their oratory. Throughout its history, the stage has provided a natural platform for stirring speeches. Beginning with the Greeks, and continuing through the Elizabethans, the French and Spanish theaters of the seventeenth century, and other European theaters at the close of the nineteenth century, playwrights wrote magnificent lines, lines which actors, having honed their vocal skills to a fine point, delivered with zest. Any performer today who intends to act in a revival of a traditional play must learn to speak and project stage verse, which requires a vocal power and breath control usually found only in opera singers.

Physical Movement on Stage

Performers are seen as well as heard. In the eighteenth and nineteenth centuries, when every stage was a proscenium or picture-frame stage, the actors were like figures in a tableau or picture. Actors in a love scene, or any scene, were very much on display. For that reason it became a rule that a performer must never turn his or her back to the audience but always face the front, even when speaking to another character. This formal approach has long since been abandoned, but there is still a necessity for a performer's physical movements to be clearly visible. An actor who remains permanently turned away from a large part of the audience, for instance, is derelict in his obligations as a performer. Because dramatic characters are symbols, every movement counts, and the performer's gestures and facial expressions must be communicated to the audience clearly and instantaneously.

As with the voice, traditional theater makes strong demands on the performer's body. In Shakespeare, for instance, actors are always running up and down steps or ramps, having to play prolonged death scenes, or meet other characters in sword fights. Anyone who has seen a first-rate sword fight on stage knows how difficult and impressive it can be. A duel, in which the combatants strike quickly at one another—clashing swords frequently without hitting each other—resembles a ballet in its precision and grace.

The equivalent activity in a modern play would be a headlong fall down a flight of stairs. Such a fall occurred in the 1972 Broadway play *That Championship Season*. The story concerns a basketball team at a reunion, trying to relive past glory with their coach, twenty years after

Figure 5-5 Physical demands of the stage. *Performers frequently must perform difficult physical feats which require training, discipline, and expert timing. The dueling scene between Cyrano and his opponent in this production of* Cyrano de Bergerac *by the American Conservatory Theater of San Francisco illustrates the point. (Photo—William Ganslen.)*

winning a championship. One actor, playing an alcoholic, was required to tumble head over heels down a full flight of stairs at every performance. He had to master the art of appearing to lose all control and yet never injure himself.

Avant-garde or experimental plays frequently make extreme demands on performers too. Earlier we mentioned a play by Eugene Ionesco called *Rhinoceros*. One of the two chief characters turns into a rhinoceros during the course of the play. The actor does not actually put on an outfit of horns and leathery hide, but must physically transform himself by means of his posture, voice, and general demeanor. Critic Walter Kerr described how actor Zero Mostel did this in the 1961 Broadway production:

Figure 5-6 A man becomes a rhinoceros. *Without benefit of makeup or costume, actor Zero Mostel transforms himself into an image of a rhinoceros in the play by Ionesco. Mostel uses his voice, his facial expressions and his body to create the change. Such effects require skill and practice. (Photo—Friedman-Abeles.)*

Now the rhinoceros beneath the skin begins to bulge a little at the eyes. The Kaiser Wilhelm mustache that has earlier adorned the supposed Mr. Mostel loses its spiky endpoints, droops, disintegrates into a tangle that makes it second cousin to a walrus. The voice starts to change. "I hate people—and I'll r-r-un them down!" comes out of a larynx that has stiffened, gone hollow as a 1915 gramophone record, and is ready to produce a trumpet-sound that would empty all of Africa. The shoulders lift, the head juts forward, one foot begins to beat the earth with such native majesty that dust—real dust—begins to rise like the afterveil that seems to accompany a safari. The transformation is on, the secret is out, evolution has reversed itself before your horrified, but nevertheless delighted, eyes.[7]

In another avant-garde play, Samuel Beckett's *Happy Days*, an actress is buried on stage in a mound of earth up to her waist in the first act, and her neck in the second. She must carry on her performance through the entire play while virtually immobile.

There are other cases requiring special discipline or training. Obviously musical theater requires talent in singing and dancing. Coordination is important too: the members of a musical chorus must sing, dance, or move together, frequently in unison. Pantomime provides another demanding category of performance: without words or props an actor or actress must indicate everything by physical suggestion, lifting an imaginary box or walking against an imaginary wind in a convincing fashion.

A similar stylization and symbolism characterizes the acting of the classical theaters of China and Japan. To achieve the absolute control, the concentration, and the mastery of the body and nerves necessary to carry out the movements, the performers of the various classical Oriental theaters train for years under the supervision of master teachers. Every movement of the performers is prescribed and

Figure 5-7 **Special problems in acting.** *Samuel Beckett's play* Happy Days *calls for the actress to play the first act buried in a mound up to her waist, and the second buried up to her neck, as shown here by actress Ruth White. Such limitations put severe pressure on the performer to convey all emotion, etc., by means of voice and facial expressions alone. (Photo—Copyright © Alix Jeffry.)*

Figure 5-8 The rigors of musicals or the New Theater. *Singers and dancers in musicals, as well as performers in much of New Theater, must train their bodies like athletes and their voices like concert singers to carry out their tasks on the stage. Here we see performers in a routine from the Broadway muscial* Company. *(Photo—Friedman-Abeles.)*

carefully controlled, combining elements of formal ballet, pantomime, and sign language. Each gesture tells a story and means something quite specific—a true symbolism of physical movement. Between the fourth and ninth centuries, Sanskrit plays became the classical plays of India. For these Sanskrit dramas, the gestures of the actors were conventionalized and rigidly adhered to. These included thirteen movements of the head, thirty-six of the eyes, seven of the eyebrows, six of the nose, five of the chest, twenty-four of the hands, thirty-two of the feet, and so forth.

THE NEW THEATER: ACTING REQUIREMENTS

Like the traditional theater of Europe and the classical Oriental theater, the modern theater movement known as the New Theater puts great stress on the development of the performer's body and voice, but for a somewhat different purpose. The New Theater stresses improvisation, ritual, and the use of the total person (mind, body, and emotions together). The voice becomes not only a means of communicating speech but emitting sounds as well. As an example, rather than a character saying "I am anguished" or expressing this feeling is a poetic phrase such as "how all occasions do inform against me," actors produce unintelligible but unmistakable cries from the soul: a "primal scream" on the stage. As with the voice, the body too becomes an instrument—like that of a dancer or acrobat—to perform feats or create aesthetic movement.

As a pioneer in the field, Jerzy Grotowski developed a training program for his actors, the purpose being not merely to condition the voice and the body, but chiefly to "discover the resistances and obstacles which hinder him in his creative task."[8] Of the voice Grotowski says, "special attention should be paid to the carrying power of the voice so the spectator not only hears the voice of the actor perfectly, but is also penetrated by it as if it were stereophonic." Further he says, "the actor must exploit his voice in order to produce sounds and intonations that the spectator is incapable of reproducing or imitating."[9] Grotowski's training requires a series of rigorous vocal exercises, some more elaborate than any dreamed of by opera singers. As for physical exercises, Grotowski has one for every part of the body in every conceivable position: headstands, handstands, shoulder stands, back bends.

Grotowski never works in isolation, however. Every exercise is associated with concepts or impressions—an animal, perhaps, or a sensation—and is designed to lead toward a further integration of the personality and development of the actor's instrument.

The demands made on performers by the New Theater is only the most recent example of the rigorous, intensive training which acting generally requires. In every age, performers must develop the sensitivity and insight to penetrate the secrets of the human soul, and at the same time, train their voices and bodies to express their feelings in such a way that they are readily apparent to the audience.

ACTOR-AUDIENCE CONTACT

Earlier we spoke of the projection of the performer's voice into the audience. In fact, the performer must project his or her total personality, because as we have said, it is the contact between actor and audience which forms the basic encounter of theater. In many types of theater the actors appear to perform as if the audience were not there; and we might ask, what of the actor-audience relationship in this situation? From the audience standpoint, it is very intense because audience members focus exclusively on the stage. The involvement is so intense that a cough or whisper, unnoticed in an ordinary room or on the street, is magnified a thousandfold. But the actors are conscious of the relationship too. They may concentrate on an object on stage or one another, as Stanislavski advised, but a part of them continually senses the audience.

In short, though actors are concentrating on one another, there is still great variation in the intensity and honesty with which they perform. If they are absorbed in a life-and-death struggle on stage, the audience will be absorbed too, like bystanders at a street corner fight. If the actors are listless and uninvolved with the play or each other, the audience will be turned off as well.

Judging Performers

As observers, we study the techniques and problems of acting so that we will be able to understand and judge the performances we see. If a performer is unconvincing in a part, we know that he or she has not mastered a technique leading to truthful acting, such as suggested by Stanislavski. We become watchful for exaggeration, overacting, and bombast. We recognize that if a performer moves awkwardly or cannot be heard clearly, the performer has not been properly trained in body movement or vocal projection. We learn, too, to notice how well performers play together: whether they listen to each other and respond properly.

If we are aware of these acting techniques, we will understand what makes one performance exciting and convincing, and another superficial and dull. In both cases, this awareness enhances our theater experience.

SUMMARY

1 Performers must make the characters they portray believable and convincing. One problem facing the performer is to avoid exaggerated gestures or speech. The tendency to "show off" destroys credibility.

2 Beginning with the end of the nineteenth century and continuing to the present, many plays have been written in a very realistic, lifelike manner. The characters in these plays resemble ordinary people in their dialogue, behavior, etc. The interpretation of the characters in these plays calls for truthful acting of a high order.

3 A Russian director, Constantin Stanislavski, developed a "system" or "method" of acting to enable performers to be truthful. His suggestions included **(a)** dealing with specific objects and feelings—a handkerchief, a glass of water, etc., **(b)** using the power of fantasy or imagination—the "magic if"—to achieve a sense of inner truth in a role, **(c)** developing a spine or through line which runs through a role from the beginning to the end of a play.

4 The stage makes demands aside from credibility in a role. Among these are **(a)** the ability to project the voice, even in a quiet, intimate scene, **(b)** the development of the voice in order to be able to speak verse and other declamatory speech, **(c)** the training of the body to fight duels, to fall down stairs, to manage physical transformations (as in the play *Rhinoceros*).

5 The New Theater makes additional demands on the performer in terms of voice and body training. The voice is sometimes used to emit odd sounds, screams, grunts, and the like. The body must perform feats of acrobatics and gymnastics.

For the audience, the most immediate and powerful impact of a theater experience is the enounter with live performers: watching actors and actresses impersonate other human beings, admiring their talent and skill, and above all, feeling the strong link, the sense of communication which develops between performers and spectators. There is a difference in the characters whom performers portray, however. Some are intended to appear as fully rounded human beings, while others are more symbolic. Also, characters in plays are not actually people; they are representatives of people. How characters function, together with an examination of various types of characters, will be the subject of the following chapter.

6

DRAMATIC CHARACTERS

Theater is art, not life, and as such it mirrors or reflects life. Key aspects of life are carefully selected by the dramatist to be emphasized, while other features are minimized or eliminated. In this fashion, dramatic characters are created. By being highly selective and incisive, the dramatist can show us in two hours the entire history of a person whom it could take us a lifetime to know in real life. In Tennessee Williams's *A Streetcar Named Desire*, for example, we come to know the leading character, Blanche DuBois, in all her emotional complexity better than we know people we see every day. The dramatist reveals to us not only Blanche's biography but her soul, and we become intimately acquainted with the inner workings of her mind.

Figure 6-1 Cleopatra: an exceptional character. The heros and heroines of traditional theater stand apart from ordinary people: in position and in personality. Shakespeare's Cleopatra—portrayed here by Janet Suzman in the Royal Shakespeare Company's production of Antony and Cleopatra—*is a complex woman. She is beautiful, vain, selfish, and desirous of immortality, all at the same time. (Photo—Max Waldman.)*

Also, the playwright has wide latitude in what to emphasize and how to present the character. A stage character can be presented in different ways: (1) drawn with a few quick strokes, as a cartoonist sketches a political figure, (2) given the surface detail and reality of a photograph, or (3) fleshed out with the more interpretive and fully rounded quality of an oil portrait. Whatever the form, however, to achieve maximum impact as an image or symbol, a dramatic character must stand out in some way. Traditionally several major types of characters have proved effective in the theater.

EXTRAORDINARY CHARACTERS

Traditional Theater

The heroes and heroines of most important dramatic works of the past are extraordinary in some way. They stand apart from ordinary people and are "larger than life." Historically, major characters have been kings, queens, bishops, members of the nobility, or other figures clearly marked as holding a special place in society. Such characters are extraordinary in the first place by virtue of their position. A queen, for instance, is accorded respect because of her authority, power, and grandeur. In the same way we respect a Supreme Court justice because of the high place he occupies.

Dramatists go one step further, however, in depicting extraordinary characters. Not only do these characters fill prestigious roles, they generally represent men and women at their worst or best, at some extreme of human behavior. Lady Macbeth is not only a noblewoman, she is one of the most ambitious women ever depicted on the stage. In virtually every instance with extraordinary characters we see men and women at the breaking point, at the outer limits of human capabilities and endurance. Antigone and Saint Joan, for example, are the epitome of the independent, courageous female, willing to stand up to male authority and suffer whatever consequences they are forced to endure. Prometheus, Oedipus, and the biblical figure Abraham are men willing to face the worst the gods can throw at them and meet it with strength and dignity. The Cid, hero of the play by Pierre Corneille (1606–1684), represents the warrior at his most noble and chivalrous. Thomas à Beckett, Archbishop of Canterbury under King Henry II of England—the subject of *Beckett* by Jean Anouilh, and *Murder in the Cathedral* by T. S. Eliot (1885–1965)—was martyred for his defiance of a king.

Among those qualifying as men and women at their worst are Medea, who murdered her own children, and the brothers of the heroine of *The Duchess of Malfi* by John Webster 91575–1638), who forbade their sister to get married so they could get her estate. When the brothers discovered she had married, they had her and her children imprisoned, cruelly tortured, and eventually strangled.

Many traditional characters fall between the poles of extreme virtue and vice, but they nevertheless possess exceptional, sometimes strongly contradictory, qualities. Faustus, treated by Christopher Marlowe in *Doctor Faustus* and by Johann Wolfgang Goethe (1749–1832) in *Faust*, was a great scholar, but so bored with his existence and so ambitious that he made a compact with the Devil forfeiting his life in return for unlimited power. Cleopatra, an exceedingly vain, selfish woman, had at the same time, "immortal longings." Electra's strong sense of family honor led her on the one hand to stand up for her murdered father, but on the other to arrange the murder of her own mother and stepfather. Queen Elizabeth I of England and Mary Queen of Scots, rivals in real life, have made admirable dramatic characters, being women of both strong virtues and telling weaknesses. In short, the heroes and heroines of traditional theater have been exceptional, not only by virtue of their station in life, but because they possess those traits common to us all—ambition, generosity, malevolence, fear, and achievement—in such great abundance.

Modern Theater

Kings and queens have continued to be treated in drama in the modern period, but beginning in the eighteenth century, ordinary people took over from royalty and nobility as the heroes and heroines of drama—a reflection of what was occurring in real life. The chief figures in drama, therefore, frequently became people without the symbolic significance of a titled or regal person. Even so, the leading figures of drama continued in many cases to be exceptional men and women at their best and worst.

The heroine of August Strindberg's *Miss Julie* is a neurotic, obsessive woman at the end of her rope. So, too, in her own way is Blanche DuBois, whom we referred to a moment ago. In *Mother Courage* by Bertolt Brecht we see the portrait of a woman who will sacrifice almost anything to survive; she even loses a son by haggling over the price of his release. *Emperor Jones*, by Eugene O'Neill (1888–1953), shows the downfall of a powerful black man who has made himself the ruler of a Caribbean island.

Among modern characters who stand for people at their worst are Joe Keller of Arthur Miller's *All My Sons* and Regina of *The Little Foxes* by Lilliam Hellman (1905–). Keller, in his insatiable desire for profit, manufactures defective airplane parts in World War II, leading

Figure 6-2 Mother Courage: a modern dramatic character. The leading figures in contemporary drama are usually not kings or queens but are frequently exceptional in another way. Brecht's Mother Courage—*played here by Viveca Lindfors—will go to any lengths to survive, even to the extent of bargaining for the life of her son. (The Arena Stage, Washington, D.C. Photo—George de Vincent.)*

to the death of several pilots. Regina, a cunning, avaricious woman, stands by while her dying husband has a heart attack, refusing to get the medicine which can save his life.

PROTOTYPICAL CHARACTERS

When ordinary characters took over from kings and queens, a new type of leading character emerged alongside the extraordinary character, a character who might be called *prototypical.* The prototypical character is not a stereotype but a fully rounded, three-dimensional character. Rather than being exceptional as the worst, the best, or some other extreme, these characters are exceptional in the way they *embody* the characteristics of an entire group: not as a caricature, but as a complete picture of a person.

A good example of a prototypical character from modern drama is Nora Helmer, the heroine of Henrik Ibsen's *A Doll's House.* A spoiled, flighty woman, she secretly forged a signature to get money for her husband who was dying and needed medical attention. All her life, first by her father, then by her husband, she had been treated like a doll, or plaything, not as a mature, responsible woman. In the last act of the play Nora rebels against this attitude; she makes a declaration of independence to her husband, slams the door on him, and walks out. It has been said that Nora's slamming of the door noted the beginning not only of modern drama, but of the emancipation of modern women. Certainly, Nora's defiance—her claim to be treated as an equal—has made her a prototype of all housewives who refuse to be regarded as house pets. She is an ordinary wife and mother in one sense, far from an Antigone or a Lady Macbeth, but she is exceptional in the way she sums up an entire group of women. *A Doll's House* was written in 1879, but today, almost a hundred years later, Nora is still a symbol of modern woman. The play is revived year after year, and Nora's message does not lose its relevance.

In Edward Albee's (1928–) *Who's Afraid of Virginia Woolf?*, the main characters are a husband and a wife, quite commonplace in a way. He is a somewhat ineffectual college professor; she, the college president's daughter. They argue and fight almost to the point of exhaustion. Another unhappily married couple? Yes. But again, they are quintessential; that is, they contain the essence of a certain type of married couple. To Albee, they represent an American type: a bitter, alienated couple, bored with themselves and each other. And to underline his point, he names them Martha and George, giving them the same first names as Martha and George Washington—America's "first couple."

Figure 6-3 Martha and George: prototypical characters. *Though not exceptional in other ways, the wife and husband in Edward Albee's* Who's Afraid of Virginia Woolf? *are typical of a married couple always at swords' points with each other. They embody to the full the characteristics of such people. (The Arena Stage, Washington, D.C. Photo—George de Vincent.)*

Another example is Jimmy Porter, the main character in *Look Back in Anger*, by John Osborne (1929–). Written in England in 1956, the play deals with a generation of working-class Englishmen, disillusioned with the "Establishment" and their prospects for the future in the period following the Second World War. On the one hand, Jimmy is a commonplace, jobless man, like thousands of other Englishmen of his day; at the same time he sums up his generation, which came to be known collectively as the "angry young men." Similarly, Willy Loman, the chief character in Arthur Miller's *Death of a Salesman*, sums up all salesmen in America, traveling in their sales territories on a "smile and a shoeshine." He has bought the false dream that by putting up a good front and being "well liked," he will be a great success and achieve material wealth.

Nora Helmer, Martha and George, Jimmy Proter, and Willy Loman: all are examples of prototypical characters who stand apart from the crowd, not by standing above it, but by summing up in their personalities the essence of a certain type of person.

STOCK CHARACTERS

Many characters in drama are not as complete as the extraordinary or prototypical characters. Rather, they symbolize in bold relief some particular type of person or some outstanding characteristic of human behavior to the exclusion of virtually everything else. They appear particularly in comedy and melodrama, though they can be found in almost all kinds of drama.

Among the stock characters, some of the most famous examples are those in *commedia dell'arte*, a form of popular comedy which flourished in Italy during the sixteenth and seventeenth centuries. In *commedia dell'arte*, there were no scripts, but rather scenarios which gave an outline of the story. The actors improvised or invented words and comic actions to fill out the play. The stock characters of *commedia* were either straight or exaggerated, and were divided into servants and members of the ruling class. In every case, however, one particular feature or trait was stressed. Wherever they appeared, these characters had the same propensities and wore the same costumes. The bragging soldier, called the *Capitano*, always boasted of his courage in a series of fictitious military victories. (A forebear of this character had appeared in Roman comedy centuries before.) The young lovers were fixtures as well. Older characters included *Pantalone*, an elderly merchant who spoke in clichés and chased young girls, and a pompous lawyer called *Dottore*, who spoke in Latin phrases and attempted to impress others with his learning. Among servants, *Harlequin* was the most popular; displaying both cunning and stupidity, he was at the heart of every plot complication. These are but a few of a full range of characters, each with his or her own peculiarities. As for other examples of stock characters in drama, we are all familiar with such figures as the lovely young heroine "pure as the driven snow," and the villain, lurking in the shadows, twirling his moustache.

Characters with a Dominant Trait

Closely related to stock characters are characters with a single trait or "humour." A theory that the body was governed by four humours, which must be kept in balance for a person to be healthy, was widely held during the Renaissance. In the sixteenth century it was extended to include psychological traits, and the playwright Ben Jonson (1572–1637) followed this notion extensively in his plays. In *Every Man in His Humour* and *Every Man out of His Humour*, for instance, he portrayed characters in whom one humour came to dominate all others, making for an unbalanced, often comic, personality. Jonson often named his characters for their single trait or humour. In *The Alchemist* he includes Subtle, Face, Dol Common, Dapper, Surly, Tribulation, Wholesome, and Dame Pliant.

During the English Restoration and after, playwrights continued to give characters names indicating their personalities. In *The Way of the World*, by William Congreve (1670–1729), one character is called Fainall, meaning he feigns all, or pretends everything. Other characters are named Petulant, Sir Willfull Witwood, Weightwell, and Lady Wishfort, the last being a contraction of "wish for it." Names of characters in other English plays of the seventeenth and eighteenth centuries included Lady Sneerwell, Careless, Snake, Sir Benjamin Backbite, Mrs. Candour, Lady Fidget, Pinchwife, Scandal, Tattle, and Mrs. Frail. The French playwright Moliere, while generally giving his characters regular names, frequently emphasized the dominant trait of the main character in the title: *The Miser, The Misanthrope, The Would-be Gentlemen*, and *The Imaginary Invalid*.

NONHUMAN PARTS

In Greece in the fifth century B.C., and in many primitive cultures, actors portrayed birds and animals, and the practice has continued tothe present. Aristophanes, the Greek comic dramatist, used a chorus of actors to play the title parts in his plays *The Birds* and *The*

Figure 6-4 *Stock characters in commedia dell'arte.* *Italian comedy of the Renaissance developed stereotype characters who were always the same; they dressed the same and played the same part. On the left is Pantalone, an elderly merchant who spoke in clichés and chased young girls. On the right is the stock character of a servant, called a Zanni. (From a contemporary engraving.)*

Frogs. In the modern period, Eugene Ionesco has men turn into animals in *Rhinoceros*; and Edmond Rostand (1868–1918), a French playwright, has written a poetic fable about a rooster called *Chantecler*. Karel Čapek (1890–1938), a Czechoslavakian dramatist, collaborated with his brother, Josef, to write *The Insect Comedy*, a picture of insect life as seen in the delirium of a dying vagabond.

Occasionally actors are called on to play other nonhuman parts. Karel Čapek also wrote a play entitled *R.U.R.* in which people play robots. The initials in the title stand for Russum's Universal Robots and it was from this play that the word "robot" derives. In the medieval morality play *Everyman*, characters represent ideas or concepts, such as Fellowship, Good Deeds, Worldly Possession, Beauty.

In certain forms of New Theater—particularly in Happenings, a free-form improvisation that combines art and dance with theater—performers might be used as objects or automatons. In the words of Michael Kirby, a commentator on Happenings, "Occasionally people are used somewhat as inanimate objects."[1] An example would be an actor performing a "task" such as climbing a stepladder over and over again, or an actor on his hands and knees serving as a bench for another actor. In such cases there is some doubt that questions of "dramatic characters" or "acting" even enter the picture. Performers are serving another purpose, in the way that dancers sometimes use their bodies as moving shapes in abstract ballets.

Dramatic characters in the guise of animals or robots are the exception rather than the rule. When they do occur, more often than not it is the human quality of the animal which is being emphasized, and sometimes the reverse: the animalistic quality of the human being, a point to be discussed in a moment.

JUXTAPOSITION OF CHARACTERS

Since characters are symbols of people, the playwright can use them in combination with one another to bring out certain qualities. From the Greek theater we have the terms *protagonist* and *antagonist*. The protagonist is the main character in the play—Othello, for instance—and the antagonist is the main character's chief opponent. In the case of *Othello*, the antagonist is Iago. It is through the contest of the two characters that their individual qualities are developed.

There are other ways in which dramatists combine characters. Sophocles created two exceptionally strong-willed, independent female characters—Antigone and Electra—each one the title character in a play. Both are young women intent on defying an older person and willing to risk death to fight for a principle. But Sophocles was not content to present them as they were on their own. Unlike other dramatists who had told the same story, Sophocles gave them sisters whose characters contrasted sharply with theirs. To Antigone he gave Ismene, a docile, compliant girl who argued with Antigone that she should obey the law and give in to authority. To Electra, Sophocles gave Chrisothemis, a meek, frightened creature who protested that as women they were powerless to act. Sophocles strengthened and clarified both Antigone and Electra by providing them with parallel characters to show off their determination and courage.

Frequently a dramatist will introduce secondary characters to act as foils or counterparts to the main characters. In *Hedda Gabler*, by Henrik Ibsen, the main character is a willful, destructive woman, bent on having her own way; Hedda wishes to possess men but is unable to love them. Mrs. Elvsted, another character in the play, is her opposite in almost every way: a trusting, warm, sincere woman, able to give of herself to others. This technique of setting parallel or contrasting characters beside one another is like putting one color next to another. A single color is sometimes difficult to judge, but the moment we put others beside it, we become aware of its relative brightness. A bright red, for instance, looks even brighter next to pink; a dark green looks much darker when it is seen next to pale green.

Major and Minor Characters

Lesser characters in a play are sometimes referred to as *minor* characters. *Major* characters are the chief characters, the ones about whom the play revolves. In *Hamlet*, major characters include Hamlet, Claudius, Gertrude, Polonius, Laertes, and Ophelia. Minor characters are those who appear briefly and serve only to further the story or to support the major characters. In *Hamlet*, minor characters include Marcellus and Bernardo, who are standing watch when the ghost appears, and Reynaldo, a servant to Polonius. Sometimes characters fall halfway between major and minor; examples in *Hamlet* are Rosencrantz and Guildenstern, or the gravedigger. In these instances the characters, each of whom has a distinctive personality, play a small but quite important part in the play.

One function of minor characters is to point very clearly to the important figures in a play. In the same way that a dramatist selects certain features of a person to emphasize and eliminates others, so the dramatist focuses on the main characters, and places others in the background. Otherwise the viewer would have no perspective and sense of proportion with regard to the various characters.

Orchestration of Characters

Anton Chekhov, the Russian dramatist, is said to have "orchestrated" his characters. The reference is to a musical composition in which the theme is played first by one section of the orchestra, such as the violins, and then by another, such as the brass or woodwinds. Not only is the theme taken up by various sections, but it can be played in different ways, first in a major key and then in a minor. In his plays, Chekhov drew a series of characters with a common problem, and each of the characters represented some aspect of the central theme. In Chekhov's *Uncle Vanya*, for example, the theme of disillusionment and frustration with life is shared by virtually every character in the play—providing the spine we mentioned previously—but each in his or her own way. Uncle Vanya has been working on an estate to help support a professor whom he discovers is a fraud. In the midst of his disillusionment Vanya falls in love with the professor's young wife, but she does not return his love. A neighbor, Dr. Astrov, has sacrificed himself as a doctor in a small rural community and grown dissatisfied with his life. He too loves the professor's wife, but nothing can come of it. Vanya's niece, a plain woman who works hard for little reward, is in love with Dr. Astrov, but he cannot return her love. And so it goes; practically everyone embodies the theme. But it is subtly and carefully done. No one person stands alone; the theme is brought out through the overall effect in which gradations and shadings of meaning are interwoven like threads in a tapestry.

Chekhov was a master at orchestrating his characters, but he is not the only dramatist to employ the technique. In one way or another, most dramatists try to arrange their characters so that they produce a cumulative effect. It is not what one character does or says, but what all characters do together.

HUMAN CONCERNS: THE SUBJECT MATTER OF THEATER

Before leaving dramatic characters, we should note their significance for the drama. Their presence indicates that human beings are the primary concern of theater. Indeed, theater is always about human subjects though different aspects are emphasized in different plays: the pretenses of men and women in society in William Congreve's *The Way of the World*; the conflict between high principle and expediency in Sophocle's *Antigone*; the terrible way in which members of one family can drive one another into desperation and despair in Eugene O'Neill's *Long Day's Journey into Night*; the alternating hope and futility of men waiting for salvation in Samuel Beckett's *Waiting for Godot*; or the celebration of life in a small town in Thornton Wilder's *Our Town*.

Drama focuses on human concerns even when actors play animals, inanimate objects, or abstract ideas. The medieval morality play *Everyman* is a good example. Though actors play abstract ideas such as Fellowship, Knowledge, Good Deeds, Beauty, and Strength, the central character is Everyman, a prototypical character if there ever was one. And the problem of the play—death coming to human beings before they want it to come—is a universal human theme. *The Insect Comedy* is another case in point. The characters in the play are insects, but the play is really about people. As John Gassner explains, its true meaning is "an expressionistic fantasy of the foibles, predatoriness, regimentation, and warring habits of the human race."[2]

Figure 6-5 Combining characters: a Chekhov grouping. *Characters in a play serve as contrasts, counterparts, or complements to one another. One group opposes or is parallel to another. Chekhov was a master at weaving a rich tapestry with a number of characters. Here a group in* The Three Sisters *poses for a photograph. (Photo—Diane Gorodnitzki.)*

The way in which gods are depicted provides a further illustration of the person-centered quality of theater. In Greek drama, the gods sometimes appeared at the end of the play to intervene and tie up loose ends of the plot. The manner of their entrance is noteworthy: they were lowered to the orchestra level from the top of the stage house by a large lever or crane, called a *machine*. The term *deus ex machina*, which means literally "god from the machine," has come to stand for any device, divine or otherwise, brought in to solve problems arbitrarily. The gods were introduced, however, at the end, after the main characters—all human beings—had been through the anguish and struggle of the play. The emphasis was on the human problem, and the appearance of a god was almost an afterthought.

Occasionally, as in *Rhinoceros* or *The Insect Comedy*, a play is metaphorical, presenting an analogy for the human condition. But whenever there are gods, animals, or insects in plays, they are there to support a central human theme, not the reverse.

In the modern world, human beings have lost the central place they once occupied in the universe. In the Ptolemaic view of the universe, which prevailed until the sixteenth century when Copernicus discovered that the earth revolved around the sun and not the reverse, it was assumed that the earth, ruled by human beings, was the center of everything. Today, we have long since given up that notion, particularly in light of recent explorations in outer space. The human being has become less and less significant, and less and less at the center of things. But not in theater. It is one area where the preoccupations of men and women, for better or worse, are still the core, the center of gravity around which other elements orbit—the center, in other words, of the dramatic universe.

In films, by contrast, the frame of reference may be quite different: an aerial shot from a helicopter will present a panorama of a whole countryside; the scale is vast and the human being hardly figures in it at all. In theater this could never happen; the human being is always center stage, literally and figuratively.

Human Beings: Form as well as Content

In addition to being about human beings, theater is also performed *by* human beings, namely, actresses and actors. This is another way of saying that human beings are both the *content* and the *form* of theater. (The subject of any art is called the *content*—*what* is being said. The *way* it is said, that is, the means by which it is communicated, is called the *form*.) This distinguishes theater from other arts in which either the content or the form of the art is not so clearly focused on human beings.

T. E. Kalem, drama critic for *Time* magazine, has written, "Art, like nature, is divided into organic entities. A rose is not a pear, and a pear is not a giraffe. Similarly, a novel is not a play, and a play is not a film."[3] One way to separate the pears from the giraffes in art is by form and content. The arts are invariably separated from one another by one or the other, and sometimes by both. The subject matter of a portrait, for example, may be a person—Abraham Lincoln or Martin Luther King, Jr.—but unlike theater, the form or medium is oil paint on canvas. An abstract painting, on the other hand, shares neither form nor content with theater; it depicts an arrangement of shapes and lines in a combination of colors with human beings as neither subject matter nor form. In a film, the story, or content, might be identical to that of a stage play—Tennessee Williams's *Cat on a Hot Tin Roof*, for instance—but the medium is different because the medium in cinema is not a live person but a photographic image projected on a screen.

In dance a story is presented primarily through movement and without words, and in opera a story is told through music. These two, however, are the closest to theater in form and content, and at times share with it the distinction of being art forms by and about human beings.

DRAMATIC CHARACTERS: IMAGES OF OURSELVES

Returning to the subject of dramatic characters, as with symbols and dreams, they sometimes seem more real than real. In fact, Luigi Pirandello (1867–1936), an Italian dramatist, wrote a play, *Six Characters in Search of an Author*, in which he argued that dramatic characters are more permanent and less of an illusion than human beings. Speaking through the character of The Father, he says, "He who has had the luck to be born a character can laugh even at death. He cannot die. The man, the writer, the instrument of the creation will die, but his creation does not die." Arguing with a theater manager in the play, The Father points out that whereas human beings are always changing, and are different from one day to the next, characters remain the same. The Manager picks up the argument, with the character of The Father:

The Manager	Then you'll be saying next that you . . . are truer and more real than I am.
The Father	But of course; without doubt! . . .
The Manager	More real than I?
The Father	If your reality can change from one day to another . . .
The Manager	But everyone knows it can change. It is always changing, the same as anyone else's.
The Father	No, sir, not ours! Look here! That is the very difference! Our reality doesn't change; it can't change! It can't be other than what is is, because it is already fixed forever.[4]

Their permanence, however, is not the only feature of the dramatic characters. When well drawn they present us with a vivid, incisive picture of ourselves. We see individuals at their best and their worst; we see them perform acts of heroic courage, acts we like to feel we ourselves are capable of; and we see deeds of cowardice and violence, again, actions we fear we might commit in moments of weakness or anger. We see outrageous cases of human folly and pretention, which make us laugh uproariously. In short, we see ourselves in the revealing and illuminating mirror theater holds before us.

We said before that the exchange between performer and spectator is the basic encounter of theater. But the dramatic characters impersonated by performers are images of ourselves. In truth, therefore, the basic encounter of theater is with ourselves. Sometimes in the midst of watching a theater event we see a part of ourselves on stage, and realize for the first time some truth about our lives. This confrontation is at the heart of the theater experience.

SUMMARY

1 Dramatic characters are symbols of people and fall in several categories; the chief characters of traditional theater are extraordinary characters, men and women at the outer limits of human behavior.

2 In modern serious theater we frequently find prototypical characters—complete, fully rounded portraits of people who embody a whole group or type. An example is Willy Loman, the salesman in *Death of a Salesman.*

3 Some characters are stereotypes. Stock characters, for instance, are predictable, clearly defined types. Other characters feature one dominant trait which overshadows all other features.

4 Occasionally performers are asked to play nonhuman parts—animals, birds, etc.—but generally with a strong human flavor.

5 Characters are placed together by the playwright in certain combinations to obtain maximum effectiveness; (a) a protagonist is opposed by an antagonist, (b) minor characters support major characters, and (c) characters are orchestrated into a whole.

6 The fact that people are both the subject matter and the instrument—the content and the form—of theater distinguishes it from the other arts in which either the content or the form is not so clearly focused on human beings.

7 Dramatic characters are symbols of people; therefore, the basic confrontation in theater is with ourselves.

We have been looking closely at dramatic characters and have determined that human beings and matters relating to the human conditions are the subject matter of theater. But how do we get to know dramatic characters? How are these images of ourselves revealed to us, and how do we come to know so intimately characters like Blanche DuBois in *A Streetcar Named Desire*? In the next section we will study dramatic structure: the means by which dramatists and performers unfold the lives of characters and give substance to drama. Structure is an important means by which a theater experience attains unity, by which we get the sense that the experience is whole or complete.

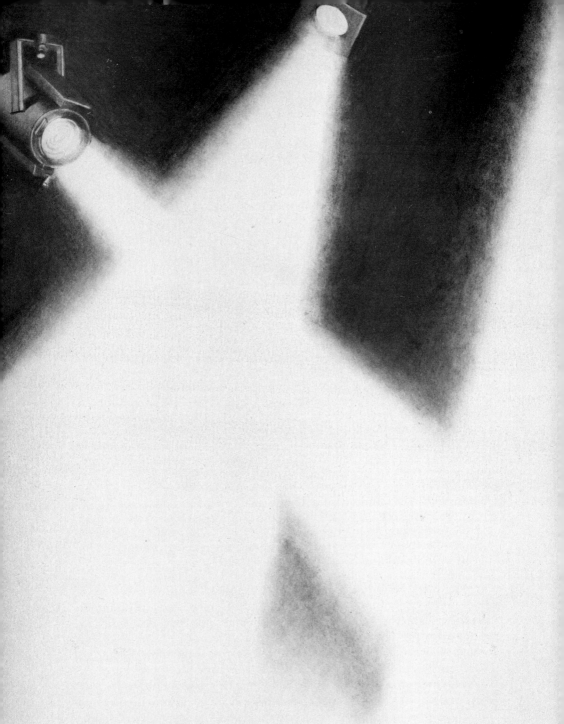

POINT OF VIEW

DRAMATIC STRUCTURE

PART THREE

DRAMATIC STRUCTURE: THE ARCHITECTURE OF A PLAY

ENVIRONMENT

PERFORMERS   AUDIENCE

7

CONVENTIONS OF DRAMATIC STRUCTURE

If we were to construct a grammar of theater, the *subject* would be people, that is, some area of human concern. But just as in grammar every subject needs a verb, in theater dramatic characters need a verb—some form of action—to define them. A noun standing alone, any noun, means nothing—or everything. We can read the word "telephone," or "box," or "toothbrush," and we know very little. When we add a verb, however, we know something: the telephone *rang*, or *fell off the table*, or *went dead*. With people, even more than objects, a verb is necessary, to tell us who they are and what they are

Figure 7-1 Characters in conflict. Marlon Brando and Jessica Tandy as Stanley Kowalski and Blanche duBois in the original production of Tennessee Williams's A Streetcar Named Desire. *The natural antagonism of Stanley and Blanche is an important part of the play's structure. (Photo—Museum of the City of New York, Theatre and Music Collection.)*

about. We do not get to know people by seeing them in a tableau or still-life picture; we get to know them from what they do and say.

The words "to act" and "to perform" are used in theater to denote the impersonation of a character by an actor or an actress, but the words also mean "to do something," "to be active." Professor Alvin B. Kernan has pointed out that the word "drama derives from a Greek root, the verb *dran*, meaning 'to do' or 'to act.'"[1] At its heart, theater involves action. Characters in plays "act" or "do something"; they do not stand on stage like statues.

ASPECTS OF DRAMATIC PLOT

One theory of history maintains that the growth and well-being of a civilization lies in its ability to respond successfully to environmental and human challenges. Without speculating on the accuracy of this as a theory of history, we can say that *people* often define themselves by the way they handle challenge and response. If they cannot face up to a challenge, it tells us one thing; if they meet it with dignity, even though defeated, it tells us another; if they triumph, it tells us something else. It is the same in our own lives. We get to know the members of our family, our friends, and our enemies by being with them over a period of time. We see how they respond to us, and to other people; we see how they meet crises in their own lives, and in ours.

In life this process can take years—in fact, it continues to unfold as long as we know a person. But in the theater we have only a few hours. The playwright, therefore, must devise means by which the characters will face challenges and be tested in a short space of time. The American playwright Arthur Miller named one of his plays *The Crucible*. Literally, a crucible is a vessel in which metal is tested by being exposed to extreme heat. Figuratively, a crucible has come to stand for any severe test of human worth and endurance—a trial by fire. In a sense, every play provides a crucible: a test devised by the playwright to show how the characters behave under conditions of stress. Through this test the meaning of the play is brought out.

The crucible of a play can vary enormously: it might be a fight for a kingdom, or in modern terms, a fight for a man's "turf," but it can just as easily be a fight over a person. It can be an intellectual or moral confrontation. There may be no overt clash at all, as in Samuel Beckett's *Waiting for Godot*, but there must be tension of some sort. In *Waiting for Godot*, for instance, there are several sources of tension or conflict: the ever-present question of whether the mysterious Godot will come or not; the friction between the two main characters who get on one another's nerves but desperately need each other; the unfolding revelation of men deluding themselves, over and over again; and on top of these, a constant probing of religious and philosophical ideas in a series of questions posed by Beckett. A play might even consist of a series of apparently disconnected events, which rub against one another, producing a jarring effect and challenging the spectator to make his or her own pattern out of the events.

Though the conflict or tension in drama may take a number of forms, its presence is essential. Every play must have kinetic energy, a magnetic field, a flow of electrical current—use whatever figure of speech you choose. This is the only way we come to know dramatic characters, to experience a play, and ultimately, to absorb its meaning.

Plot Distinguished from Story

Traditionally, the most widely employed means of providing the dynamics of theater has been the dramatization of a story; a character or a group of characters move through a series of episodes seeking goals, facing obstacles, and making choices. Stories, being narrative accounts of what people do, are as old as men and women: they form the substance of daily conversation, of newspapers and television, of novels and films. However, every medium presents a story in a different form.

In theater, the story must be presented by living actors on a stage in a limited period of time, and this requires selectivity. In presenting a play about Abraham Lincoln, for example, the playwright must make choices. Does the dramatist include scenes in Springfield, Illinois, where Lincoln served as a lawyer and held his famous debates with Stephen A. Douglas? Or does everything take place in Washington after Lincoln became President? Are there scenes with Lincoln's wife, Mary Todd, or only with government and military officials?

The selection and order of scenes in a play is the *plot*. It is important to remember that plot differs from story. A story is a full account of an event, or series of events, usually told in chronological order. The story of Abraham Lincoln begins with his being born in a log cabin and continues to the day he was shot at Ford's Theater in Washington, D.C. Plot, as opposed to story, is a selection and arrangement of scenes taken from a story for presentation on the stage. Plot is what actually happens on stage and the *way* it is made to happen. The plot of a play about Abraham Lincoln and his wife, Mary Todd, would include scenes and characters related primarily to their lives. The plot of a play about the Lincoln-Douglas debates would include scenes relating chiefly to that subject.

Plot is the responsibility of the playwright; he or she decides at what point in the story the plot will begin and what characters will participate. Also, he or she decides what scenes will be included and in what sequence they will occur. Even in a fictional story, invented entirely by the playwright, the characters and scenes must be selected and the sequence determined. Along with making these selections, the playwright must *dramatize* the material—transform it into action and conversation, the latter referred to as *dialogue,* because ultimately everything on stage must be acted or spoken by a performer. There are other questions to be determined as well: How long will each scene last? What is the main conflict, and when does it arise? How is the conflict resolved?

A playwright designs a play just as an architect designs a building. The script is the blueprint from which the director, actors, and designers construct a production. Unlike a building occupying space, however, a production is a series of events and confrontations moving through time. Though we cannot see it as we see a building, it has a structure all the same. We build it in our minds. The scenes and characters at the beginning form a foundation; following that, images and impressions accumulate and reinforce one another. In Ibsen's *Hedda Gabler,* the heroine gives a gun to a man suggesting that he shoot himself, and later in the play he does. Her first action leads to the second, just as the ground floor of a building supports the second.

Importance of the Opening Scene

The formation of a play's structure begins with the first scene, which sets the tone and style of the play. It tells us whether we are going to see a serious play or a comic one, and whether the play will deal with affairs of everyday life or some fantasy. The opening scene is a cue or signal as to what lies ahead; it also sets the wheels of action in motion, giving the characters a shove and hurtling them toward their destination.

The playwright provides this initial shove by posing a problem to the characters, establishing an imbalance of forces or a disturbance in their equilibrium which compels characters to respond. Generally this imbalance occurs just before the play begins or arises immediately after it opens. In *King Oedipus*, for example a plague has hit the city just prior to the opening of the play. In *Hamlet*, "something is rotten in the state of Denmark" before the play opens, and early in the play the ghost of Hamlet's father appears to tell Hamlet that he must seek revenge. At the beginning of *Romeo and Juliet*, the Capulets and

Montagues are at one another's throats in a street fight. Strindberg's *Miss Julie* is set on Midsummer's Eve and opens with Miss Julie acting "wildly," obviously on the verge of some precipitous act. In the opening of *A Streetcar Named Desire*, Blanche DuBois arrives in the apartment of her sister and brother-in-law, where she is an unwanted guest.

As these examples suggest, the opening scene initiates the action. Characters are presented with a challenge and thrust into a situation which provides the starting point for the entire play.

Obstacles and Complications

Having met the initial challenge of the play, characters then move through a series of steps alternating between achievement and defeat, between hope and despair. The moment they seem to accomplish one goal or reach a plateau of satisfaction, something cuts across the play to upset the balance and start them on another path. A series of hurdles or challenges is thrown up before them. In theater these are referred to as *obstacles* or *complications*. The former is an impediment put in a character's way; the latter is some outside force, or new twist in the plot, introduced at an inopportune moment.

Shakespeare's *Hamlet* provides numerous examples of obstacles and complications. Once Hamlet has confirmed the guilt of King Claudius by seeing the King's reaction to the play-within-the-play, Hamlet's way to revenge seems clear; he has but to kill Claudius. But when Hamlet goes to carry out his mission, he discovers Claudius at prayer. An obstacle has been thrown in his path, and he faces a dilemma: if he kills Claudius while praying, Claudius may go to heaven rather than hell, where Hamlet wishes him to go, and so Hamlet does not kill him. Later, Hamlet is in his mother's bedroom when he hears a noise behind a curtain. Surely Claudius is lurking there, and Hamlet can kill him instantly. But when Hamlet puts his sword through the curtain, he finds that he has killed Polonius instead. This complicates matters because it provides Claudius with an excuse to send Hamlet to England with Rosencrantz and Guilden-stern, whom Claudius has instructed to murder Hamlet. Hamlet gets out of that trap and returns to Denmark. Now, at last he can carry out his revenge. But upon his return he discovers that Ophelia has killed herself while he has been away, and her brother, Laertes, is seeking revenge on Hamlet. This complicates the situation once again; Hamlet is prevented from meeting Claudius head on because he must also deal with Laertes. In the end Hamlet does carry out his mission, but only after many interruptions.

Dramatic characters have objectives or goals they are strongly

Figure 7-2 An obstacle in Hamlet's path. *Obstacles and complications confronting the main characters prolong the action and heighten the tension in traditional plot structure. When Hamlet finds the King at prayer he is unable to kill him: one of many such impediments Hamlet encounters before carrying out his final revenge. (Photo—The New York Public Library at Lincoln Center, Theatre Collection. Astor, Lenox and Tilden Foundations. Photo by Vandamm.)*

motivated to obtain. Macbeth wants to become king; Miss Julie wants to conquer the servant, Jean; Blanche DuBois wants to find a safe haven. But there are obstacles to achieving these goals, and other characters oppose their wishes and interfere with their plans. The result is an inevitable tension and conflict. In most plays the characters confront a series of crises—some less complicated than Hamlet's, some more complicated—until a final climax in which the issues of the play are resolved. In living through their experiences, the characters provide those of us in the audience with an experience of our own. In our mind we live through their adventures with them.

DRAMATIC CONVENTIONS: SIMILAR TO RULES IN SPORTS

In order to ensure that events on stage will be dynamic and that characters will face a meaningful test, a series of conventions or "ground rules" have evolved in dramatic structure. A good analogy in this regard would be the ground rules in sports contests which assure maximum results for both participants and spectators. There are several obvious similarities between theater and sports: many sports have a playing area similar to the stage, and spectators at a sporting event are comparable to the audience in a theater. More important, however, is the parallel in the events themselves. In sports, the spectators want to see a strong, sustained contest. To achieve this end, each sport has a set of ground rules, designed to test to the maximum the ability and finesse of the participants. Theater is more varied and complex than most sports events, and the ground rules are not so clearly defined or consciously imposed. Nevertheless there are similarities which point up the ways in which a play achieves maximum impact.

Limited Space

Most sports have a limited playing area. In some cases this consists of a confined space: a boxing ring, a basketball court, or a baseball field. Invariably there is some kind of "out of bounds." The combatants cannot run away; they must stand there and face one another. The playing area is clearly defined, and both players and spectators know a fair ball from a foul.

Theater is limited to a stage, but we are speaking here of a limit within the play itself. The action of a play is generally confined to a "world" of its own, that is, to a fictional universe which contains all the characters and events of the play, and none of the characters or actions moves outside the orbit of that world. Sometimes the world of a play is restricted to a single room. In his play *No Exit*, Jean Paul Sartre (1905–), a French existentialist, confines three characters to one room, from which, as the title suggests, there is no escape. The room is supposed to be Hell, and the three characters—a man, Garcin, and two women, Estelle and Inez—are confined there forever. Estelle loves Garcin, Garcin loves Inez, and Inez, a lesbian, loves Estelle. Each one, in short loves the one who will not reciprocate, and by being confined to the one room, they face a form of permanent torture, in other words, a form of Hell.

The neoclassical writers in France, such as Jean Racine (1639–1699), a great tragic dramatist, set their plays in one room, generally the hall or vestibule of a palace. Writers like Ibsen and Strindberg frequently confined their plays to one room as well. Among modern plays, there are numerous instances in which the action takes place in a single room. Even those plays not so closely contained usually occupy a restricted area. The action might be in one castle and its environs, as in *Hamlet*, or the general area of a battlefield, as in Bertolt Brecht's *Mother Courage*. But the sense of a private universe, with outer limits, is always there.

A Time Limit

Sports puts some limit on the duration of action. In the case of football or basketball, there is a definite time limit. In golf, there is a given number of holes, and in baseball or tennis, a minimum number of innings or games. Theoretically, those sports which are open-ended, such as baseball or tennis, can go on forever, but fans get impatient with this arrangement as indicated by the move in tennis in recent years to establish a "sudden death" or tie-breaker playoff when a set reaches six-all. A time or score limit ensures that spectators can see a complete event; they can live through a total experience in miniature with a clear winner and loser, and no loose ends.

The longest theatrical productions about which we have records are medieval cycle plays. A series usually lasted several days, and one, at Valenciennes, France, in 1547, went on for twenty-five days. Generally, however, these presentations comprise a group of separate plays—one on Adam, another on Noah, a third on Abraham and Isaac, etc.—each one complete in itself, with the series strung together like beads on a chain.

We spoke earlier of Greek drama festivals. The principal one, the *City Dionysia*, held in March each year, went on for four days following several days of preliminary preparation. One day of the festival, however, was devoted to individual comedies, and on each of the other three days, a trilogy of tragedies, followed by a satyr play, was presented. A trilogy is a group of three plays joined together by a common theme or subject. Even if we count a Greek trilogy as one play, it lasted only the better part of a day. In most instances, however, theatrical performances last only one, two, or three hours. More often than not, a play compresses the events of a lifetime into a matter of minutes.

Aside from the actual playing time of a performance, many plays contain within them a time limit or deadline as a condition the characters must face. At the end of the second act of Ibsen's *A Doll's House*, the heroine, Nora, is trying desperately to get her husband to put off until the following evening the opening of a letter which she fears will establish her as a forger and will threaten their marriage. When her husband agrees, Nora says to herself, "thirty-one hours to live." In Thornton Wilder's *Our Town*, the young girl, Emily, is given only one day to return to earth to relive her experiences.

Strongly Opposing Forces

Most sports involve two teams, or two individuals, opposing each other. This ensures clear lines of force: the good guys and the bad

Figure 7-3   Rival gangs in West Side Story. *Traditional plot structure calls for strongly opposing forces in a play. The antagonist opposes the protagonist; one group opposes another, like the two families in* Romeo and Juliet *or the two gangs shown above in the musical* West Side Story *derived from* Romeo and Juliet. *(Photo—The New York Public Library at Lincoln Center, Theatre Collection. Astor, Lenox and Tilden Foundations. Photo by Vandamm.)*

guys, the home team and the visitors. The contest is straight and simple, like a shoot-out on main street at high noon between the sheriff and the outlaw. (Imagine what a hockey game would be like if there were five teams playing in one game?) The musical *West Side Story* features two opposing gangs, not unlike opposing teams in sports. In the simplest dramatic situations, one character directly opposes another—the protagonist against the antagonist.

In a manual on playwrighting, the critic Kenneth MacGowan emphasized that "characters must be so selected and developed that they include people who are bound to react upon each other, bound to clash. . . . "[2] In the vast majority of dramas, playwrights have followed this approach. A perfect example of characters bound to clash are the man and women, Julie and Jean, in Strindberg's *Miss Julie.* Julie, an aristocrat, is the daughter of the owner of an estate. She has had an unhappy engagement and is deeply suspicious of men, but at the same time, sexually attracted to them. Jean, an aggressive male, is a servant with dreams of escaping his life of servitude and becoming a hotel owner. These two, drawn together by strong forces of repulsion and attraction, meet on Midsummer's Eve in a climactic encounter. A similar confrontation occurs in Tennessee Williams's *A Streetcar*

Named Desire, between Blanche DuBois and Stanley Kowalski. Stanley, crude and outspoken, is the person most inimical to Blanche, a faded Southern belle trying desperately to hold on to her gentility. On his side, Stanley is insecure about his lack of education and refinement, and Blanche with her superior airs provokes him almost to the breaking point.

An Equal Contest

Rules ensuring that the contest will be as equal as possible without coming to a dead draw are a feature of most sports. Everyone wants his or her team to win, but would rather see a close, exciting contest than a runaway; nothing is duller to a sports fan than a lopsided game. The struggle, as much as the outcome, is the source of pleasure. And so rules are set up, with handicaps or other devices, to equalize the forces. In basketball or football, the moment one team scores, the other team gets the ball so that it will have an opportunity to even the score.

In theater, a hard-fought and relatively equal contest is implicit in what has been said about opposing forces: Jean stands opposite Miss Julie, and Blanche opposite Stanley. Even in the somewhat muted, low-key plays of Anton Chekhov, there is a balance of forces among various groups. In *The Cherry Orchard*, those who own the orchard are pitted against the man who will acquire it; in *The Three Sisters*, the sisters of the title are opposed in the possession of their home by their acquisitive sister-in-law.

A device frequently used by dramatists to guarantee friction or tension between forces is the restriction of characters to members of one family. Relatives have built-in rivalries and affinities: parents versus children, sisters versus brothers. Being members of the same family, they have no avenue of escape. Mythology, on which so much drama is based, abounds with familial relationships. The story of Agamemnon, the basis of a trilogy by the Greek playwright Aeschylus, is a good example. In simple outline, Agamemnon sacrifices his daughter Iphigenia, thinking the gods have ordered it. Later, when he returns home from the Trojan War, his wife, Clytemnestra, and her lover, Aegisthus, slay him to avenge the daughter's death. Following that, Clytemnestra's children, Electra and Orestes, murder their mother to avenge their father's death. Because family pride and honor run so strong, one member after another feels compelled to commit murder in a chain reaction of revenge.

Shakespeare frequently set members of one family against each other: Hamlet opposes his mother; Lear opposes his daughters; Jessica opposes her father, Shylock, in *The Merchant of Venice*. In

Figure 7-4 Members of a family in conflict. *Drama frequently puts members of the same family in confrontation with one another. In the Negro Ensemble Company production of Joseph Walker's* The River Niger, *the father sits between his wife and son as friends of the family look on. (Photo—Bert Andrews.)*

modern drama, virtually every writer of note has dealt with close family situations: Ibsen, Strindberg, Chekhov, Williams, Miller, and Albee, to mention a few. The American dramatist Eugene O'Neill—who used the Agamemnon myth in his *Mourning Becomes Electra*—wrote what many consider his finest play, *Long Day's Journey into Night*, about the four members of his own family. A powerful play about a black family, *The River Niger* by Joseph Walker (1935–), concerns a son, his father, mother, fiancée, and old friends. In plays where families are not directly involved the characters are usually in close proximity, fighting for the same turf, the same throne, the same woman or man.

A Prize or Goal

In sports, to guarantee the participants will play their hardest in an intensive, hard-fought contest, a prize is offered. In professional sports it is money; in amateur sports, a cup. In addition, there is the glory of winning, the accolades of TV and the press, and the plaudits of family and friends.

For its part, good drama never lacks incentive or motivation for its characters: Macbeth wishes desperately to be king; Antigone fights for her family's honor; St. Joan wishes to save France; and Blanche DuBois must find protection and preserve her dignity in order to survive.

DEVELOPING A PLOT

The playwright uses the tools we have discussed—the initial imbalance of forces in a play, the motivations and goals of the characters, obstacles and complications, and the conventions of dramatic construction—to develop a plot. In developing a dramatic plot, however, the playwright has something specific in mind. He or she wants to show us a special world, to portray an unusual character, to emphasize a particular point of view, to underscore a theme. In short, the playwright wants to provide a specific experience for the audience.

A playwright decides, for example, to focus on one character, as Edmond Rostand did in *Cyrano de Bergerac,* or on a group of characters, as Anton Chekhov did in such plays as *The Three Sisters* or *The Cherry Orchard.* A playwright can emphasize a particular character trait in one play, and its opposite in another. This is what Henrik Ibsen often did. In his *Brand* the leading character is a stark, uncompromising figure who will sacrifice everything—family, friends, love—for his principles. "I am stern in my demands," Brand says. "I require all or nothing. No half-measures." On the other hand, Ibsen's Peer Gynt from the play of the same name is always compromising, always running away. In the dark forest Peer meets an unseen force called The Boyg, which advises him not to meet life directly. "Go roundabout, Peer," the voice says over and over again, advice which he follows throughout his life.

It is up to the playwright to determine how to interpret the characters or story, and in doing so he or she sometimes even changes the order of events. A good example is the way the three prominent tragic dramatists of Greece in the fifth century B.C. treated the Electra myth. The story, referred to above, concerns Electra's revenge on her mother, Clytemnestra, and her stepfather, Aegisthus, for having murdered her natural father, Agamemnon. In carrying out her revenge, Electra enlists the help of Orestes, her brother, who has just returned from exile.

In the versions by Aeschylus (525–406 B.C.) and Euripides (525–426 B.C.), the stepfather is murdered first, and the mother, Clytemnestra, murdered last. This puts emphasis on the terror of murdering one's own mother. But Sophocles saw the story differently. He wished to emphasize that Electra and her brother were acting honorably and to play down the mother's murder. And so he reversed the order of the murders and had the mother killed first, then built up to the righteous murder of the stepfather as the final deed. The change made by Sophocles indicates the latitude writers have in altering events to suit their artistic purposes. The manner in which a play unfolds is up to the playwright and is controlled by his or her individual approach.

Whatever the approach, however, playwrights make choices aimed at providing the maximum dramatic impact. A playwright selects the scenes, characters, words, and actions to engage the spectator, excite the imagination, and communicate a total experience. The goal is a plot which will be the ultimate crucible, or verb, for that particular play.

SUMMARY

1   We learn about dramatic characters by what they do and say, the same way we learn about people in everyday life.

2   The action of a play frequently consists of a test or crucible for the characters in which their true nature is defined.

3   The most usual test for a character is being enmeshed in activities or events—a dramatic plot.

4   A dramatic plot is not the same as a story. The story tells the complete account of an episode or sequence of events, but plot is what we see on stage. In a plot the events have been selected from a story and arranged in a certain sequence.

5   A play generally begins with an imbalance of forces, or a loss of equilibrium by one of the characters; this in turn propels the characters to action.

6   As a play progresses, the characters meet a series of complications as they attempt to fulfill their objectives or realize their goals. These encounters produce the tension and conflict of drama.

7   Dramatic conventions, ensuring a strong plot and continuation of tension, are analogous to ground rules in sports: (a) a limited space or playing area, (b) a time limit imposed on the action, (c) strongly opposing forces, (d) an evenly matched, equal contest, and (e) a prize or goal for the participants.

8   In developing a plot, the playwright uses the conventions and tools of dramatic construction to emphasize specific characters or other elements. The same story can be told in different ways, an example being the three different versions of the Electra myth as told by Aeschylus, Sophocles, and Euripides.

In this chapter we have been discussing the development of plot which thrusts characters into action. So far we have examined general principles; when we look at dramatic construction more closely, we discover that certain forms have recurred throughout theater history. In the next chapter we will examine individual forms of dramatic structure.

8

FORMS OF DRAMATIC STRUCTURE

Throughout theater history, whatever the country or period, we find basic dramatic forms reappearing. A form adopted in Greece in the fifth century B.C. emerges, somewhat altered, in France in the seventeenth century. This same form shows up once more, again with variations, in Norway in the late nineteenth century. From the Greek period to the twentieth century there have been two basic approaches to plot: the *climactic* and the *episodic*. During that time one or the other of the two forms has been the dominant dramatic structure. A third approach, where dramatic episodes are strung together without

Figure 8-1 ***The* Caucasian Chalk Circle: *an episodic play.*** *The dramatist Bertolt Brecht generally uses the loose, multiscene structure referred to as episodic. In* The Caucasian Chalk Circle, *Grusha, the character shown here, goes through many adventures in a series of scenes. This form contrasts with the more compressed* climactic *structure. (Photo—The Arena Stage, Washington, D.C. Photo by George de Vincent.)*

any apparent connection, has shown up at times in the past, and in the modern period has emerged in a new guise. A fourth approach, the absurdist approach, is a more modern phenomenon. The fifth, a ritual or pattern, is both old and new. The characteristics of the basic forms will be clearer when we look at each one separately, beginning with the form which first developed in Greece twenty-five hundred years ago.

CLIMACTIC PLOT

Plot Begins Late in the Story

The first hallmark of climactic drama is that the plot begins quite late in the story; Sophocles's *King Oedipus* illustrates how late. The story, as is well known, concerns a man born in Thebes who is put on a mountaintop to die because of a prophecy that he will murder his father and marry his mother. He is saved by the King of Corinth, however, who raises him as his own son. In later life, hearing the prophecy, Oedipus flees Corinth so that he will not kill the man he believes to be his father. On the road he meets his real father, and without knowing his identity, kills him. Again, in ignorance, he marries his mother and rules Thebes. All we have recited so far, as important as it is in the story, is not part of the plot. The play has not begun; it begins at the very end of the story when a plague hits Thebes and Oedipus must unravel his past to save the city.

If we drew a time curve of the play it would look like Figure 8-2. The play begins when all the roads of the past converge at one crucial intersection of the present—at the climax, in other words.

Ibsen's *Ghosts*, written in 1881, affords a more recent example. Before the play begins, the following has occurred: Mrs. Alving has married a dissolute husband who fathers an illegitimate child by another woman and contracts a venereal disease. Discovering this early in her marriage, she nevertheless stays with her husband out of a Victorian sense of duty, sending her own son away to escape the father's influence. When her husband dies, Mrs. Alving builds an orphanage in his honor to camouflage his true character. As with *King Oedipus*, the play still has not begun; it begins later, when the son returns home and the facts of the past are unearthed, precipitating the crisis of the play. In climactic drama, with the play beginning so late, it is frequently necessary to find out what has gone before by having one character report the information to another. The technical term for this revelation of background information is *exposition*.

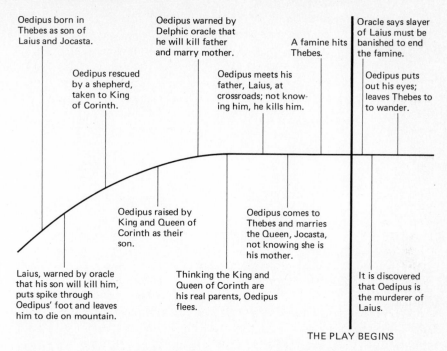

Oedipus born in Thebes as son of Laius and Jocasta.

Oedipus warned by Delphic oracle that he will kill father and marry mother.

A famine hits Thebes.

Oracle says slayer of Laius must be banished to end the famine.

Oedipus rescued by a shepherd, taken to King of Corinth.

Oedipus meets his father, Laius, at crossroads; not knowing him, he kills him.

Oedipus puts out his eyes; leaves Thebes to to wander.

Oedipus raised by King and Queen of Corinth as their son.

Oedipus comes to Thebes and marries the Queen, Jocasta, not knowing she is his mother.

Laius, warned by oracle that his son will kill him, puts spike through Oedipus' foot and leaves him to die on mountain.

Thinking the King and Queen of Corinth are his real parents, Oedipus flees.

It is discovered that Oedipus is the murderer of Laius.

THE PLAY BEGINS

Figure 8-2 Climactic plot begins late in the story. In Oedipus *by Sophocles the events in the chart to the left of the vertical line occur before the play begins. Only the events to the right occur during the play. Prior events must be described in exposition.*

Because climactic plots begin so late in the story, the time span in a climactic play is usually brief. The action of Racine's plays, for example, takes place in a few hours. At the most, events in a climactic play cover a few days. Some playwrights, attempting to push events as near the climax as possible, have stage time (the time we imagine is passing when we are watching a play) coincide with real time (that is, clock time). An example is Tennessee Williams's *Cat on a Hot Tin Roof*: the events depicted in the story last the same 2 1/2 hours as the play itself.

Limited Scenes, Locales, and Characters

A limited number of long segments, or acts, mark climactic drama. In Greek plays there were generally five episodes separated by choral interludes. The French neoclassicists invariably used five acts. For

Figure 8-3 Climactic drama: confined in time and space. Most climactic drama is tightly compressed—with few characters, a short time-span, and confinement of physical space. The setting for Ibsen's Ghosts, shown here, is one room, where the entire action of the play takes place. (Photo—The New York Public Library at Lincoln Center, Theatre Collection. Astor, Lenox and Tilden Foundations. Photo by Vandamm.)

much of the nineteenth and twentieth centuries, three single acts were standard.

Limited scenes in a play usually means a restricted locale as well. In the previous discussion of ground rules of drama, we spoke of confining the action to a single room, as in Sartre's *No Exit*. Such close confinement is a hallmark of climactic drama. Along with locale, there is a restriction of characters. Aside from the chorus, Greek drama generally has four or five principal characters. Racine never had more than seven or eight, and the modern realistic dramatists rarely go above that number.

Tight Construction

Because it is carefully constructed, a well-made or climactic play fits tightly together, with no loose ends. It is like a chain indisolubly linked in a cause-and-effect relationship. As in a detective story, A leads to B, B to C, which causes D, leading in turn to E, and so on. Just as the space and the time frame affords no exit, so the event chain is locked in; once action begins, there is no stopping it.

To give an illustration: in Racine's *Phaedra*, the heroine, Phaedra, is secretly in love with her stepson, Hippolytus. When she hears (A) that her husband, Theseus, is dead, she (B) confesses her love to Hippolytus, causing him (C) to react in horror and disgust. Theseus, unknown to Phaedra, is not dead, however, and when he returns home, Phaedra, fearing disclosure of her incestuous love, (D) allows her nurse to tell Theseus that Hippolytus has made advances to her. Whereupon Theseus (E) invokes a god to punish Hippolytus. Hippolytus (F) is slain, leading Phaedra (G) to poison herself, confessing the truth to Theseus before she dies.

Anouilh, in his *Antigone*, compares tragedy to the workings of a machine:

> The spring is wound up tight. It will uncoil of itself. That is what is so convenient in tragedy. The least little turn of the wrist will do the job. . . . The rest is automatic. You don't need to lift a finger. The machine is in perfect order; it has been oiled ever since time began and it runs without friction.[1]

Anouilh claims this notion applies only to tragedy but, in fact, it fits every play in the climactic form; the aim always is to make events so inevitable that there is no escape—at least not until the very last moment when a *deus ex machina* may intervene to untangle the knot. Because a climactic drama is so carefully and tightly constructed, in the modern period it has frequently been referred to as the *well-made* play.

Clearly, the method of climactic drama is one of compression. Every element—characters, locale, events—is severely restricted. As if by centripetal motion, everything is forced to the center, in a tighter and tighter nucleus, making the ultimate eruption that much more explosive. It is like the cylinder in an automobile engine: a mixture of gasoline and air is compressed by the piston in the cylinder to such extreme intensity that when a spark is introduced, the resulting detonation pushes the piston out, thereby providing power for the car. And so it is with climactic drama; since the story begins near its conclusion, people and events are forced together in a sort of compression chamber, making an explosive confrontation inevitable.

A Popular Plot Structure

The countries and periods (together with the names of a few well-known playwrights) in which the climactic structure has been the dominant form include Greece, fifth century B.C. (Aeschylus, Sophocles, Euripides); Rome, third to first centuries B.C. (Plautus, Terence); France, seventeenth century (Corneille, Racine, Molière); France, nineteenth century (Scribe, Sardou); Europe and America, nineteenth and twentieth centuries (Ibsen, Strindberg, O'Neill, Williams, Miller).

THE EPISODIC PLOT

When we turn to examples of the episodic plot, we see the contrast in construction. Episodic drama begins relatively early in the story, and rather than compressing action, expands it.

Proliferation of People, Places, and Events

The typical episodic play covers an extensive period of time, sometimes many years, and ranges over a number of locations. In one play we can go anywhere: to a small antechamber, a large banquet hall, the open countryside, and mountaintops. Short scenes, some only a half page or so in length, alternate with longer ones. The following examples, giving the number of characters and scenes in each play, indicate the extended nature of episodic drama:

Shakespeare's *Antony and Cleopatra*: thirty-four characters, forty-plus scenes
Lope de Vega's *The Sheep Well*: twenty-six characters, seventeen scenes
Goethe's *Goetz von Berlichingen*: forty-plus characters, fifty-six scenes
Ibsen's *Peer Gynt*: forty-plus characters, thirty-nine scenes
Brecht's *The Caucasian Chalk Circle*: fifty-plus characters, approximately seventeen scenes.

Unlike climactic drama, episodic plays do not necessarily follow a close cause-and-effect development. Both the methods and the effects of climactic drama are different from those of episodic. Rather than

Figure 8-4   Episodic drama: many characters, places, and events. *The drama* Marat/Sade *has a play within a play. It moves back and forth in time, covers a number of incidents, and involves many characters—all typical of episodic structure. (Photo—The Williamstown Theatre Festival, Williamstown, Mass.)*

centripetal, the forces are centrifugal, moving out to embrace additional elements. The possibilities of the episodic or extended approach are discussed by John Gassner in the following description of Bertolt Brecht's work:

> He favors a type of dramatic composition that grasps the various facets of man's life in society without limiting itself to unity of time, place, and action. Some of his plays . . . even have the extensiveness of an Elizabethan chronicle such as *Henry IV, Parts I* and *II* and as much variety of action and tone. One scene may convey a realistic situation while another may symbolize it; or the scene may take the form of a debate or narration; or there may be no scene at all, only a song or recitation, at points in the play. But the episodes, combined with narrative and lyrical passages, and augmented with pantomime, dance, signs or placards, slides and motion-picture sequences if necessary—all following one another in rapid succession or alternation—will form one rich tumultuous play. . . . [2]

Parallel Plot or Subplot

In place of compression, as Gassner suggests, episodic drama offers other techniques. One is the parallel plot or subplot. In Shakespeare's *King Lear*, the title character has three daughters. The two evil daughters have convinced their father that they are good and that their sister is wicked. In the subplot—a counterpart to the main plot—the Earl of Gloucester has two sons, and one son has deceived his father into thinking he is the loyal son when the reverse is true. In both cases the old men have misunderstood their children's true worth, and in the end they are punished for their mistakes: Lear is bereft of his kingdom and his sanity, Gloucester loses his eyes. The Gloucester plot, with complications and developments of its own, is a mirror image and reinforcement of the Lear plot.

In Brecht's *The Caucasian Chalk Circle*, we are two-thirds into the play when what appears to be a brand new drama begins. In the first portion, we follow the story of Grusha, a peasant girl who, in the midst of a revolution, flees to the mountains with an abandoned child, who happens to be a prince. After following Grusha through several episodes, we suddenly leave her entirely and shift back in time to the point where the play began. We pick up the story of a reprobate named Asdak and trace his misadventures to the point where he becomes an enlightened judge. Although their stories are seemingly unrelated, Grusha and Asdak are two sides of the same coin: one is a rascal, the other a simple peasant, but both are decent people caught in the injustices of a corrupt political system. In the end their stories come together when Asdak presides at the trial which allows Grusha to keep the child and marry her fiancé. The plot is not nearly so tidy as in a climactic drama but the tapestry is richer. Two plots running side by side provide the kind of strength which results when strands of steel cable or threads in a rope are intertwined.

Juxtaposition and Contrast

Another technique of episodic drama is juxtaposition or contrast. Rather than moving in linear fashion, the action alternates between elements. We identify colors by relating one color to other colors, and in music we identify notes by relating one note to another. We determine size in the same way: a man 6 feet tall is of no particular significance unless he is surrounded by other men, who are shorter by contrast—then he stands out.

To develop its theme and story and to provide contrast, episodic drama employs a number of alternations and juxtapositions:

1 Short scenes alternate with longer ones. *King Lear* begins with a short scene between Kent and Gloucester, goes to a long scene in

which Lear divides his kingdom, then returns to a brief scene in which Edmund declares his intention to deceive his father.

2   Public scenes alternate with private ones. In *Romeo and Juliet*, full-blown scenes, such as the street fight between the Capulets and Montagues, and the Capulets' ball, stand in contrast to the intimate scenes between Romeo and Juliet. In Brecht's *The Caucasian Chalk Circle*, the first bustling scene of revolution in the town square contrasts with a quiet scene between the two lovers, Grusha and Simon, which follows immediately.

3   We move from one group to an opposing group. In the early sections of Goethe's *Goetz von Berlichingen*, the hero is waging war against the Bishop of Bamberg, and the scenes move from Goetz, to the Bishop, and back again. We can view both sides as they prepare for a confrontation.

4   Comic scenes alternate with serious scenes. In *Macbeth*, just after Macbeth has murdered King Duncan, there is a knock on the door of the castle. It is one of the most serious moments of the play, but the man who goes to open the door is a comical character, a drunken porter, whose speech is a humorous interlude in the grim business of the play. In *Hamlet,* the gravedigger and his assistant are preparing the grave for Ophelia when Hamlet comes on the scene. The gravediggers are joking about death, but for Hamlet, who soon learns the grave is Ophelia's, it is a somber moment. This juxtaposition of the comic with the serious may seem incongruous, but properly handled, it can bring out the irony and poignancy of an event in a way rarely achieved by other means.

There are of course other forms of alternation in episodic drama, but the above illustrations give an indication of the ways in which this technique can be used to create dramatic effects.

Overall Effect

As for cause and effect in episodic drama, the impression created is of events piling up: a tidal wave of circumstances and emotions sweeping over the characters. Rarely does one letter, one phone call, or one piece of information determine the fate of a character. Time and again, Hamlet has proof that Claudius has killed his father, but it is a rush of events which eventually leads him to kill Claudius, not a single piece of hard evidence. The corruption in the court of Denmark is pervasive, and it is the combined weight of incidents and atmosphere that makes the outcome inevitable rather than a single precipitating incident. Episodic drama, by developing a series of extensions, parallels, contrasts, juxtapositions—in fact a whole web or network of characters and events—achieves a cumulative effect all its own, at its best creating what Gassner referred to as a "tumultuous play."

The countries and periods (together with prominent playwrights) in which the episodic form has predominated include England, late sixteenth and early seventeenth centuries (Shakespeare, Marlowe); Spain, late sixteenth and early seventeenth centuries (Lope de Vega, Calderon); Germany, late eighteenth and early nineteenth centuries (Goethe, Lessing, Schiller, Büchner); and Europe and America, late nineteenth and twentieth centuries (Ibsen, Brecht, Genet).

It will be noted that in modern theater both climactic and episodic forms have been adopted, sometimes by one playwright. This is characteristic of the diversity of our age. Ibsen, for example wrote a number of well-made plays—*Ghosts, Hedda Gabler*, etc.—but also several episodic plays, such as *Brand* and *Peer Gynt*.

COMPARING CLIMACTIC AND EPISODIC FORMS

The following table outlines the chief characteristics of the two major forms and illustrates the differences between them:

	CLIMACTIC	EPISODIC
1	Plot begins late in the story, toward the very end or climax.	Plot begins relatively early in the story and moves through a series of episodes.
2	Covers a short space of time, perhaps a few hours, or at most a few days.	Covers a longer period of time: weeks, months, and sometimes many years.
3	Contains a few, solid extended scenes, such as three acts with each act comprising one long scene.	Many short, fragmented scenes; sometimes an alternation of short and long scenes.
4	Occurs in a restricted locale, one room or one house.	May range over an entire city, or even several countries.
5	Number of characters severely limited, usually no more than six or eight.	Profusion of characters, sometimes several dozen.
6	Plot is linear, and moves in a single line with few subplots or counterplots.	Frequently marked by several threads of action, such as two parallel plots, or scenes of comic relief in a serious play.

CLIMACTIC	EPISODIC
7 Line of action proceeds in a cause-and-effect chain. The characters and events are closely linked in a sequence of logical, almost inevitable development.	Scenes are juxtaposed to one another. An event may result from several causes, or no apparent cause, but arises in a network or web of circumstances.

It is clear that the climactic and episodic differ from each other in their fundamental approach. The one emphasizes constriction and compression on all fronts; the other takes a far broader view and aims at a cumulative effect, piling up people, places, and events.

COMBINING CLIMACTIC AND EPISODIC FORMS

There is no law which says a play must fall exclusively in the episodic or climactic form. They are not watertight compartments. It is true that during certain periods, one form or the other has been predominant. And it is not easy to mix the two, because as we have seen, each has its own laws and its own inner logic.

The two forms have been mixed successfully, however, particularly in the modern period. There are plays which fall primarily in one category, but incorporate features of the other. *Cyrano de Bergerac*, by Edmond Rostand, has the traditional five acts of climactic drama; at the same time it has a multitude of characters—well over fifty—and between the fourth and fifth acts there is a gap of fifteen years. Chekhov, who generally writes about one principal action and sets his plays in one household, usually has more characters than is customary in climactic drama—fifteen in *The Cherry Orchard*, for instance. Frequently, too, Chekhov's plays cover a period of several months or years.

Arthur Miller in *Death of a Salesman* has combined the two forms in still a different way. The main frame of the story is in climactic form and covers the last hours of Willie Loman's life. Events from the past, however, are not described in exposition as is usually the case, but presented as full-fledged scenes. Rather than hearing about the past, we see it enacted in a series of flashback scenes. In this way Miller achieves the finality of the climactic play but opens his drama up in the fashion of an episodic drama.

DRAMATIC DEVICES USED WITH PLOT

Before leaving climactic and episodic plots, we should note two dramatic devices which frequently occur in conjunction with plot structure.

Juxtaposition of Chorus or Narrator to the Main Action

A technique used in many plays is a *dialectic* or *counterpoint* between a party outside the play and characters in the central action. ("Counterpoint" is a term from music denoting a second melody that accompanies or moves in contrast to the main melody.) Good examples of the device are the chorus in Greek drama or a narrator in a modern play. In Greek drama, the chorus is rarely part of the plot itself, but stands outside the action, arguing with the main characters, making connections between present events and the past, warning the main characters of impending danger, and drawing conclusions from what has occurred.

In the modern play *Our Town*, author Thornton Wilder used a Stage Manager to comment on the action. Wilder set up a counterpoint between the episodes of the play—most of them mundane, everyday events—and the more general, universal observations of the Stage Manager. By setting one element next to the other, he gave broader meaning to specific episodes and, at the same time, a concrete, down-to-earth reality to philosophical observations. As an example, at the opening of the play, Joe Crowell, Jr., while delivering the morning paper, sees Doc Gibbs, and talks to him about such things as the marriage of Joe's schoolteacher and his trick knee—perfectly ordinary topics of conversation. But later in the play, the Stage Manager gives a broader perspective to Joe's life when he tells us that after graduating from high school with honors, Joe won a scholarship to MIT, only to die shortly thereafter in France fighting in World War I. As the Stage Manager observes, "All that education for nothing."

Bertolt Brecht used a narrator, and sometimes singers, in more drastic fashion. He wanted to startle members of the audience by a sudden shift from the main story to a foreign element. In *The Caucasian Chalk Circle*, Grusha, the innocent, peace-loving peasant woman, steps out of character at one point to sing a song extolling the virtues of a general who loves war. Grusha, in other words, is asked to sing a song with a point of view opposite to her own. This wrenching of characters and attitudes is deliberate on Brecht's part: to make us think about war and the ravages of war. The pieces are not meant to fit together in the play itself, but rather in the minds of the spectators.

Figure 8-5 Thornton Wilder as narrator in Our Town. *The author of* Our Town, *standing at the left, plays the narrator-stage manager in a Williamstown Theatre Festival Production. Generally, the narrator in a play stands apart from the action, comments on it, and gives it perspective. (Photo—The Williamstown Theatre Festival, Williamstown, Mass.)*

Intellectual or Conceptual Conflicts

A second device used in conjunction with traditional plot structure is an intellectual debate. This occurs particularly in a type of drama called the *play of ideas*, whose main conflict or problem is intellectual. It is worth pointing out that the purely intellectual approach to theater can be dangerous. When carried to extremes, it concentrates entirely on abstruse arguments, leaving behind flesh-and-blood characters. It ignores completely the foundation of theater, namely, the experience embodied in the actor-audience relationship. Occasionally writers present a discourse or debate in play form. But this is really a subterfuge. Such a play is a treatise in disguise, and no more related to the experience of theater than the description of the valves of the heart would be to falling in love. Ideas, insight, and perception are essential to meaningful drama, but they must serve the play and not the other way around. Philosophy is one thing, theater another. Ideas in a play must be incorporated into the fabric of the work and must be as much a part of the whole, or as wedded to the whole, as a person's soul or mind is to the body.

At times a playwright successfully gives theatrical form to an intellectual concept. A good example is *Six Characters in Search of an Author*, by the Italian playwright Luigi Pirandello. Pirandello establishes an opposition between actors rehearsing a play and a group of fictional characters who are not real people but creations like Hamlet or Hedda Gabler. The characters urge the actors to perform their story, which has never been presented in final form, and in the process of this confrontation Pirandello raises questions of appearance versus reality, and fiction versus fact.

NONSENSE AND NONSEQUITUR: THEATER OF THE ABSURD

Following World War II a new type of theater emerged in Europe and America. Critic Martin Esslin has called it the *Theater of the Absurd*. Although dramatists whose work falls in this category do not write in identical styles and are not really a "school" of writers, they do share enough in common to be considered together. Esslin took the name for this form of theater from a quotation in *The Myth of Sisyphus* by the French writer, dramatist, and philosopher Albert Camus (1913–1960). Camus maintains that in the present age we have lost the comfort and security of being able to explain the world by reason and logic. As he puts it in *The Myth of Sisyphus*:

> A world that can be explained by reasoning, however faulty, is a familiar world. But in a universe that is suddenly deprived of illusions and light, man feels a stranger. His is an irremediable exile, because he is deprived of memories of a lost homeland as much as he lacks hope of a promised land to come. This divorce between man and his life, the actor and his setting, truly constitutes the feeling of Absurdity.[3]

Camus is saying that the modern world is absurd; it makes no sense. One cannot explain the injustices, the inconsistencies, and the malevolence of today's world in terms of the moral yardsticks of the past.

Plays falling in the Theater of the Absurd category express the ideas articulated by Camus and others like him. In one way or another they convey a sense of alienation and of people having lost their bearings in an illogical, unjust, and ridiculous world. Although serious, this viewpoint, generally, is depicted in plays with considerable humor; an ironic note runs through much of the Theater of the Absurd. For example, in Samuel Beckett's *Waiting for Godot*, the chief characters frequently say one thing and do just the opposite. One says to the other, "Well, shall we go?" and the other says, "Yes, let's go." But having said this, they don't move; they sit stone still, and the contrast between their words and deeds is funny.

Theater of the Absurd plays suggest the ideas of absurdity both in what they say—their content—and in the way they say it—their form. Their structure, for instance, is a departure from dramatic structures of the past.

Structure in Theater of the Absurd

Traditional plot arrangements in drama proceed in a logical way from a beginning through the development of the plot to a conclusion. This in turn suggests an ordered universe. Even violent or disordered events, such as Macbeth's murder of Duncan or King Lear's madness, are presented in a rational framework. The same was true of writers in the 1920s and 1930s: many of their plays *described* absurdity, but the structure of their plays did not *demonstrate* absurdity. The dramatists of the Theater of the Absurd set about correcting this discrepancy so that their plays not only proclaimed absurdity, they embodied it.

An example is *The Bald Soprano*, by Eugene Ionesco. The very title of the play is nonsense; a bald soprano is mentioned once in the play, but with no explanation, and it is clear that the bald soprano has nothing whatever to do with the play as a whole. The absurdity of the piece is manifest the moment the curtain goes up. A typical English couple is sitting in a living room when the clock on the mantle strikes seventeen times and the wife's first words are, "There, it's nine o'clock." At one point a fire chief, dressed in full uniform, bursts into the living room. He claims to be looking for fires, but when he finds no fires, he stays to tell stories to the two couples present. It is obvious that there is no logical explanation for his being there. We have mentioned other Ionesco plays with equally ridiculous elements, such as *Amedee*, in which a long-dead corpse continues to grow and finally crashes through the wall of the apartment on stage during the course of the play.

Edward Albee, an American playwright, has also written plays in the absurd form. His *The American Dream*, a study of the banality and insensitivity of American family life, introduces a handsome young man of around twenty as the embodiment of the American Dream. The Mommy and Daddy of the play wish to adopt him because he seems perfect to them. We learn, however, that he is only half a person; he is all appearance, with no inner feelings. He is the other half of a child Mommy and Daddy had mutilated and destroyed years before when the child began to have feelings, to want to touch things, and to express curiosity about the world around him. Obviously Mommy and Daddy care more for appearance than true human emotions. To further underscore the absurdity of Mommy's and Daddy's world, Albee has them return from a search of their house to report that an entire room has suddenly disappeared.

It should be noted that not every play in the absurdist form abandons traditional plot structure altogether. At the same time that they contain elements of nonsense, a few Theater of the Absurd plays adopt a conventional approach in developing the incidents of the play. The characters move through a series of episodes, increasing in tension to the point where they reach a climax, and then conclude. In Ionesco's *The Lesson* a professor is teaching a student math. As he moves to linguistics he becomes increasingly agitated; he torments the student with growing menace until finally he stabs her to death in a climactic moment. In another Ionesco play, *The Chairs*, an old couple sets up chairs for a group of imaginary visitors, and the pace of the arrival of guests builds to the climax. Harold Pinter's plays, such as *The Birthday Party* and *The Homecoming*, also develop in the manner of more traditional plays. In Theater of the Absurd plays where the structure is familiar, the dislocation and disruption which we associate with the form occurs in the behavior of the characters, in unexpected incidents, and in language.

Verbal Nonsense

Events and characters are frequently illogical in the Theater of the Absurd and so too is language. "Nonsequitur" is a Latin term meaning that one thing does not follow from what went before, and it perfectly describes the method of Theater of the Absurd, including the use of language. Sentences do not follow in sequence, and words do not mean what we expect them to mean. As Esslin says, there is a tendency "toward a radical devaluation of language."

A passage from Ionesco's *The Bald Soprano* in which two couples are talking will illustrate the point:

Mrs. Smith: The car goes very fast, but the cook beats batter better.
Mr. Smith: Don't be turkeys; rather kiss the conspirator.
Mrs. Smith: I'm waiting for the aqueduct to come see me at my windmill.
Mr. Martin: One can prove that social progress is definitely better with sugar.
Mr. Smith: To hell with polishing![4]

The majority of the dialogue in the play is equally irrelevent and based on just such nonsequiturs.

Figure 8-6 **Existential characters in** Waiting for Godot. *The characters in Samuel Beckett's play have no real past—only a present. The structure of the play does not unfold like the typical narrative. Events occur, patterns are repeated, rather than moving from the beginning of a story to its resolution. (Photo—Diane Gorodnitzki.)*

Another example of the irrationality or debasement of language is found in Samuel Beckett's *Waiting for Godot.* The character Lucky does not speak for most of his time on stage, but at the end of the first act, he delivers a long speech of incoherent, religious, legalistic jargon. The opening lines offer a small sample:

Lucky: Given the existence as uttered forth in the public works of Puncher and Wattmann of a personal God quaquaquaqua with white beard quaquaquaqua outside time without extension who from the heights of divine apathia divine athambia divine aphasia loves us dearly with some exceptions for reasons unknown but time will tell. . . .[5]

One could multiply the examples of such language many times over, not only in the plays of Ionesco and Beckett, but in those of most absurdist writers.

Existential Characters

A significant feature of the structure of absurdist plays lies in the handling of characters. Not only is there an element of the ridiculous in their actions, they frequently exemplify an *existential* point of view toward human behavior. Most traditional philosophies hold that essence precedes existence, that is, that there is a quality for everything which is present even before it exists. There is a quality for apples, for instance, before an individual apple appears on a tree, and in personal terms, a *self* for each person preceding his or her existence. *Existentialism*, on the other hand, holds that existence precedes essence; a person creates himself or herself in the process of living. Beginning with nothing, the person develops a self—an essence—in taking action and making choices.

When applied to theater, existentialism suggests that characters have no personal history before the play begins: no background and therefore no specific causes for their actions. This is contrary to the practice of most traditional drama. Take the case of Blanche DuBois in *A Streetcar Named Desire.* We learn in the play that Blanche has come from an aristocratic Southern background, has had several unfortunate experiences with men, and has lost both money and prestige at home. These facts explain why she is so desperate when she arrives in New Orleans to stay with her sister and brother-in-law.

By contrast, the two main characters in Beckett's *Waiting for Godot* are devoid of biographies and personal motivation. We are told nothing of their backgrounds, or their family life, or their occupations. As characters they exist; they *are*, but without explanation. They meet every night at a crossroads to wait for Godot, but how long they have been coming there, or what they do when they are not there, remains a mystery. They exist for the moment, in the here and now.

This lack of concern for background and motivation has an effect on structure. In the Theater of the Absurd we see characters for whom little or no explanation is offered. We catch them in midair, or midstream, and this is what the dramatist wants. There is no preoccupation with the past, no solving of riddles as in *Oedipus*. The structure does not lead us to seek solutions but to confront a view of modern life, a view both existential and absurd.

NONSEQUITUR IN THE NEW THEATER

Like the absurdists, certain practitioners of the New Theater abandon logic in putting scenes together. Their argument—similar to the one for multifocus theater—is that life itself is unstructured and therefore art should be too. To this extent, the viewpoints of the absurdists and the New Theater exponents are related, but there are essential differences in focus and intent. The dramatists of the Theater of the Absurd wish to create an absurd world in their art, whereas the exponents of abandoning structure in the New Theater wish to avoid art or creation altogether. With the latter the emphasis is more on the random, disconnected quality of life than the absurd, ridiculous quality. Rather than writing a single play such as *The Bald Soprano* or *The American Dream*, they advocate stringing together a series of unrelated activities or events. In Happenings, for instance, various arts, such as painting, film, and music, are combined, as well as various activities.

Michael Kirby, an expert on Happenings and the New Theater, describes a typical sequence of events offered to an audience in this type of presentation:

> A piano is destroyed. The orchestra conductor walks on stage, bows to the audience, raises his baton, and the curtain falls. A formally dressed man appears with a french horn under his arm; when he bows, ball bearings pour forth from the bell of a horn in a noisy cascade. A person asks if La Monte Young is in the audience; when there is no answer, he leaves. A man sets a balloon on stage, carefully estimates the distance as he walks away from it, then does a backward flip, landing on the balloon and breaking it.[6]

John Cage, an avant-garde composer also active in creating Happenings, describes the purpose behind a lack of structure in a theater presentation:

> The structure we should think about is that of each person in the audience. In other words, his consciousness is structuring the experience differently from anybody else's in the audience. So the less we structure the theatrical occasion and the more it is like unstructured daily life, the greater will be the stimulus to the structuring faculty of each person in the audience.[7]

Cage is saying that if the audience is given a series of unrelated events, or several events simultaneously, each member of the audience will put them together like a personal jigsaw puzzle. Perhaps, too, Cage is suggesting that it will be more meaningful because it will belong to the individual audience member and to no one else.

Of course, making spectators more aware, raising their consciousness, is important, but the argument for a totally unstructured work of art is debatable. Just as there is a distinction between the roles of the performer and the spectator, so is there a distinction between the roles of the creators of theater—writers, directors, designers, as well as actors—and the observer. We go to the theater to see a different vision of life from the one we carry with us every day.

Reflecting life in an imaginative way—the job of the artist—is not the same thing as simply duplicating it. Besides, any attempt to demonstrate the random quality of life in a theatrical context always takes on a special aura because it is being "presented."

We have been describing an extreme, however. Most New Theater pieces and the major portion of the Theater of the Absurd present an illogical structure, or a series of nonsequiturs, with a definite artistic purpose in mind. There is sense to the nonsense. Such presentations, while not necessarily leading to logical conclusions, do create dramatic tension and lead us to ask why such puzzling material is being shown to us. For some dramatists this is enough—for us to ask questions. At the very least, this technique creates uncertainty and expectancy in wondering what will happen next or what it all means. At its best, however, it does much more than that; it brings us face to face with a view of the world which many feel accurately reflects the chaos and uncertainty of the modern world. When this is done with intelligence and inventiveness—and with humor, as it often is—this type of theater is fulfilling the ancient function of the art in providing us with a unique experience of ourselves and our world.

RITUAL OR PATTERN AS DRAMATIC STRUCTURE

Thus far, we have discussed two forms of traditional structure—the climactic and the episodic—and two more contemporary forms—the Absurdist and random arrangements such as we find in Happenings. We turn now to two other forms of structure which are used in combination with other forms, or serve as the basis of structure by themselves—ritual and pattern.

Ritual

Like acting, ritual is a part of everyday life of which we are generally unaware. Basically, ritual is the repetition or reenactment of a proceeding or transaction which has acquired special meaning. It may be a simple ritual like singing the national anthem before a sports contest, or a deeply religious one such as the Mass in the Roman Catholic church or the Kaddish for the dead in the Jewish faith. Every one of us in our personal or family life develops rituals: a certain meal we eat with the family once a week, or a routine we go through every time we take an examination in school.

Occasions like Thanksgiving, Christmas, or Passover become family rituals, with the same order of events each year, the same menu, and perhaps even the same conversation. Rituals give continuity, security, and comfort to human beings. Often, as in the case of primitive tribes, those performing a ritual assume that by carrying out a ceremony faithfully they will be blessed or their wishes granted. Conversely, they assume that a failure to follow the ritual to the letter will lead to punishment.

In the theater, ritual is an area where the old and new come together. Traditional plays are full of rituals: coronations, weddings, funerals, and other ceremonies. And in the modern theater, ritual has been rediscovered and given new life. The British playwright David Storey (1933–) has incorporated a type of ritual in the structure of his plays *The Contractor* and *The Changing Room*. In each play a group of men go about a task or repeat a routine they have been through many times before. In *The Contractor* a crew of laborers erects a tent for the wedding of their employer's daughter. In the first act they set up the tent, in the second act they decorate it, and in the third act they take it down. Their individual jobs—putting in stakes, unfolding canvas, tying ropes—become ritualized through repetition. *The Changing Room* develops in a similar way. In the first act we see a semiprofessional English rugby team in the locker room preparing for a Saturday afternoon match. In the second act we see the team at half time, and in the third, we see the exhausted players after the game. The symbolic values the men attach to small routines, and the sustenance they draw from them, are brought sharply into focus in both of these plays.

Ritual has structure. Actions are repeated in a set fashion; they have a beginning, middle, and end, and there is a natural progression of events. Storey has made the structure of ritual a part of the structure of his plays. The New Theater movement has made a conscious attempt to develop new rituals or revive old ones. The Performance Group's *Dionysus in 69* included a birth ritual adopted from an Asmat New Guinea ritual. In *The Serpent*, the Open Theater created a ritualistic version of the assassination of President John F. Kennedy. The scene is the car in which the President and Mrs. Kennedy and Governor John Connally of Texas and his wife rode. There are twelve frozen scenes or tableaux representing various stages in the assassination, beginning with the actors waving to the crowds. We move from this to a still-life scene of the President being shot in the neck, then to the Governor being shot, then to the President falling against his wife, and so forth. The actors assume the twelve poses as numbers from one to twelve are shouted out, and once the actors have gone through the sequence, they repeat it in reverse order. This "stop action" lets us concentrate on individual moments in the incident; it clothes the event in a ritual which can be repeated. At the same time, this method of presentation evokes images of single frames from a movie film, or "freeze frames" on television.

Patterns

Related to ritual is a pattern of events. In Samuel Beckett's *Waiting for Godot*, the characters have no personal history, and the play does not build to a climax in the ordinary way. But if Beckett has sacrificed traditional plot structure, he has replaced it with a repeated sequence of events containing its own order and logic. The play has two acts, and in each act a series of incidents is duplicated. Each act opens with the two chief characters coming together on a lonely crossroads after having been separated. Then in both acts a similar sequence of events occurs: they greet each other; they despair of Godot's ever coming; they attempt to entertain themselves. Two other men, Pozzo and Lucky, appear, and following a lengthy scene, disappear. The men are left alone once more. The two acts continue to follow the same sequence: a small boy comes to tell them that Godot will not come that day; the boy leaves, and the men remain together for another night. There are important differences between the two acts—differences which give the play meaning and resonance—but the identical sequence of events in each act achieves a pattern which takes on a ritualistic quality.

The Serpent, which contains within it such rituals as the Kennedy assassination, also develops a pattern of action. It opens with a contemporary scene, then moves back in time to the Garden of Eden in biblical times. It returns to the present, then moves once more to Adam and Eve, and so on—alternating between Old Testament times and the present. With their regularity and rhythm, such patterns provide us with a sense of structure which takes the place of plot development in a traditional play.

When ritual occurs in theater, we might ask, where are the dynamics and tension? Does ritual not deteriorate into dull routine or hollow repetition? It can, of course, but ritual, though sometimes known by heart, is not static. Remember, it is a reenactment, or reliving, of an episode or occasion, and as such, is active, not passive. Beyond that, ritual has special powers; it carries with it the magic or mystery of a meaningful, almost holy act. This can be its source of energy in theater, as it is in life.

A SERIES OF INDIVIDUAL THEATER EVENTS

A different kind of structure is a series of acts or episodes offered as a single presentation. In this case, individual segments are strung together like beads on a necklace. Sometimes a central theme or common thread holds the parts together; sometimes there is little or

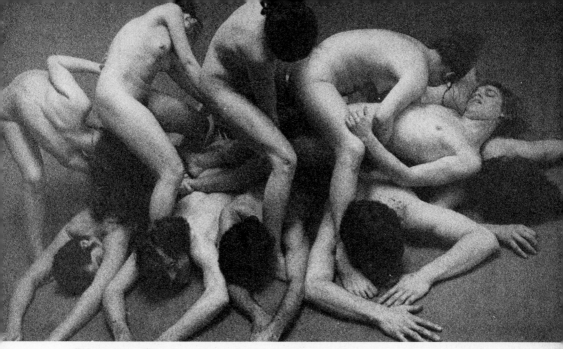

Figure 8-7 Ritual on stage. *The Performance Group incorporates an Asmat birth ritual from New Guinea in its production of* Dionysus in 69. *The man at the right symbolically emerges from the womb. Through repetition and formalization, ritual gives significance to events and a secure feeling to those who take part or observe. (Photo—Max Waldman.)*

no connection among the various parts. The musical revue is a case in point. In the revue, short scenes, vignettes, skits, dance numbers, songs, and possibly even vaudeville routines are presented on a single program. There may be an overall theme, such as political satire or the celebration of a certain year from the past. Sometimes a master of ceremonies provides continuity to the various segments. In a revue for which there is no visible connection of the parts, the primary consideration is the pace and variety of the acts. A song is usually followed by a dramatic scene, a serious number by a comic one, and so forth.

The short play, often called the one-act, is the basic unit for many theatrical programs. The structure of short plays can follow any one of the plot developments outlined above. A short play can be climactic or episodic or written in the style of the New Theater or the Theater of the Absurd. The exact form will be dictated by general theater practice and the preferences of the individual dramatist.

Plays in the medieval period were in the short form. A cycle of brief plays depicted a series of biblical stories. A play about Adam and Eve would be followed by one about Cain and Abel; these would be followed by plays about Abraham and Isaac, Noah, and so on. Although they had a common religious theme, each play in the series was self-contained. Some were serious and others contained strong elements of humor. In the Oriental theater a series of short plays strung together is the rule rather than the exception. For centuries in India, China, and Japan, theater practice has leaned to this form. The Noh theater of Japan, for instance, features from two to five short plays on a program, each play being separated from the others by a brief comical interlude.

In today's theater we frequently see a program of short plays. Sometimes there will be a bill of one-act plays by the same author, but at other times two or three plays by different authors. Also, on some occasions an attempt is made to relate the separate plays to a central theme, but on others the plays are chosen simply to complete an evening's entertainment.

SIGNIFICANCE OF STRUCTURE

The Foundation of Drama

Every work of art has some kind of structure. Whether it is loosely connected or tightly knit is not important; what is important is that a framework exists. There is a loose analogy or parallel between the structure of a play and that of a building. An architect and an engineer are like a playwright and a director. The architect and engineer plan a skeleton or substructure which will provide the inner strength for the building. They determine the depth of the foundation, the weight of the support beams, and the stress on the side walls. In a similar fashion the playwright and director establish a premise for the play which serves as its foundation; they introduce various stresses and strains in the form of conflicts; they establish boundaries and outer limits to contain the play; they calculate the dynamics of the action. In short, they "construct" a play.

Buildings vary enormously in size and shape: they can be as diverse as a skyscraper, a cathedral, and a small cottage. Buildings can come in clusters, such as homes in a suburban development or the buildings on a college campus. And engineering requirements will vary according to the needs of individual structures: a gymnasium roof must span a vast, open area, and this calls for a different construction from that of a sixty-story skyscraper. These in turn call for something different from a ski lodge on the side of a mountain. Plays, too, vary; they can be climactic, episodic, ritualistic, or randomly arranged. The important point is that each play, like each piece of architecture, has its own internal laws, its own framework, which give it its shape, strength, and meaning. Without structure, a theater event falls apart, just as a building collapses which has been put together improperly.

Naturally, structure manifests itself differently in theater from the way it manifests itself in architecture. A play is not a building. It unfolds through time rather than occupying space. It evolves and develops like a living organism, and we become aware of its structure as we sense the underlying pattern and rhythm of the production. The repeated impulses of two characters in conflict or the tension which mounts as the pace quickens: these insinuate themselves into our subconsciousness like the throb of a silent drum beat. Moment by moment we see what is happening on stage, but below the surface we sense a substructure, giving the event meaning and purpose.

Problems of Structure

Frequently we see a production in which most elements—the acting, the costumes, the scenery, the words, even the situation—appear correct. But somehow the play does not seem to progress; it becomes dull and repetitious. Or perhaps the play becomes confusing and diffuse, going off in several directions at once. When this happens, the chances are that the problems are structural. Either no clear structure existed to begin with or the structure which did exist was violated along the way. This suggests two principles of dramatic structure: (1) every theatrical event must have an underlying pattern or organization, and (2) once the pattern or organization is established, it must be true to itself—it must be organic and have integrity. A plot in the climactic form which suddenly becomes episodic two-thirds of the way through the play will cause confusion. Conversely, a play cast in the random mold of a Happening which suddenly takes on the rigid structure of a climactic drama becomes overly artificial and contrived.

Sometimes a basically acceptable pattern is repeated too often and becomes repetitous. *La Ronde*, by the Austrian playwright Arthur Schnitzler (1862–1931), is a clever theater piece in ten scenes, each of which is a seduction scene. As the play progresses, one person from a preceding scene is paired with a new partner in the next scene in a kind of "round dance." In spite of its originality, however, the play eventually is predictable because the action underlying each scene remains the same. Quite often, plays with a less obvious pattern than *La Ronde* have a similar problem: though the characters and events appear to change and develop, underneath they remain essentially the same.

Although sometimes less apparent than the performances of the actors and actresses or less obvious than the words and actions of the play, structure is no less important.

Structure as Part of the Theater Experience

We said earlier that for the audience theater is an experience of the imagination and that it involves particularly the encounter between spectators and performers. But no matter how stimulating a performance on stage might be, it is not complete theater experience if it has no form or shape. Structure provides the necessary shape and form, the profile or contour into which the experience can fit. Art stands apart from life by selecting materials from life and organizing them into an artistic whole—a process that involves structure. By furnishing the framework which holds the experience together, structure becomes an integral part of the theater experience.

SUMMARY

1 There are several basic types of dramatic structure. The form adopted by the Greeks and used frequently since then is the *climactic* form. Its characteristics are a plot beginning quite late in the story; a limited number of characters; a limited number of locations and scenes; little or no extraneous material; tight construction, including a cause-and-effect chain of events.

2 The *episodic* form of dramatic structure involves a plot covering an extended span of time; numerous locations; a large cast of characters; diverse events, including the mixing of comic and serious episodes; parallel plots or subplots. Shakespeare's plays are good examples of the episodic form.

3 The climactic and episodic forms can be combined, as they have been in the modern period in the works of Anton Chekhov, Arthur Miller, and others.

4 Nonsense or nonsequitur, a feature of the Theater of the Absurd, can be the basis of dramatic construction. Events do not logically follow one another, suggesting the chaos and absurdity of the world in which we live.

5 The New Theater sometimes arranges events in a random way to suggest the random or haphazard manner in which life unfolds in everyday situations.

6 Ritual often is used as the basis of dramatic structure. Words, gestures, and events are repeated; they have a symbolic meaning acquired both through repetition and through the significance invested in them from the past.

7 In certain cases theater events are strung together to make a program. This could include a group of unrelated one-act plays, or a

group of skits and songs in a revue. In this case structure is within the individual units themselves. Among the units the only structure might be the separate elements unfolding; or there can be a common theme uniting them.

8 Structure of some kind is essential in the theater. Whether carefully wrought or developed in some less organized way, the skeleton of a piece—its construction—communicates an important part of its meaning. Without structure of any kind, we do not have art.

We have examined three significant areas contributing to the theater experience: the audience; the performers and their parts; and the dramatic structure. We come now to a fourth: the point of view or perspective with which we view a production. Point of view provides signposts telling us how to approach the characters and the story. As we watch events unfold on stage, we need a clue as to what they mean and how we are to take them. A simple story, or a group of characters taken alone, might be interpreted in many ways, and we need guidance. For example, is what we see on stage to be taken seriously, or is it all in fun? Is the story something which might actually happen in life, or is it simply a fantasy? Point of view addresses itself to these questions. It tells us what attitude and frame of mind we should adopt as we watch a theater production. This important aspect of the theater experience is the subject of the next section.

POINT OF VIEW

DRAMATIC STRUCTURE

ENVIRONMENT

PERFORMERS   AUDIENCE

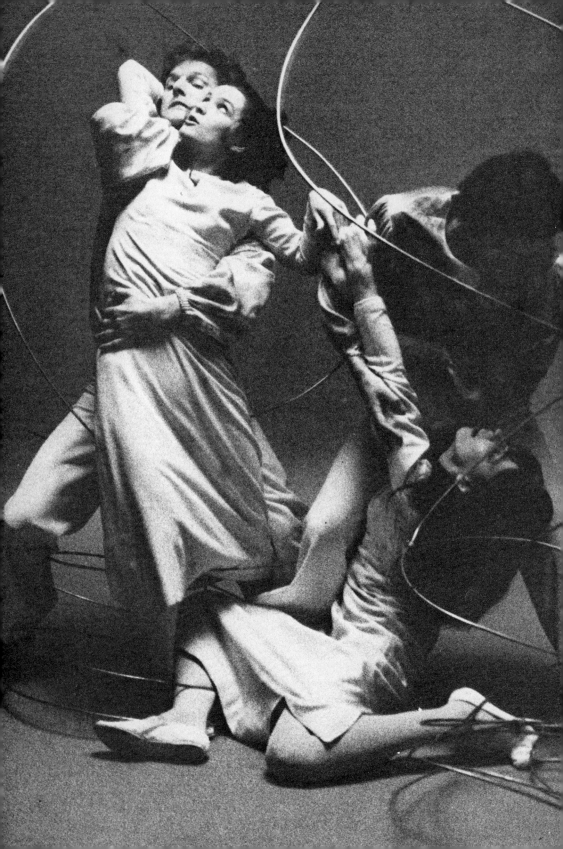

9
SUBJECT MATTER: DIFFERENT APPROACHES

People and events can always be interpreted in widely different ways. How we perceive them depends on our point of view. There is the familiar story of two people looking at a bottle half filled with wine; the optimist will say that the bottle is half full, but the pessimist will note that the same bottle is half empty.

Anyone familiar with evidence given in a court trial involving an automobile accident knows that different witnesses, each of whom may be honest and straightforward, will describe the same accident in different terms. One will say that she saw a yellow car go through a

Figure 9-1 A modern view of Shakespeare. In his production of A Midsummer Night's Dream, *director Peter Brook, along with his scenic and costume designer, brought a new point of view to Shakespeare's comedy. The coiled wires suggest the intrigues in which the characters are caught. A clear point of view is essential to all art, including theater. (Photo—Max Waldman.)*

stoplight and hit a blue car; another will say that he remembers clearly that the blue car pulled out before the light had changed and blocked the path of the yellow car. The same variation in viewpoint affects our assessment of politicians and other public figures. To some people, a certain politician will be a dedicated, sincere public servant, interested only in what is best for the people. But to others, that same politician will be a hypocrite and a charlatan, that is, a fake, concerned exclusively with personal gain.

Point of view influences the way we look at virtually everything in life, but it plays a particularly important role in the arts. Under ordinary circumstances, those who attempt to determine our point of view, such as advertisers or politicians, frequently disguise their motives, employing subtle and indirect techniques to convince us that they are not trying to impose their views on us, but we know that that is exactly what they are trying to do. In the arts, on the other hand, the imposition of a point of view is direct and deliberate. Rather than being disguised, it is emphasized. The artist makes it clear that he or she is looking at the world from a highly personal point of view, perhaps turning the world upside down, or looking at it from an unusual angle.

A good example can be found in films, where we have become familiar with the various points of view, angles of vision, and perspectives which the camera selects for us. In a close-up we do not see an entire room, or even an entire person; we see one small detail: a hand putting out a cigarette or a finger on the trigger of a gun. In a medium shot we see more—a couple embracing, perhaps—but still only part of their bodies. In an exterior scene we might view a panorama of the vast plains of the Russian steppes or a full military parade. The camera also predetermines the angle from which we see the action. In a scene emphasizing the strength of a figure, the camera will look up from below to show a man looming from the top of a flight of stairs. In another scene we might look down on the action. The camera might be tilted so that a scene looks off balance; a scene might be shot out of focus so that it is hazy or blurred; or it might be filmed through a special filter.

Whereas in everyday life we resist having someone tell us how to look at things, greeting an advertisement or a political speech with a certain skepticism, in the arts our reaction is just the opposite. We value art precisely because it presents its own point of view, giving us a fresh look at ourselves and the world around us.

As with the other arts, point of view is an important ingredient of theater. It tells us how to interpret the words and actions of the characters we see on stage; it provides a key to understanding the entire experience. In a successful theater production, point of view permeates the work. It is reflected in the script, in the actions of the performers, in the design of the costumes, scenery, and lighting. So strong is it that it takes us inside the work and permits us to see the subject through the artists' eyes. Their world becomes our world. This sharing of a point of view is an absolutely essential element of the experience.

Basically, there are two areas of theater in which point of view is particularly significant. One is the area of tragedy and comedy, and the other is the area of realism and nonrealism, to which we turn first.

REALISM AND NONREALISM

In theater it is always possible to look at a subject *realistically* or *nonrealistically*. Initially, we spoke of realism when we discussed acting and the techniques of Constantin Stanislavski. What do we mean by *realism* and *nonrealism*? At the outset it is essential to know that realism, when applied to the theater, denotes a special application of what we call genuine or real. The division between realism and nonrealism does not imply that one is genuine and the other is not. Rather, realism and nonrealism are two different ways of presenting "reality." Realism in the theater refers to what is recognizable from everyday life. In one sense it implies photographic realism; we call those elements of theater realistic which conform to our observations of people, places, and events. Another way of putting the difference is to say that in realism, events follow an observable cause-and-effect sequence, whereas in nonrealism they may not. We are referring here to such things as the law of gravity, or to the fact that it takes a person a certain length of time to travel from one place to another, or to accepted rules of human behavior. Realism must generally observe these principles, but nonrealism is not compelled to.

Realism and nonrealism are also known as *representational* and *presentational* theater, respectively. These terms come from the fact that in realism an actress *represents* the character she plays; she attempts to do all in her power to merge her personality with the character's and to convince the audience that she is not merely playing the character, but *is* the character. In the same way, a stage set in realism *represents* the real thing: a hospital room appears to be a true hospital room, in every respect. By contrast, *presentational* theater makes no attempt to be the person or thing; it frankly *presents* its subject. An illustration of presentational theater is the convention in the Elizabethan period in England of having women's parts played by

Figures 9-2a and 9-2b   Realism and nonrealism. *These two stage settings illustrate the differences between two approaches to reality. The room seen at the top in* That Championship Season *is "real" in that the walls, lamps, and furniture look just as they would in someone's home. The set for* Androcles and the Lion *shown below, however, is unmistakably "unreal"—the trees are cutouts, and the outline of the four columns stand for an entire building. Nonrealism offers possibilities for fantasy and the imaginative not available in realism. (Photo on left—George E. Joseph. Photo on right—The New York Public Library at Lincoln Center, Theatre Collection. Astor, Lenox and Tilden Foundations. Photo by Vandamm.)*

boy actors. All Shakespeare's heroines—Desdemona, Lady Macbeth, Cordelia—were played not by women, as they are today, but by young boys. Obviously, no one in the audience at an Elizabethan theater thought that the young boys *were* women; instead it was understood that a boy was *presenting* an impression or imitation of a woman. Presentational theater says quite honestly to its audience: "What you see is a symbol, an image, a suggestion of life, not a substitute for it."

A wide range of techniques and devices in the theater falls in the nonrealistic or presentational category. A good example is the soliloquy in which a character speaks alone to the audience, expressing in words an unexpressed thought. In real life, we might confess some of our inner fears or hopes to a priest, a psychiatrist, or our best friend, but we do not announce such fears out loud for the world to hear as Hamlet does when he says, "To be or not to be. . . ." Another example of nonrealism is pantomime, in which performers pretend to be using articles that do not actually exist, such as pouring a cup of coffee or opening an umbrella. Many aspects of musical comedy are nonrealistic. A street gang walking in an alley does not suddenly break into a carefully rehearsed dance routine as the performers in *West Side Story* do. Nor do people burst into song in someone's living room or in a classroom. One could say that any activity or scenic device which transcends or symbolizes reality tends to be nonrealistic.

The concept of realism and nonrealism will be clearer if we cite specific examples. The two approaches manifest themselves in every

Figure 9-3 **Walking an imaginary tightrope.** *Pantomime, as practiced by Marcel Marceau, is an excellent example of nonrealistic acting. The pantomimist pretends he has coffee to pour, stairs to climb, or a rope to walk when none of these actually exists. (Photo—Ronald A. Wilford Associates.)*

area of theater, and the following table illustrates the contrast between them:

REALISM	NONREALISM
Story	
Events taken from everyday life which the audience knows have happened or might happen: Blanche DuBois in Tennessee Williams's *A Streetcar Named Desire* goes to New Orleans to visit her sister and brother-in-law.	Events which do not occur in real life, but only in the imagination: Emily in Thornton Wilder's *Our Town*, after she has died, appears alive and returns to visit the earth for one day.
Structure	
Action confined to real places; time passes normally as it does in everyday life: in *The Little Foxes* by Lillian Hellman the activity occurs over several days in Regina's house as she takes control of her family's estate.	Arbitrary use of time and place: in Strindberg's *The Dream Play*, walls dissolve, characters are transformed, as in a dream.
Characters	
Recognizable human beings such as the family—mother, father, and two sons—in O'Neill's *Long Day's Journey into Night*.	Unreal figures like the Ghost of Hamlet's father in *Hamlet*, the Three Witches in *Macbeth*, or the people who turn into animals in Ionesco's *Rhinoceros*.
Acting	
Performers portray people as they behave in daily life: Nora Helmer in Ibsen's *A Doll's House* leaves her husband and an unsatisfactory marriage in a believable, forthright manner.	Performers act as ghosts and animals; they also engage in singing, dancing, acrobatics and gymnastics in a musical comedy or a New Theater piece.

REALISM	NONREALISM

Language

Ordinary dialogue or conversation: the Gentleman Caller in Williams's *The Glass Menagerie* tells Laura about his future in the language of an optimistic young salesman.	Poetry such as Romeo speaks to Juliet in Shakespeare's play; or the song "Tonight" sung to Maria in the musical *West Side Story*.

Scenery

The rooms of a real house, as in Chekhov's *The Cherry Orchard*.	Abstract forms and shapes on a bare stage—for a Greek play, for example, such as Sophocles's *Electra*.

Lighting

Light on stage appears to come from natural sources—a lamp in a room, or sunlight, as in Ibsen's *Ghosts*, where the sunrise comes through a window in the final scene.	Shafts of light fall at odd angles; also, an arbitrary use of colors in the light. Example: a single, blue spotlight on a singer in a musical comedy.

Costumes

Ordinary street clothes, like those worn by the characters in Walker's *The River Niger*.	The bright costumes of a chorus in a musical comedy; the strange outfit worn by Caliban, the half-man, half-beast in Shakespeare's *The Tempest*.

Makeup

The natural look of characters in any domestic play.	Masks worn by characters in a Greek tragedy or in a modern play like van Itallie's *American Hurrah*.

Advantages of Realism

Both realism and nonrealism offer distinct advantages. As for realism, every type of theater that is not pure fantasy has an element of realism; it is an essential link with recognizable human behavior, without which theater would lose all grounding in reality. But the degree and quality of realism have varied, and it was not until fairly recently, during the nineteenth century, that strict realism became a predominant form of theater. Prior to that time the emphasis in serious drama had been on heroic or romantic drama, with the leading characters being legendary figures who bore little resemblance to the people whom the ordinary theatergoer knew.

We discussed the rise of realism in the section on realistic acting. During the latter part of the nineteenth century and the early part of the twentieth century, a number of significant artists and critics decided that theater, in order to be more meaningful, should be more closely identified with the life most people knew and understood. This movement gave rise to characters such as the housewives of Ibsen's plays, the quarreling couples of Strindberg's, and the dispossessed families of Chekhov's. Here were characters who spoke, dressed, and behaved as one expected people to, and because the characters and situations were so easily recognizable, they seemed truer. This kind of theater resembles life so closely, one assumes that it must *be* life. When we are able to verify what we see before us so readily from our own observations and experience, we are likely to accept its authenticity that much more quickly, and so realism appears to offer a direct approach to fundamental truths about human beings. Because of this direct appeal, realism has become a major form of theater in the past one hundred years, and it seems likely to remain so. A good example is found in the black theater movement which emerged in America following the Second World War, in which the primary approach of many black playwrights was realistic.

Realism takes several forms. At one extreme is *naturalism*, a kind of superrealism. Naturalism attempts to put on stage as exact a copy of life as possible, down to the smallest detail. In a naturalistic stage set of a kitchen, for instance, an actress can actually cook a meal on the stove; the toaster makes toast, the water tap produces water, and the light in the refrigerator goes on when the door opens. Characters

Figure 9-4   Nonrealism: the mask. Masks—used in theater almost from the beginning—are one of several traditional nonrealistic devices. The men in the Greek drama shown here represent the many faces of one man—Creon. Masks can freeze the face into a single expression and give an outer appearance to an inner feeling. (Photo—Kenn Duncan Ltd.)

speak and act as if they had been caught unobserved by a camera and tape recorder. In this sense, naturalism is supposed to resemble an undoctored documentary film. Naturalism is sometimes called *slice-of-life* drama, as if a section had been taken from life and transferred to the stage.

At the other extreme of realism is *heightened realism*. Here the characters and their activities are intended to resemble life, but a certain license is allowed. The scenery, for example, might be skeletal, that is, incomplete and in outline, although the words and actions of the characters are realistic. Or perhaps a character is allowed a modern version of a soliloquy in an otherwise realistic play. All art calls for selectivity, and the idea that slice-of-life theater can fulfill the total artistic requirements of the theater by itself is impractical. Heightened realism recognizes the necessity for the artist to inject selectivity and creativity into the process. Realism itself occupies the middle ground and includes the extremes at each end.

Advantages of Nonrealism

The notion of heightened realism suggests the basis for nonrealism. The argument is that the surface of life—a real conversation or real room in a house—can never convey the whole truth of life, because so much of life occurs in our heads, in our imagination. If we are deeply depressed and we tell a friend that we feel "lousy" or "awful," we do not begin to communicate the depths of our feelings. It is doubtful that the words we use everyday can ever convey the basic human emotions which play such a crucial role in our lives. It is because of the inadequacy of ordinary words that people turn to poetry, and because of the inadequacy of other forms of daily communication that they turn to music, dance, art, sculpture, and the entire range of symbols and metaphors discussed earlier. In theater, symbolic expression takes the form of nonrealistic techniques. The chorus in a Greek play can express ideas, feelings, and emotions which could never be included in a strictly realistic presentation. The feeling of being haunted by the past can never be as vividly portrayed in a simple description as it can by a figure like the ghost of Hamlet's father, or Banquo's ghost appearing before Macbeth. The opportunity for the presentation of these inner truths—of the reality that is "realer than real"—is what nonrealism offers in the theater.

Two well-known types of nonrealism are *allegory* and *expressionism*. *Allegory* is the representation of an abstract theme or subject through the symbolic use of characters, actions, or other elements of a production, such as scenery. Good examples are the medieval morality plays in which characters personify ideas in order to teach an intellectual or moral lesson. In *Everyman* actors play the parts of Good Deeds, Fellowship, Worldly Goods, etc. In less direct forms of allegory a relatively realistic story serves as a parable or lesson. Arthur Miller's play *The Crucible* is about the witch hunts in Salem, Massachusetts, in the late seventeenth century, but it can also be regarded as dealing with specific investigations by the United States Congress in the early 1950s which Miller and others felt treated ordinary citizens unfairly, becoming modern "witch hunts."

Although *expressionism* was at its height in art, literature, and the theater during the first quarter of the twentieth century, traces of it are still found today, and contemporary plays using its techniques are termed *expressionistic*. In simple terms, expressionism gives outward expression to inward feelings. In Elmer Rice's *The Adding Machine*, the feelings of Mr. Zero when he is fired from his job are conveyed by having the room spin around in a circle amid a cacophony of shrill sounds such as loud sirens and whistles.

Realism and Nonrealism: Both Are Essential

There have been times when critics or theoreticians have argued about the relative merits of realism and nonrealism, but the truth is that each offers advantages, and the theater needs them both. Each can accomplish something the other cannot, and beyond that, they are not mutually exclusive. There are ways in which they can be combined, with the assets offered by each incorporated in a final result. Arthur Miller's *Death of a Salesman*, for example, is basically realistic, but has flashbacks, fantasies, and dramatizations of events which occur only in Willy Loman's mind. Tennessee Williams's *The Glass Menagerie* is also largely realistic, but the son, Tom, steps out of the action of the play to tell the audience his own inner feelings and to describe events not shown on stage. For the audience it is important to be aware of the relative strengths and limitations of both realism and nonrealism, to understand when one or the other is being used by the playwright, director, or designer.

SERIOUS OR COMIC POINT OF VIEW

In addition to incorporating a point of view regarding realism, every theatrical production reflects a serious or comic outlook. (As with realism and nonrealism, sometimes the two points of view are combined.) We do not know why, but there is no question that individual artists look at the world through different eyes. Horace Walpole, an English author of the eighteenth century, wrote: "This world is a comedy to those that think, a tragedy to those that feel." There may or may not be truth in Walpole's epigram, but the chief point it underlines is that people see the world differently. Just why some people look at the world and weep, and others look at it and laugh, is difficult to say, but there is no question that they do. This is especially true in art, with its possibilities of selectivity. Like artists in other fields, the dramatist adopts a particular attitude toward his or her subject matter. In a serious play, for instance, the playwright says: "I know the world is not always somber; there are pleasant moments. Life is not made up exclusively of violence, treachery, and alienation. But at times it seems that way, and so for the duration of this play I will deal only with the serious side of life and put everything else aside."

Another writer might take what is ordinarily a serious subject and treat it humorously. A good example is Arthur Kopit (1937–), who, in his play *Oh, Dad. Poor Dad. Mama's Hung You in the Closet, and I'm Feelin' So Sad*, gave a comic twist to a man who has hanged himself. The title itself, with its mocking tone and its unusual length, makes it clear from the beginning that Kopit wants us to laugh at his subject.

Society's View

The most important single factor in determining the point of view of a particular play is the outlook of those who create it, especially the playwright, but also the director, the designers, and the actors. In arriving at that point of view, however, these same people are deeply influenced by the outlook of the society in which they live. We spoke earlier of the close relationship between theater and society: this manifests itself particularly in the point of view artists adopt toward their subject matter.

Tragedy, for example, occurs only in periods when society as a whole assumes a certain attitude toward people and the universe in which they live. Two periods conducive to the creation of tragedy were the Golden Age of Greece in the fifth century B.C. and the Renaissance. Both periods incorporated two ideas essential to tragic drama: on the one hand, the notion that human beings are capable of extraordinary accomplishments, and on the other, that the world is potentially cruel and unjust. A closer look at these two periods will demonstrate how they reflected these two viewpoints.

In both the fifth century B.C., in Greece, and the Renaissance (the fourteenth through the sixteenth centuries) in Europe and England, human beings were exalted above everything else, and neither the gods nor nature were given as prominent a place in the scheme of things. A look at the history of the two periods shows that men and women of the time considered the horizons for human achievement unlimited. In the fifth century B.C., Greece was enjoying its Golden Age in commerce, politics, science, and art; nothing seemed impossible in the way of architecture, mathematics, trade, or philosophy. The same was true in Europe and England during the Renaissance. Columbus had discovered the New World in 1492, and the possibilities for trade and exploration appeared infinite. Science and the arts were on the threshold of a new day as well.

In sculpture, the human figure was glorified as it rarely had been before or has been since. Fifth-century Greece abounded in statues—on friezes, in temples, in public buildings—of heroes, athletes, and warriors. And during the Renaissance, Michelangelo was only one of many who gave inimitable grace and distinction to the human form.

The celebration of the individual was apparent in all the arts, including drama. The Greek dramatist Sophocles exclaimed:

> Numberless are the wonders of the world,
> but none
> More wonderful than man

And in the Renaissance, Shakespeare has Hamlet say:

> What a piece of work is man! How noble
> in reason! how infinite in faculty!
> in form, in moving, how express and
> admirable! in action how like an angel!
> in apprehension how like a god!

The credo of both ages was expressed by Protagoras, a fifth-century B.C. Greek philosopher:

> Man is the measure of all things.

But there is another side to the tragic coin. Along with this optimistic and highly humanistic view, there was a simultaneous awareness of what life can do to men and women: a faculty for admitting, unflinchingly, that life can be—and in fact, frequently is—cruel and unjust. Shakespeare put it this way in *King Lear*:

> As flies to wanton boys, are we to the gods;
> They kill us for their sport.

And in *Macbeth*, he expressed it in these words:

Out, out brief candle!
Life's but a walking shadow, a poor player
That struts and frets his hour upon the stage
And then is heard no more; it is a tale
Told by an idiot, full of sound and fury,
Signifying nothing.

These periods of history—the Greek Golden Age and the Renaissance—were expansive enough to encompass both strains: the greatness of human beings on the one hand, and the cruelty of life on the other. These two attitudes form two indispensable sides of the tragic equation; without them, the possibilities for traditional tragedy are virtually nonexistent.

To clarify the distinction between tragic and other points of view, we need only to examine other periods in history when one or both of the attitudes forming the tragic equation were absent or expressed in a quite different way. In Europe and Great Britain, the eighteenth century was known as the Age of Enlightenment, and the nineteenth century as the Century of Progress. The French and American revolutions were under way, and the industrial revolution as well; the merchant class and the middle class were in the ascendancy. The glorification was not of single men and women—alone and unafraid—but of groups, or masses, beginning to stir and throw off the yokes of the past. Enlightenment and progress: together they express the philosophy that men and women can analyze any problem—poverty, violence, disease, injustice—and by applying their intelligence to it, solve it. It was an age of unbounded optimism, in which no problem was thought insurmountable and feelings of moral justice ran strong. This is not the soil in which tragedy can grow.

To underscore the effect such an age has on art, in 1681 a man named Nahum Tate rewrote the ending of Shakespeare's *King Lear* so that Lear's daughter does not die as she does in Shakespeare's play, but remains alive, thus softening the tragic effect. This version of the play was performed in England throughout the eighteenth and much of the nineteenth centuries. The critic Dr. Samuel Johnson, a cold-eyed realist in many respects, preferred the Tate version and wrote in 1765 that he found the death of Cordelia in Shakespeare so painful that he had been unable to bring himself to read the original play for many years. In times such as the eighteenth and nineteenth centuries it is difficult for any dramatist, no matter what his personal inclinations, to produce tragedy.

Personal Vision

As important as it is, however, the outlook of society serves as the background in creating theater. In the foreground stands the point of view of the individual artist. Proof of this is the variation among playwrights within the same era. At the same time that Euripides was writing tragedies in ancient Greece, Aristophanes was writing satirical farces. In France in the seventeenth century, Molière was writing comedies when Racine was writing tragedies. In the modern period particularly, we have a multiplicity of viewpoints expressed in drama.

THE PROBLEM OF CATEGORIES

By combining the two elements—the view of society and the individual outlook of the artist—a wide range of serious and comic points of view are incorporated in individual plays. When we try to separate and organize these various kinds of plays, however, we raise the spectre of categories, which presents serious problems to a free and open understanding of theater. Shakespeare made fun of this problem in *Hamlet* when he had Polonius announce that the players who had come to court could perform anything: "tragedy, comedy, history, pastoral, pastoral-comical, historical-pastoral, tragical-historical, tragical-comical-historical-pastoral." In spite of the absurdity of this, there are those who continue to try to pigeonhole or label every play that comes along. The attempt to assign plays to given categories, however, is a dangerous pursuit. In the first place, more often than not, plays do not fit neatly into categories. As the quotation from Polonius suggests, different dramas intersect and overlap: a few plays are pure tragedy, but some are heroic drama with tragic elements, and others are serious drama with no elements of tragedy. Also, the serious and the comic sometimes overlap.

Dramatists do not write categories or types of drama; they write individual plays. The dramatist, as well as everyone else concerned with producing a theater event, deals with a specific play—and so should members of the audience. A preoccupation with establishing categories diverts our attention from the main purpose of theater, namely, to *experience the play in performance*. What we sense, feel, and comprehend as we sit in a theater is the important point—not a definitive judgment as to a play's classification. As important as an awareness of point of view is, to the extent that our concern with it interferes with our immediate response to a theater event, theater is done a disservice.

The reason we learn the various forms of drama is not to spend our time pinning labels on plays, but to understand that writers, as well as those responsible for the production of a play, take a point of view with regard to their material. Members of the audience must be aware of that point of view if they are to understand a performance properly. A play which aims at a purely melodramatic effect, for instance, should be looked at differently from one which aspires to tragedy. A lighthearted comedy should not be judged by the same standards as a philosophical play. It is to understand these differences, and to grasp the various ways in which playwrights have traditionally approached their material, that we study categories into which groups of plays frequently fall.

SUMMARY

1 Point of view is the way we look at things: the perspective or angle of vision from which we view people, places, and events.

2 In the arts, the establishment of a point of view is direct and deliberate; it is an integral part of a performance or work of art, providing a clue to the audience as to how to interpret and understand what is being seen and heard.

3 Point of view is important in the area of realism and nonrealism. Realistic theater conforms to observable reality: details of what happens on stage resemble what we see and hear in the world around us. Nonrealistic theater, on the other hand, employs symbol and metaphor to go beneath the surface of daily life to suggest inner states and deeper truths.

4 Both realism and nonrealism have advantages; they can also be combined in a single work.

5 Whether a theater piece is serious, comic, or some combination of the two depends on the point of view of the artists who create it.

6 The viewpoint of society also affects the outlook of individual artists in terms of tragedy, comedy, etc.

7 In studying various types of drama—tragedy, comedy, farce—an overemphasis on labels and categories must be avoided; otherwise, theater is robbed of its immediacy and spontaneity.

Having observed how a production is infused with a point of view with regard to realism and nonrealism, as well as tragedy and comedy, we are now in a position to examine specific manifestations of serious and comic treatments of drama.

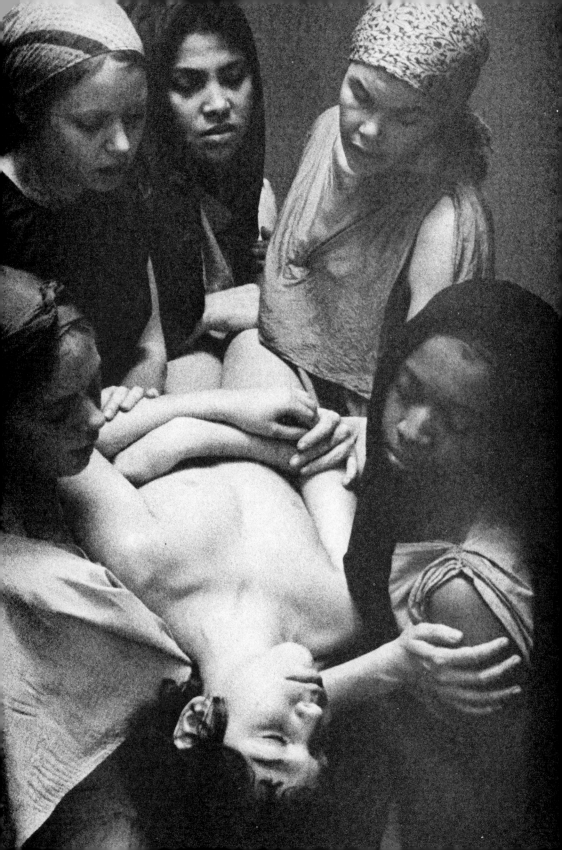

10
TRAGEDY AND OTHER SERIOUS DRAMA

"There is nothing either good or bad, but thinking makes it so," Shakespeare wrote in *Hamlet*, to which could be added a parallel statement: "There is nothing either funny or sad, but thinking makes it so." One's point of view determines whether one takes a subject seriously or laughs at it, whether it is an object of pity or of ridicule.

Once adopted, a point of view is transmitted to others in innumerable ways. In everyday life, for instance, we telegraph to those around us the relative seriousness of a situation by the way we behave. Anyone coming into a scene where a person has been hurt in an accident will immediately sense that the situation is no laughing

Figure 10-1 The faces of tragedy. Serious drama emphasizes the somber aspects of life as in this scene from the Greek tragedy The Trojan Women *by Euripides. The women shown here are mourning the death of a young man. (Photo—Max Waldman.)*

matter. The people looking on will have concerned expressions on their faces, and their voices and actions will reflect tensions and urgency. In contrast, a person coming into a group where a joke is being told will notice an air of pleasurable expectancy among the spectators and a teasing, conspiratorial tone on the part of the storyteller.

A similar thing happens in the theater. Point of view begins when a dramatist takes a strong personal view of a subject, deciding that it is grave, heroic, or humorous. The view reflects the writer's special angle of vision but includes as well the view of society discussed in the previous chapter. Then the dramatist incorporates this point of view in the play itself, giving the characters words to speak and actions to perform which convey that attitude. In a serious work the writer will choose language and actions suggesting sobriety and sincerity. Take the lines spoken by Othello:

> O, Now for ever
> Farewell the tranquil mind! Farewell content!
> Farewell the plumed troop and the big wars
> That make ambition virtue!

These words express Othello's profound sense of loss in unmistakable fashion.

The director and the performers in turn must transmit the dramatist's intentions to the audience. The actor playing Othello, for example, must deliver his lines in a straightforward manner and move with dignity, that is, without the exaggerations or excesses of comedy. By combining a series of gestures, vocal inflections, and activities on the part of performers with the words and ideas of the dramatist—and setting them in an appropriate visual environment established by the designers—a world is created in a theatrical production. It might be a sad world, a bittersweet world, a hopeful world, or a tragic world. If it is fully and properly created, however, the audience becomes aware of it instantly and enters that world, living in it for the duration of the performance. Entering and inhabiting a world which reflects a particular point of view is an indispensable part of the theater experience.

Historically, the elements which create the world of a play—specific language, characters, and actions—have clustered together to form a group. The characteristics of one group distinguish them from other groups. Frequently a group of plays which forms a single type is called a *genre*, after a French word which means "category" or "type." Tragedy and comedy are the best known genres, but there are others. Certain serious plays have common characteristics, as do certain kinds of comedies. In this chapter we will examine genres reflecting a serious attitude, and in the following chapter we will turn to comedy and mixed forms.

Serious drama takes a thoughtful, sober attitude toward its subject matter. It puts the audience in a frame of mind to think carefully about what it sees and to become involved with the characters on stage: to love what they love, fear what they fear, and suffer what they suffer. Serious drama takes several forms, of which tragedy is perhaps the best known.

TRAGEDY

Tragedy asks the most basic questions about human existence. Why is the world sometimes so unjust? Why are men and women called on to endure such suffering in their lives? What are the limits of human suffering and endurance? In the midst of cruelty and despair, what are the possibilities of human achievement? To what heights of courage, strength, generosity, and integrity can human beings rise?

Tragedy assumes that the universe is indifferent to human concerns, and often cruel or malevolent. Sometimes the innocent appear to suffer while the evil prosper. In the face of this, some human beings are capable of despicable deeds, but others can confront and overcome adversity, attaining a nobility which places them "a little lower than the angels." We can divide tragedy into two basic kinds: traditional and modern. Modern tragedy generally includes plays of the last one hundred years. Traditional tragedy includes works from several significant periods of the past.

Traditional Tragedy

Three noteworthy periods of history in which tragic drama was produced are Greece in the fifth century B.C., England in the late sixteenth and early seventeenth centuries, and France in the seventeenth century. The tragedies which appeared in these three ages had several characteristics in common, characteristics which help define traditional tragedy. They include the following:

1 Generally the hero or heroine of the play is an extraordinary person: a king, queen, general, or nobleman—that is, a person of stature. In Greek drama, Antigone, Electra, Oedipus, Agamemnon, Creon, and Orestes were members of royal families. In Shakespeare, Hamlet, Claudius, Gertrude, Lear, and Cordelia also were royalty; Julius Caesar, Macbeth, and Othello were generals; and others—

Figure 10-2 Othello: a tragic hero. The heroes and heroines of traditional tragedy are generally extraordinary people, due to a combination of outstanding characteristics—position, power, personality, passion, intelligence, or the like. When tragic heroes fall it has special significance. In this scene, Othello, played by James Earl Jones, has just killed Desdemona, thereby sealing his own doom as well as hers. (Photo—George E. Joseph.)

Ophelia, Romeo and Juliet—were members of the nobility. Because the heroes and heroines are important, the plays in which they appear have added importance; the characters of tragedy stand not only as individuals, but as symbols for an entire culture or society. The idea is expressed in *Julius Caesar* as follows:

> Great Caesar fell
> O! what a fall was there my countrymen;
> Then I, and you, and all of us fell down.

2 The central figures of the play are caught in a series of tragic circumstances: Oedipus, without realizing it, murders his father and marries his mother; Phaedra falls hopelessly and fatally in love with her stepson, Hippolytus; Othello is completely duped by Iago; and Lear is cast out by the very daughters he benefited. In traditional tragedy, the universe seems determined to trap the hero or heroine in a fateful web.

3 The situation becomes irretrievable: there is no turning back, no way out. The figures of tragedy find themselves in a situation from which there is no honorable avenue of escape; they face a tragic fate and must go forward to meet it.

4 The hero or heroine shows a willingness and an immense capacity to suffer. This is true whether the individual is praiseworthy or villainous; he or she endures the calamities suffered and fights back. Heroic figures accept their fate: Oedipus puts out his eyes; Antigone dies; Othello kills himself. One who suffers immensely, King Lear, lives through personal humiliation, a raging storm on a heath, partial insanity, and the death of his daughter, and finally faces his own death. A statement by Edgar in *King Lear* applies to all tragic figures: "Men must endure their going hence even as their coming hither."

5 The language of traditional tragedy is verse. Because it deals with lofty and profound ideas—with men and women at the outer limits of their lives—tragedy soars to the heights and descends to the depths of human experience, and many feel that such thoughts and emotions can be expressed only in poetry. Look at Cleopatra's lament upon the death of Mark Antony:

> O, wither'd is the garland of war,
> The soldier's pole is fall'n! Young boys and girls
> Are level now with men. The odds is gone,
> And there is nothing left remarkable
> Beneath the visiting moon.

The sense of admiration for Antony, and of desolation now that he is gone, could never be conveyed so tellingly in less poetic terms.

Effects of Traditional Tragedy

When the elements of traditional tragedy are combined, they appear to produce two contradictory reactions simultaneously. One is pessimistic: the hero is "damned if he does and damned if he doesn't," and the world is a cruel, uncompromising place, a world of despair. When one sees *Hamlet*, for instance, one can only conclude that people are avaricious and corrupt, and the world unjust. Claudius, Gertrude, Polonius, Rosencrantz, Guildenstern, and even Ophelia, are part of a web of deception, in which Hamlet is irrevocably caught. And yet, in the bleakest tragedy—whether *Hamlet, Medea, Macbeth*, or *King Lear*—there is affirmation: the other side of the tragic coin. One source of this positive feeling is the drama itself. It has been pointed out that

Sophocles, Euripides, Shakespeare, and Racine, though telling us that the world is in chaos and utterly lost, at the same time have affirmed just the opposite by creating such carefully shaped and brilliant works of art. Why bother, if all is hopeless, to create a work of art at all? The answer must be some residual hope in the midst of the gloom.

Another positive element resides in the persons of tragic heroes and heroines. They meet their fates with such dignity and such determination that they defy the gods. They say, "Come and get me; throw your worst at me and I will not only absorb it, but fight back. Whatever happens, I will not surrender my individuality and my dignity." In Aeschylus's play *Prometheus*, the title character, one of the first tragic heroes, says: "On me the tempest falls. It does not make me tremble." In defeat, the men and women of tragedy triumph. They lose, but in losing, they win. This paradox gives traditional tragedy much of its resonance and meaning and explains why we are both devastated and exhilarated by it.

As for the deeper meanings of individual tragedies there is vast literature on the subject, and each play has to be looked at and experienced in detail to obtain the full measure of its meaning. Certain tragedies seem to hold so much meaning, to contain so much in substance, in echoes and reverberations, that one can spend parts of a lifetime studying them.

Modern Tragedy

Tragedies of the modern period, that is, of the last one hundred years, do not have queens or kings as central figures, and they are written in prose not poetry. For these reasons, as well as more philosophical ones, a debate has raged for some time over whether they are true tragedies. Small men and women, the argument runs, lack the stature of tragic figures. A traveling salesman such as Hickey in O'Neill's *The Iceman Cometh*, or Willy Loman in Miller's *Death of a Salesman*, a nymphomaniac Southern woman like Blanche DuBois in Williams's *A Streetcar Named Desire*, and a housewife who shoots herself, like Ibsen's Hedda Gabler, lack the grandeur of princely rulers.

Similarly, it is argued that the lofty ideas of tragedy can never be adequately expressed in the language of ordinary conversation. A third argument holds that the present world view, in our industrialized, computerized age, looks at the human being as a helpless victim of society. How is it possible for a hero to show his defiance of the gods when he is not free to act on his own, but is controlled by social or mechanical forces?

All these arguments are to a certain extent irrelevant; they blame the present age for not being the past. We have no kings or queens:

neither in a mythology, nor for all practical purposes, in real life. Does this mean, however, that no one can stand for other people, or be symbolic of a whole group or culture? Certainly not. As for language, there is no doubt that poetry can convey thoughts and feelings to which prose can never aspire. Some prose, however, approaches the level of poetry, and beyond that, there is nonverbal expression: the structure of the plot, the movements and gestures of actors, the elements of sound and light. These have a way of communicating meanings below the surface of the words themselves. Speaking of the importance of nonverbal elements in theater, Friedrich Nietzsche, in the *Birth of Tragedy*, wrote:

> The myth by no means finds its adequate objectification in the spoken word. The structure of the scenes and the visible imagery reveal a deeper wisdom than the poet himself is able to put into words and concepts.[1]

Stanislavski, whom we discussed in the chapter on acting, stressed what he called the *subtext* of a play, by which he meant the emotions, tensions, and thoughts not expressed directly in the text. Such feelings often appear much stronger than the surface expressions, and when properly presented are abundantly clear to the audience.

Some modern dramatists have attempted to re-create Greek or Elizabethan tragedies, featuring royal figures and written in blank verse. But the results are more often than not anachronistic and archaic. They tend to be reproductions or imitations, rather than fresh creations. These attempts at re-creating traditional tragedy provide a strong argument against imitation of the classics as a means of achieving modern tragedy.

Regarding the modern world view, the question is not whether we view the human condition in the same way as the French in the seventeenth century or the Greeks in the fifth century B.C.—the truth is that they did not view life in the same way either—but whether our age allows for a tragic view on its own terms. The answer seems to be yes. Compared with either the eighteenth or the nineteenth century—the ages of enlightenment, progress, and unbounded optimism—our age has truly tragic vision. In spite of a supposedly mechanistic approach to life, our dramatic heroes and heroines fight to the end. If there is sometimes less exaltation or exhilaration at the end of a modern tragedy than at the end of some classic tragedies, this does not negate the total effect. Besides, certain classical tragedies, *Medea*, to name one, provide very little exhilaration or uplift themselves.

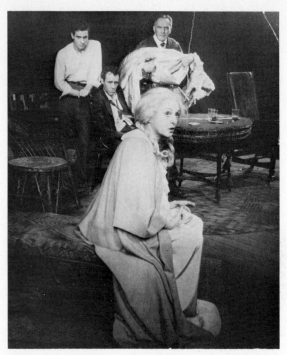

Figure 9-3 **Modern tragic figures.** *The family in Eugene O'Neill's* Long Day's Journey into Night *lack the scale and grandeur of tragic figures from the past, but their suffering has meaning for us today and speaks more directly to us, creating a form of modern tragedy. In this scene from the original production, Jason Robards plays the oldest son, Fredric March his father, and Florence Eldridge his mother. (Photo—Museum of the City of New York, Theatre and Music Collection.)*

Modern tragic dramatists probe the same depths and ask the same questions as their predecessors: why do men and women suffer? Why is there cruelty and injustice in the world? And perhaps most fundamental of all, what is the meaning of our lives? Naturally they do it on their own terms, but many dramatists of the recent past have looked at life with the same level gaze, and the same sense of awe, as those before. In these terms, Ibsen, Strindberg, Lorca, O'Neill, Williams, and Miller—to mention a few—can lay claim to legitimate modern tragedy. Part of this, of course, is a question of semantics, or definitions. The ultimate test of a play is not whether it meets someone's definition of tragedy, but the effect it produces in the theater, and the way in which it subsequently stands up to continued scrutiny. Eugene O'Neill's *Long Day's Journey into Night* takes as bleak a look at the human condition, with, at the same time, as compassionate a view of human striving and dignity, as it seems possible to take in our day. We might *hope* for more—in an exalted language which O'Neill lacks—but it is difficult to see how we can *expect* more.

HEROIC DRAMA

The term *heroic drama* is not a commonly used term like *tragedy* or *comedy*, but there is a wide range of plays with common characteristics which are not tragedies and for which heroic drama seems an appropriate name. We will use the term specifically to indicate serious drama of any period which features heroic, or noble, figures, and which includes other traits of traditional tragedy—dialogue in verse or elevated language, extreme situations, etc.—but which differs from tragedy in important respects. Such serious drama may differ on the one hand in having a happy ending, and on the other in assuming a basically optimistic world view, even when the ending is sad. In the case of the happy ending, the chief characters go through many trials and tribulations, but emerge victorious at the end. The threatening events of the play turn out to have been narrow escapes, but escapes nevertheless. We agonize with the hero or heroine, knowing all the time that the play will end well.

Several Greek plays, ordinarily classified as tragedies, are actually closer to what we are calling heroic drama. In Sophocles's *Electra*, for instance, Electra suffers grievously, but at the end of the play she and her brother Orestes triumph. Corneille's *The Cid*, written in France in the seventeenth century, has a hero who leads his men to victory in battle and in the end, rather than being killed, wins a duel over his rival, Don Sanchez. In *Life Is a Dream*, by the Spanish playwright Calderon (1600–1681), Prince Segismundo, after numerous misfortunes, emerges as a generous and dignified king. In the late seventeenth century in England, a form of drama developed which was called specifically "heroic drama," or "heroic tragedy," and it was precisely the type of which we are speaking—the serious play with the happy ending for the hero or heroine.

Many plays in Oriental drama—from India, China, and Japan—though resisting the usual classifications and involving a great deal of dance and music as part of the presentation, bear a close resemblance to heroic drama. Frequently, for example, the hero goes through a series of dangerous adventures, emerging victorious at the end. The vast majority of Oriental dramas end happily.

A second type of heroic drama involves the death of the hero or heroine, but neither the events along the way nor the final conclusion could be thought of as tragic. Several of Goethe's plays follow this pattern: *Egmont* depicts a much-loved count who fights for freedom and justice. He is imprisoned and dies, but not before he sees a vision of a better world to which he is going, to be a free man. In *Goetz von Berlichingen*, the lead character wages war against an unjust bishop and the emperor; and though he dies, he dies in triumph, with the word "freedom" on his lips. Many of Goethe's plays, along with those of his contemporaries in the late eighteenth and early nineteenth centuries, form a subdivision of heroic drama, referred to as *romantic drama*. *Romanticism* was a literary movement which took hold in Germany at the time and spread to France and throughout much of Europe. It celebrated the spirit of hope, personal freedom, and natural instincts.

A number of plays in the modern period fall in the category of heroic drama. *Cyrano de Bergerac*, written by Edmond Rostand in 1897, is a good example. The title character of the play dies at the end, but only after the truth of his love for Roxanne, hidden for fifteen years, is revealed. He dies a happy man, declaring his opposition to oppression and secure in the knowledge that he did not love in vain. Some might find the play sentimental, but it could not be called tragic. *St. Joan* by George Bernard Shaw (1856–1950), is another example: Joan's burning at the stake is actually a form of triumph, and as if that were not enough, Shaw provides an epilogue in which Joan appears alive after her death.

History plays, such as Shakespeare's *Richard II, Henry IV, Parts 1* and *2*, and *Henry V*, also fall in the genre of heroic dramas. In the modern period the Swedish dramatist August Strindberg wrote a number of history plays about his native land, and there have been others by modern writers about historical figures in a similar vein.

In the history of theater, the group of plays we are calling heroic drama occupies a large and important niche, cutting, as it does, across the Orient and Western civilization, and across periods from the Greek Golden Age to the present.

MELODRAMA

The word *melodrama* means "music drama" or "song drama." It comes from the Greek, but its modern form was introduced by the French in the late eighteenth century and applied to plays which employed background music of the kind we hear in movies: ominous chords underscoring a scene of suspense, and lyrical music underscoring a love scene.

Melodrama is exaggerated theater, and we have come to use the term *melodramatic* as an expression of disdain or disapproval. When taken to extremes, melodrama is laughable; we have all seen silent movies where a heroine with curly blond hair, pure as the driven snow, is being pursued by a heartless villain, a man with a sinister moustache and penetrating eyes who will foreclose the mortgage on the home of the girl and her mother unless she will let him have his way with her. This is a caricature, however, for melodrama is an ancient and honorable form of serious drama. It does have a measure of exaggeration, but so does most theater. Actually, melodrama has much in common with all forms of serious drama, and in many cases the difference lies more in degree and emphasis than anything else.

Melodrama puts a premium on effects. It is dedicated to results and will sacrifice reality and logic in order to achieve them, but it should be made clear that there is nothing inherently wrong with this.

Among the effects for which melodrama generally strives is fright or horror. It has been said that melodrama speaks to the paranoia in all of us: the fear that someone is pursuing us or that disaster is about to overtake us. How often we have the sense that others are ganging up on us or the premonition that we have a deadly disease. Melodrama brings these fears to life; we see innocent victims tortured, or people terrorized, as a family is in *The Desperate Hours*, a play of the 1950s in which a family is held captive by a group of escaped convicts. Murder mysteries and detective stories almost invariably are melodramas because they stress suspense and a close brush with danger. This type of melodrama usually ends in one of two ways: either the victims are maimed or murdered (in which case our worst paranoiac fears are confirmed) or after a series of dangerous episodes, they are finally rescued (in which case the play is like a nightmare or a bad dream from which we awaken the following morning to realize we are safe in our beds and everything is all right).

Although the term was not used at the time, many plays written in England during the Jacobean period (the reign of James I, 1603–1625) were melodramas. John Webster's *The White Devil* and *The Duchess of Malfi*, John Marston's *The Malcontent*, and Cyril Tourneur's *The Revenger's Tragedy* could well qualify as revenge or horror melodramas.

Still another form of melodrama argues a case or presents a strong point of view. One of the hallmarks of melodrama is that characters tend to be simple and whole, rather than complex and divided, as they are in tragedy. Melodrama invariably shows us the good guys against the bad guys. When a playwright, therefore, wishes to make a case, he or she will often write a melodrama in which the good characters represent the author's point of view.

Lillian Hellman, in order to depict the predatoriness of greedy

Figure 10-4 Melodrama. *Another form of serious drama, melodrama, is designed to frighten us or stir us up. It generally has less depth than tragedy but at its best is no less theatrical. Here we see Paul Newman confronting his victim, Karl Malden, in the original Broadway production of* The Desperate Hours. *(Photo—Museum of the City of New York, Theatre and Music Collection.)*

Southern materialists, wrote a forceful melodrama called *The Little Foxes.* The play takes place at the close of the Civil War, when the leading character, Regina Giddens, wishes to take control of the family cotton mills so she can have wealth and move to Chicago. She will do anything to obtain her objectives: flirt with a prospective buyer, blackmail her own brothers, and even allow her husband to die. In a terrible scene, she stands by while her husband has a heart attack, refusing to go for the medicine which would save his life.

As with horror or suspense, melodramas arguing strongly for a point of view employ striking dramatic devices like the scene noted above. Miss Hellman has exaggerated the good qualities of the good people and the bad qualities of the bad. This technique is characteristic of all melodrama. To put it in gambling terms, those who write melodrama "load the dice" or "stack the deck."

A list of significant melodramas would range over most of theatrical history and would include writers from Euripides through

Figure 10-5   Didactic melodrama: The Little Foxes. *Tallulah Bankhead stars in Lillian Hellman's play condemning a group of predatory Southerners determined to take over a family business empire. (Photo—The New York Public Library at Lincoln Center, Theatre Collection. Astor, Lenox and Tilden Foundations. Photo by Vandamm.)*

Shakespeare and his contemporaries to dramatists throughout Europe and America in the modern period. Other types of serious drama, tragic and nontragic, frequently have strong melodramatic elements as well.

BOURGEOIS OR DOMESTIC DRAMA

There is still another group of serious plays which has neither the profundity of tragedy, the loftiness of heroic drama, nor the sensationalism of melodrama. These plays are known as *bourgeois* or *domestic* dramas. *Bourgeois* refers to people of the middle or lower-middle classes rather than the aristocracy, and *domestic* means that the plays often deal with the problems of the family or the home rather than great affairs of state. In the Greek, Roman, and Renaissance periods, ordinary people served as the main characters only in comedies; they rarely appeared as the heroes or heroines of serious plays. Beginning in the eighteenth century, however, as society changed, there was a call for serious drama about men and women with whom members of the audience could identify and who were like themselves. In England in 1731, George Lillo wrote *The London Merchant*, a story of a merchant's apprentice who was led astray by a prostitute and who betrayed his good-hearted employer. This play, like others after it, overstated the case for simple working-class virtues, but it dealt with recognizable people from the daily life of Britain, and audiences welcomed it. In Germany, Gotthold Lessing (1729–1781) followed the same ideas in *Miss Sara Sampson*, a play which takes the Medea legend and translates it into commonplace terms, focusing on a young girl who is the victim of an older woman's anger. From these beginnings, bourgeois or domestic drama developed through the balance of the eighteenth century and the whole of the nineteenth, until it achieved a place of prominence in the works of Ibsen.

A typical modern domestic drama is *A Raisin in the Sun*, by Lorraine Hansberry (1930–1965). The play concerns a black family living in a poor section of Chicago, Illinois. The son, on whom both his mother and wife pin their hopes, falls prey to the scheme of a con man who takes from him the money with which the family had planned to buy a new home. The family seems defeated, but in the end the son, having matured, determines to lead them to a better life. Problems with society, struggles within a family, dashed hopes, and renewed determination are frequent characteristics of domestic drama.

Included in the general category of bourgeois dramas are plays in which the hero is not one person but an entire group, such as the people in a village or those forming their own small society. Examples include *The Sheep Well* by the Spanish playwright Lope de Vega (1562–1635), and in the modern period, *The Weavers*, by the German writer Gerhart Hauptmann (1862–1946), and *The Lower Depths*, by the Russian dramatist Maxim Gorki (1868–1936). In one form or another, bourgeois or domestic drama has become the predominant form of serious drama throughout Europe and America during the last one hundred years.

Although tragedy is the best known type of serious drama, it should be clear that other forms, such as domestic drama, are significant in their own ways. In terms of a variety of theater experiences, we are more likely to encounter heroic drama, melodrama, or domestic drama than we are pure tragedy. It is hoped, however, that in our theatergoing we will have the opportunity to encounter them all.

SUMMARY

1 Tragedy attempts to ask the most basic questions about human existence: Why do men and women suffer? Is there justice in the world? What are the limits of human endurance and achievement? Tragedy presupposes an indifferent and sometimes malevolent universe in which the innocent suffer and there is inexplicable cruelty. It also assumes that certain men and women will confront and defy fate, even if they are overcome in the process.

2 Tragedy can be divided into traditional and modern. In traditional tragedy the chief characters are kings, queens, persons of stature, and nobility; the central figure is caught in a series of tragic circumstances which are irrevocable; the hero or heroine is willing to fight and die for a cause. The language of the play is verse.

3 Modern tragedy involves ordinary people, not nobility, and is written generally in prose rather than verse. The deeper meanings of tragedy are explored in its modern form by nonverbal elements and by the cumulative or overall effect of events as well as by verbal means.

4 There are several kinds of nontragic serious plays, the most notable being heroic drama, melodrama, and bourgeois or domestic drama.

5 Heroic drama has many of the same elements as traditional tragedy—frequently dealing with high-born characters and being written in verse. In contrast to tragedy, it is marked by a happy ending, or an ending in which the deaths of the main characters are considered a triumph and not a defeat.

6 Melodrama features exaggerated characters and events arranged to create horror or suspense or present a didactic argument for some political, moral, or social point of view.

7 Bourgeois or domestic drama deals with ordinary people in a serious but nontragic manner. It stresses the problems of the middle and lower classes, and has become a particularly prominent form in the past century.

In this chapter we have seen that within the realm of serious drama, many different theater experiences are open to us. We observe people very much like ourselves and people far removed from our own lives; we see characters to admire and characters to abhor; we become deeply involved emotionally with the action on stage, or we probe the philosophical depths of what we see. As always, the direction the experience takes depends on the point of view established in the theater event itself by the playwright and those who implement the script on stage.

In the following chapter, when we turn to points of view reflected in comedy and tragicomedy, we will find a variety of experiences as well.

11
COMEDY AND TRAGICOMEDY

Aside from a basically serious point of view, there are two other fundamental approaches to dramatic material. One is comedy, with its many forms and variations, and the other is a mixture of the serious and the comic, usually called tragicomedy.

COMEDY

Those who create comedy are not necessarily more frivolous or less concerned with important matters than those who create serious works; they may be extremely serious in their own way. Aristopha-

Figure 11-1 Comedy: mostly for fun. In pure comedy no one gets hurt too seriously, an example being the victim on the floor in this scene from Molière's School For Wives *by the Trinity Square Repertory Company of Providence, R. I. (Photo—William L. Smith.)*

nes, Molière, and George Bernard Shaw cared passionately about human affairs and the problems of men and women. But those with a comic view look at the world differently: with a smile, or a deep laugh, or an arched eyebrow. They perceive the follies and excesses of human behavior and develop a keen sense of the ridiculous, with the result that they show us things which make us laugh. How does comedy work? In the following pages, we will attempt to find out.

The Contrast Between Social Order and the Individual in Comedy

The comic viewpoint stems from a basic assumption about society against which the writer places other factors, such as the characters' behavior or the events of the play. Comedy develops when these two elements—the basic assumption about society and the events of the play—cut against each other like the blades on a pair of scissors. As an example, most traditional comic writers accept the notion of a clear social and moral order in their society. They appear to believe that it is not the laws of society which are at fault when something goes wrong but the defiance of those laws by individuals. In their comedies, the excesses, the frauds, the hypocrisies, and the follies of men and women are laughed at mercilessly, but they are laughed at against a background of normality and moderation. The comic writer (or the comic actor) is saying, in effect, "This character I show you is amusing because he is an eccentric individual; he goes beyond the bounds of common sense and turns ordinary moral values upside down." This view, we should note, is in contrast to the view of many serious plays, particularly tragedies, which assume that society itself is upside down, or that the "time is out of joint."

In Molière's comedy *Tartuffe,* the chief character is a charlatan and hypocrite who pretends to be pious and holy, going so far as to wear clerical garb. He lives in the house of Orgon, a foolish man who trusts Tartuffe implicitly. The truth is that Tartuffe is trying to take Orgon's wife as well as his money away from him, but Orgon, blind to Tartuffe's true nature, is completely taken in by him. The audience as well as other members of Orgon's family are aware of what is going on; they can see how ludicrous these two characters are, and in the end both Tartuffe's hypocrisy and Orgon's gullibility are exposed. But it is the individual who is held up to ridicule; neither religion nor marriage is assailed by Molière. Rather, it is the abuse of these two basic institutions which is criticized.

Many modern comedies, especially Theater of the Absurd comedies, reverse the positions of the scissor blades: the basic assumption is that the world is not orderly but absurd or ridiculous. Society, rather than providing a moral or social framework, offers only chaos. Against this background, ordinary people—like the husband and wife in Ionesco's *The Bald Soprano*—are set at odds with the world around them. The comedy in this case results from normal people being thrust into an abnormal world.

Suspension of Natural Laws

A characteristic of most comedy, both traditional and modern, is the temporary suspension of the natural laws of probability and logic. Actions do not have the consequences they do in real life: in comedy, when a haughty man walking down the street with his nose in the air steps on a child's roller skate, and goes sprawling on the sidewalk, we do not fear for his safety or wonder if he has any bruises. The focus in comedy is on the man's being tripped up and getting his comeuppance.

In burlesque, a comic character can be hit on the backside with a fierce thwack and we laugh, because we know it does not hurt anything but his pride. At one point in stage history a special stick made of two thin slats of wood held close together was developed to make the sound of hitting someone even more fearsome. When this stick hits someone, the two pieces of wood slap one another, making the sound of the whack twice as loud as normal. The stick is known as a *slapstick*, a name which came to describe all kinds of raucous, knockabout comedy.

Prime examples of the suspensions of natural laws in comedy are film cartoons and silent movies. Characters falling from buildings or jumping from moving trains are flattened temporarily, but soon get up, with little more than a shake of the head. There are no thoughts in the audience of real injury, of cuts or bruises, because the cause-and-effect chain of everyday life is not in effect.

Under these conditions, murder itself can be viewed as comic. In Joseph Kesselring's *Arsenic and Old Lace*, two sweet little old ladies, thinking they are being helpful, give elderberry wine containing arsenic to lonely, homeless old men, resulting, of course, in the men's deaths. The two sisters let their brother, who thinks he is Teddy Roosevelt, bury the bodies in the cellar, where the brother is digging his own version of the Panama Canal. Altogether, these innocent-seeming ladies murder twelve men before their scheme is uncovered. But we watch these proceedings with amusement; we do not really think of it as murder, and we have none of the feelings one usually has for victims. The idea of suffering and harm has been suspended, and we are free to enjoy the irony and incongruity of the situation.

The Comic Premise

The suspension of natural laws in comedy, together with the scissor effect of setting a ridiculous person in a normal world, or vice versa, makes possible the development of a *comic premise*. The comic premise is an idea or concept which turns the accepted notion of things upside down and makes this inverted notion the basis of a play. As an example, in *Arms and the Man*, George Bernard Shaw gave a complete twist to the idea that the most important attributes in war are courage and honor. Shaw says that survival is more important and that the smart soldier leaves behind some of his ammunition in order to carry chocolate into battle—after all, if a soldier does not eat, he will not be around to fight. The comic playwright uses the comic premise as the foundation on which to build the entire play. It can provide thematic and structural unity to the play and can serve as the springboard from which comic dialogue, comic characters, and comic situations develop.

Aristophanes, the Greek satiric dramatist, was a master at developing a comic premise on which to build a play. We have already mentioned *The Clouds*, where he sets up a school in the air taught by Socrates suspended in a basket, and *The Birds*, in which two citizens, tired of life in Athens, decide to migrate to a city in the sky run by birds. In another play, *Lysistrata*, Aristophanes has the women of Greece agree to go on a sex strike: they will not make love to their husbands until the husbands stop fighting and sign a peace treaty with their opponents.

The comic premise of *The Madwoman of Chaillot*, by Jean Giraudoux (1882–1944), is that a group of impractical madwomen—three in all—are smarter than hardheaded businessmen and bankers; as a corollary, Giraudoux develops a further premise that the fantasy world of the madwomen and their friends is more realistic than the workaday world of everyday life.

TECHNIQUES AND FORMS OF COMEDY

The suspension of natural laws and the establishment of a comic premise in comedy involve exaggeration and incongruity. In a way uniquely its own, comedy emphasizes the discrepancy between a norm, referred to above, and some aberration or excess. The contradictions of comedy arising from exaggeration and incongruity show up in several areas—in verbal humor, in characterization, and in comic situations.

Verbal Humor

Verbal humor can be anything from the pun to the most sophisticated verbal discourse. Close to the pun, for instance, is the *malaprop*—a word which sounds like the right word but actually is something quite different. The term comes from Mrs. Malaprop, a character in *The Rivals* by the English playwright Richard Brinsley Sheridan (1751–1816). Mrs. Malaprop wishes to impress everyone with her education and erudition but ends up doing just the opposite because she constantly misuses long words. As an example, she uses "supercillious" when she means "superficial," and she insists that her daughter is not "illegible" for marriage, meaning that her daughter is not "ineligible" for marriage. Frequently a character who wishes to appear to be more learned than he or she really is uses the malaprop. In Sean O'Casey's (1880–1964) *Juno and the Paycock*, the chief character is Captain Boyle, a man always pronouncing the last word on any subject. Throughout the play he complains that the world is "in a state of chassis," using the word "chassis" when he means "chaos." The more pompous the speaker who uses the wrong word in this way, the more humorous the effect.

A man devoted to verbal humor, Oscar Wilde (1854–1900) often turned accepted values upside down in his epigrams: "I can resist anything except temptation," says one of his characters, and "a man cannot be too careful in the choice of his enemies," says another. Displays of verbal virtuosity are hallmarks of comedy from various periods: English Restoration comedy of the late seventeenth century—*The Country Wife*, by William Wycherly (1641–1716), and *The Way of the World*, by William Congreve; comedies of manners of the eighteenth century in England—*She Stoops to Conquer*, by Oliver Goldsmith (1730–1774) and *The Rivals*, by Richard Brinsley Sheridan; and more recently, George Bernard Shaw's plays. Modern French playwrights like Anouilh and Giraudoux also use verbal wit extensively in their plays.

Comedy of Character

In comedy of character the discrepancy or incongruity lies in the way a character sees himself or pretends to be, as opposed to the way he actually is. A good example is a person who pretends to be a doctor—using obscure medicines, hypodermic needles, and Latin jargon—but who is actually a fake. Such a person is the chief character in Molière's *The Doctor in Spite of Himself*. Another example of incongruity of character is Molière's *The Would-Be Gentleman,* in which the title character, Monsieur Jourdain, a man of wealth, but

Figure 11-2 Comedy of the upper classes. *Verbal wit, plot complications, and character types—all hallmarks of high comedy or comedy of manners—are found in Sheridan's* The School for Scandal. *The play, as seen in a production by the City Center Repertory Company, satirizes those who thrive on scandal and gossip. (Photo—Diane Gorodnitzki.)*

without refinement, is determined to learn courtly behavior. He hires a fencing master, a dancing master, and a teacher of literature (the last tells him, to his great delight, that he has been speaking prose all his life). In every case Jourdain is made a fool of: he dances and fences awkwardly and even gets involved in a ridiculous courtship with a noblewoman. All along he is blind to what a ridiculous figure he makes, until the end, when his follies and pretenses are exposed. Comedy of character is a basic ingredient of Italian *commedia dell'arte* and all forms of comedy where stock characters, stereotypes, and characters with dominant traits are emphasized.

Plot Complications

Still another way in which the contradictory or the ludicrous manifests itself in comedy is in plot complications, including coincidences and mistaken identity. A time-honored comic plot is Shakespeare's *The Comedy of Errors*, based on *The Menaechmi*, a play of the late third century B.C. by the Roman writer Plautus. *The Comedy of Errors* in turn was the basis of a successful American musical comedy, *The Boys from Syracuse,* with songs by Richard Rodgers and Lorenz Hart.

In *The Comedy of Errors,* identical twins and their identical twin servants were separated when young, with one master and servant growing up in Syracuse, a Greek city, and the other growing up in Ephesus. As the play opens, however, both sets of masters and servants—unknown to one another—are in Ephesus. The wife and mistress of one master, as well as a host of others, mistake him and his servant for their counterparts in a series of comic encounters (with people making romantic advances to the wrong person, etc.) leading to ever-increasing confusion, until all four principals appear on stage at one time to clear up the situation.

A classic scene of plot complication occurs in Sheridan's *The School for Scandal* written in 1777. Surface, the main character in the play, is thought to be an upstanding man but is really a charlatan, whereas Charles, his brother, is mistakenly considered a reprobate. In this scene, called the "Screen Scene," the popular images are reversed and the truth comes out. As the scene opens, Lady Teazle, a married woman, is visiting Surface secretly. When her husband, Sir Peter Teazle, unexpectedly appears, she quickly hides behind a floor screen, but shortly after Sir Peter has come, Surface's brother Charles arrives as well, and in order not to be seen by Charles, Sir Peter starts for the screen. Sir Peter notices a woman's skirts behind the screen, but before he can discover it is his wife, Surface sends him into a closet. Once Charles has come into the room, he learns that Sir Peter is in the closet and flings it open. As if this discovery were not enough, he also throws down the screen and in one climactic moment reveals both the infidelity of Lady Teazle and the treachery of Surface. The double, even triple, comic effect is due to the coincidence of the wrong people being in the wrong place at the wrong time.

A master of the device of characters hiding in closets and under beds was George Feydeau (1862–1921), a French dramatist who wrote over sixty farces in his lifetime. Variations of this form—complications and revelations arising from coincidences and mistaken identity—are found in plays from Roman times to the present, and this device, along with verbal wit and exaggerated characters, has been used as a major weapon of the comic dramatist.

Comic Forms

Comedy takes various forms depending on the dramatist's intent and on the comic techniques emphasized. Most plays discussed in the previous section on plot complications are farces. *Farce* has no

Figure 11-3   In farce everything happens at once. *Plot complications are at the heart of bedroom farce, which was carried to a high art by the French dramatist Feydeau. In this scene from* A Flea in Her Ear, *discoveries, intrigues, and disasters are occurring on several fronts simultaneously. A Hilberry Theatre Repertory Company production directed by Richard Spear, designed by William Rowe, costumes by Stephanie Schoelzel, and lights by Gary M. Witt. (Photo— Wayne State University.)*

intellectual pretentions, but aims rather at entertainment and provoking laughter. In addition to excessive plot complications, its humor results from ridiculous situations and strong physical humor, such as pratfalls or horseplay. It relies less on verbal wit than more intellectual forms of comedy. Mock violence, rapid movement, and accelerating pace are hallmarks of farce. In *bedroom farce*, marriage and sex are the objects of fun, but medicine, law, and business can also be its subject matter.

Burlesque also relies on knockabout, physical humor, as well as gross exaggerations and sometimes vulgarity. Historically, burlesque was a ludicrous imitation of other forms of drama or of an individual play. A modern musical like *The Boy Friend* is a burlesque of the boy-meets-girl musicals popular earlier in the twentieth century. In the United States, the term *burlesque* has come to describe a type of variety show featuring low comedy skits and attractive women.

A form related to traditional burlesque, but with more intellectual and moral content, is *satire*. Satire employs wit, irony, and exaggeration to attack or expose evil and foolishness. Satire can attack one figure, in the way that *Macbird* attacked the late President Lyndon Johnson, or it can be more inclusive as in the case of Molière's *Tartuffe*, which ridicules religious hypocrisy generally.

Comedy of manners is concerned with pointing up the foibles and peculiarities of the upper classes. Against a cultivated, sophisticated background, it uses verbal wit to depict the charm and expose the social pretentions of its characters. Rather than horseplay, witty phrases and clever barbs are at a premium in the comedy of manners. In England a line of comedies of manners runs from Wycherley, Congreve, and Goldsmith in the seventeenth and eighteenth centuries, to Oscar Wilde in the nineteenth and Noel Coward in the twentieth. Many plays of George Bernard Shaw could be put under a special heading, *comedy of ideas*, for Shaw used comic techniques to debate intellectual propositions and to further his own moral and social point of view.

In all its forms, however, comedy remains a way of looking at the world in which basic values are asserted but natural laws suspended in order to underline the follies and foolishness of men and women— sometimes with a rueful look, sometimes with a wry smile, and at other times with an uproarious laugh.

TRAGICOMEDY

Comedy is usually set in juxtaposition to tragedy or serious drama: serious drama is sad, comedy is funny; serious drama makes people cry, comedy makes them laugh; serious drama arouses anger, comedy causes a smile. True, the comic view of life differs from the serious, but the two are not always as clearly separated as this polarity suggests. As we noted earlier, many comic dramatists are serious men: "I laugh to keep from crying" applies to many comic writers as well as to certain clowns and comedians. A great deal of serious drama has comic elements in it. Shakespeare, for instance, employed comic characters in several of his serious plays. The drunken porter in *Macbeth*, the gravedigger in *Hamlet*, and Falstaff in *Henry IV, Part 1*, are examples.

In medieval plays, comic scenes are interpolated in the basically religious subject matter. In a play about Noah and the ark, Noah and his wife argue like a bickering couple on television, with Mrs. Noah refusing to go aboard the ark with all those animals. Finally, when the floods come, she relents, but only after she has firmly established herself as a shrewish, independent wife. One of the best known of all medieval plays, *The Second Shepherd's Play*, concerns the visit of shepherds to the manger of the newborn Christ child. While they stop in a field to spend the night, Mak, a comic character, steals a sheep and takes it to his house, where he and his wife put it in a crib, pretending that it is their baby (a parody of Christ lying in the manger). When the shepherds discover what Mak has done, they toss him in a blanket, and after this horseplay the serious part of the story resumes.

The alternation of serious and comic elements is a practice of long standing, particularly in episodic plays, but when we speak of *tragicomedy*, we are not speaking of plays which shift from serious to comic and back again. In such cases the plays are predominantly one or the other—comic or serious—and the change from one point of view to the other is clearly delineated. We are speaking, rather, of a point of view which itself is mixed—the overview, or the prevailing attitude, is a synthesis or fusion of the serious and the comic. It is a view in which one eye looks with a comic lens and the other with a serious lens, and the two points of view are so intermingled as to be one, like food which tastes sweet and sour at the same time.

In addition to his basically serious plays and his basically comic ones, Shakespeare wrote three plays which seem to be neither one nor the other: *Measure for Measure, All's Well That Ends Well,* and *Troilus and Cressida.* By not fitting neatly into one category or the other, these plays have proved troublesome to critics—so troublesome that they have been officially dubbed "problem plays." The "problem," however, arises largely because of the difficulty in accepting the tragicomic point of view, for these plays have many of the attributes of the fusion of the tragic and comic. In all three plays, there is a sense of comedy pervading the play, the idea that all will end well and that much of what happens is ludicrous or ridiculous; at the same time, however, the serious effects of a character's actions are not dismissed. Unlike true comedy, in which the fall on the sidewalk, or the temporary threat of danger, has no serious consequences, the actions in these plays appear quite serious. And so we have tragicomedy. In *Measure for Measure,* for instance, a man named Angelo—a puritanical, austere creature—condemns young Claudio to death for having made his fiancée pregnant. When Claudio's sister, Isabella, however, comes to plead for her brother, Angelo is overcome by passion and tries to make the lady his mistress. Angelo's sentencing of Claudio is deadly serious, but the bitter irony which arises when he proves to be guilty of even worse "sins of the flesh" than Claudio is comic. The result is that we have tragic and comic situations simultaneously.

Modern Tragicomedy

It is in the modern period, however, during the last one hundred years or so, that tragicomedy has become a predominant form, the primary approach, in fact, of many of the best playwrights of our day. As suggested before, these writers are not creating in a vacuum; they are part of the world in which they live, and ours is an age which has adopted a tragicomic viewpoint more extensively than most previous ages. As if to keynote this attitude and set the tone, the Danish philosopher Soren Kierkegaard made the following statement in 1842: "Existence itself, the act of existence, is a striving and is both pathetic and comic in the same degree." The plays of Anton Chekhov, written at the end of the nineteenth century, reflect the spirit described by Kierkegaard. Chekhov labeled two of his major plays, comedies, but Stanislavski, who directed them, called them tragedies: an indication of the confusion arising from Chekhov's mixture of the serious and the comic.

As an illustration of Chekhov's approach, there is a scene in the third act of *The Cherry Orchard*, written in 1904, in which Madame Renevsky, the owner of the orchard, talks to an intense young graduate student about love and truth. She tells him that people should be charitable and understanding of those in love; no one is perfect and truth is not absolute, she argues. The student, however, insists that reason is all and that feelings must be put aside. She retorts that he is motivated not by purity but by "simple prudery." He is not above love, as he claims, but is actually avoiding it, and she insists that he should have a mistress at his age. He is incensed. Declaring that he cannot listen to such talk, he runs offstage. The stage directions say that a moment later he is heard falling down a flight of stairs. A crash is heard, women scream, and then, after a pause, they laugh. The women scream because they fear he is hurt—not the spirit of comedy—but once they learn he is all right, they laugh, realizing that the fall of this pompous lad is extremely comic. Here we have the perfect blend: a part of the scene is deadly serious, another part, genuinely comic.

A comparable, and even more significant, scene occurs at the end of the third act of Chekhov's *Uncle Vanya*, produced in 1899. Vanya and his niece, Sonya, have worked and sacrificed for years to keep an estate going to support her father, a professor. At the worst possible moment, just when Vanya and Sonya have both been rebuffed by people they love, the professor announces that he wants to sell the estate, leaving Vanya and Sonya with nothing. Sonya explains how cruel and thoughtless this is, and a few moments later Vanya comes in to shoot the professor. He waves his gun in the air like a madman and shoots twice, but misses both times, and then collapses on the floor. In this scene, Vanya and Sonya are condemned to a lifetime of drudgery and despair—a serious fate—but Vanya's behavior with the gun (there is doubt that he honestly meant to kill the professor) is wildly comic. Once again, the serious and comic elements are inextricably bound together.

Sean O'Casey, an Irish playwright, wrote plays with a similar outlook. In his *Juno and the Paycock*, mentioned above, Captain Boyle and his friend Joxer are complete comic figures, bragging about imaginary exploits, pretending bravery where none exists, and promising to go to work with no real intention of doing so. During the play, Boyle thinks he has received an inheritance and begins spending money with abandon, only to find it is a hoax. Other misfortunes strike: his daughter is left abandoned by her fiancé, his son has been dragged away to be shot as a traitor to the Irish cause, and the family is destitute. But since Boyle has never made provisions for his family or taken the problems of life seriously, he is of no help in this crisis. Instead he comes in at the end of the play with his buddy, Joxer, drinking and carrying on just as they did earlier in the play—but it is not funny now. Their jokes ring hollow and serve only to underline the sadness of what has occurred.

About a century after Kierkegaard wrote about the pathetic and the comic, the French philosopher and writer Albert Camus described the "divorce between man and his life, the actor and his setting," and "the feeling of Absurdity," referred to earlier. As for the Theater of the Absurd whose name came from this notion, many plays in this category are tragicomic. They probe deeply into human problems and cast a dark eye on the world, and yet they are also imbued with a comic spirit, containing juggling, acrobatics, clowning, and verbal nonsense, among other traditional manifestations of humor.

Samuel Beckett has given us one of the finest expressions of man's loneliness and futility ever written in *Waiting for Godot*. There is nothing bleaker nor more desolate than two tramps waiting on a barren plain every night for a supreme being called Godot, whom they think will come, but who never does. But they themselves are comic. They wear the baggy pants of burlesque comedians, and they engage in any number of vaudeville routines, including one in which they

Figure 11-4   Tragicomedy: funny and sad at the same time. *Walter Matthau
and Jack Lemmon play Captain Boyle and his friend Joxer in Sean O'Casey's
tragicomedy,* Juno and the Paycock. *These characters are comic but also
pathetic because their lack of responsibility brings about great misery for others.
(Photo—Courtesy of the Center Threatre Group, Mark Taper Forum, Los
Angeles. Photo by Steven Keull.)*

grab each other's hats in an exchange where the confusion becomes
increasingly compounded.

The plays of Harold Pinter, another writer associated with the
Theater of the Absurd, have been called "Comedies of Menace,"
combining in the phrase the idea of a theater simultaneously terrifying
and entertaining. Eugene Ionesco's plays afford a third example. In
The Lesson, a professor victimizes a young woman pupil. The play
contains a great deal of nonsense about words and their meanings,
with elements of slapstick as well, but in the end, the professor, with
an authoritarian fanaticism, plunges a knife into the pupil, making it a
macabre farce, humorous, but thoroughly unsettling.

Not only Beckett, Pinter, and Ionesco, but Genet, Adamov,
Arrabal, Albee, Grass—all of whom are included in the Theater of the
Absurd—have written plays in a similar vein. But there are other
recent writers, too, not considered absurdists, who adopt the tragi-

comic attitude. *The Visit,* by Friedrich Dürrenmatt (1921–) a Swiss dramatist, is an example. A wealthy woman returns to her birthplace, a small village which is poverty stricken. She offers money—a billion marks—to the town on the condition that the citizens murder a storekeeper in the village who wronged her when she was young. The townspeople express horror at the idea, but at the same time they begin buying expensive objects on credit, some buying from the man's own store. There is a comic quality in these scenes: the man's wife, for instance, shows up in a flashy fur coat. The conclusion, however, is not funny, for the man is eventually murdered by his greedy neighbors.

In tragicomedy, a smile is frequently cynical, chuckles may be tinged with a threat, and laughter is sometimes bitter. Whereas in the past the attitude which produced these combinations was the exception and not the rule, in our day it seems far more prevalent, not to say relevant. As a result, tragicomedy has taken its place as a major form alongside the more traditional approaches.

THE SIGNIFICANCE OF GENRE

The combination of forms in tragicomedy reminds us that individual plays rarely fall completely in one category. Some plays are pure examples of their form, but many have characteristics of two genres, and some include more than two. Frequently a play combines tragedy with heroic drama, or a melodrama overlaps with tragedy or heroic drama. In tragicomedies, the serious and the humorous intersect, and within comedy, burlesque crosses into farce, and farce into satire.

In discussing the major forms of theater, we end where we began, with the notion that we should never rush to pigeonhole or label a play. Genre can be an aid or guide telling us how to interpret and understand a play, but it should never be an end in itself. The struggle should be less to discover what genre a play belongs to than to understand it. The important lesson of genre is that in a worthwhile production, a world is created which reflects a definite point of view. For spectators, entering and living in that world is central to the theater experience.

Unlike certain arts in which point of view is established largely by a single device—the brush strokes of the artist in painting, or the use of the camera in films—in theater, point of view results from a collaborative effort of many artists. The creation of a viewpoint in theater is the responsibility not only of the dramatist, who establishes it and incorporates it in the script, but of a director, designers, and performers who must add to, reinforce, and underline the dramatist's point of view. As an example, in a production of Molière's comedy *Tartuffe*, the designers must strike just the right note of exaggeration and comment in the costumes and the scenery. There should be wit as well as elegance in the lines of the costumes and in the shapes and forms of the scenery. The color of the lighting, as well as the colors of the costumes and scenery, should be warm and bright—except, of course, for Tartuffe's black clerical costume, which stands in somber contrast to everything else and emphasizes his hypocrisy. The performances, too, must capture the dead seriousness of Molière's words but with an awareness of the underlying humor and comment the words imply. The actions of the performers will be exaggerated without being excessive, comic without being ludicrous. The total effect of script, performances, and visual effects will be a comic world, with undertones of seriousness.

If any segment of a production fails to maintain a consistent viewpoint, the result will be confusion on the part of the audience. If the scene design suggests comedy when the play is serious, or a performer is too realistic in a nonrealistic play, the spectators will lose their sense of direction. It is the responsibility of every artist working on a production to understand and follow through on the intentions and perspective of the playwright and director. Like structure, point of view is not visible to the audience in the way that a piece of scenery is, but it is an essential element of theater. Without a point of view which permeates and informs a production, members of the audience have no compass to know where they are headed and no key to unlock the play's meaning. Whatever world we are introduced to in a theatrical production—a real world or a make-believe world, a despondent world or a carefree world—the point of view which produces it must color and illuminate everything on stage. It must cut across the production like a giant spotlight cutting across the stage, throwing on every object the same light and shadow.

SUMMARY

1 Comedy takes a different approach from serious forms of drama. It sees the humor and incongruity in people and situations. Comic dramatists accept a social and moral order, and suspend natural laws (the man who falls flat on his face but does not really hurt himself).

2 Comedy is developed in several spheres: **(a)** verbal humor—turning words upside down, creating puns, malapropisms, and inversions of meaning; **(b)** comedy of character—men and women who take extreme positions, make fools of themselves, or contradict themselves; **(c)** physical comedy—slapstick and horseplay; **(d)** plot complications—mistaken identity, coincidences, and people who turn up unexpectedly in the wrong house or the wrong bedroom.

3 From the foregoing, the dramatist fashions various kinds of comedy. Depending on the degree of exaggeration, a comedy can be *farce* or *comedy of manners*; the former, for instance, features strong physical humor, while the latter relies more on verbal wit. Depending on its intent, comedy can be designed to entertain, as with *farce* or *burlesque*, or to correct vices, in which case it becomes *satire*.

4 Serious and comic elements can be mixed in theater. Many tragedies have comic relief: humorous scenes and characters interspersed in serious material.

5 Authentic tragicomedy fuses, or synthesizes, two elements—a serious and a comic. We laugh and cry at the same time. Plays from the works of Chekhov, Brecht, Dürrenmatt, and writers of the Theater of the Absurd employ tragicomedy. Some commentators feel that it is the form most truly characteristic of our time.

6 Many plays have elements of more than one genre; therefore genre should not be overstressed. It is a guide or an aid to understanding a theater experience.

7 Ideally, a clear point of view should inform and permeate every aspect of a theatrical production. It should create in each play a world which the spectators can enter and inhabit. Point of view tells the audience how to approach what they are seeing and how to assess its meaning.

Point of view is an essential element of theater, but like other components of theater, it comes to life only in a particular setting. It does not exist in the abstract, any more than the structure of a play or the performers themselves. Everything occurs in a visual framework, and the visual elements—the physical environment of the theater building, the appearance and style of the scenery, the texture and design of the costumes, the color and intensity of the lights—are an integral part of the theater experience. We turn to the visual side of theater in the following section.

POINT OF VIEW

DRAMATIC STRUCTURE

ENVIRONMENT

PERFORMERS   AUDIENCE

12
STAGE SPACES

For those who create theater, the experience begins long before the actual event. The dramatist spends weeks, months, or perhaps years writing the play; the director and designers plan the production well ahead of time; and the performers rehearse intensively for several weeks before the first public performance. Though not on the same scale, for the spectator, too, the experience begins ahead of time. Members of the audience read or hear reports of the play, they anticipate seeing a particular actress or actor perform, they purchase tickets and make plans with friends to attend, and at the time of the performance, gather ahead of time outside the theater with other members of the audience.

Figure 12-1 Environment for a play. For the Trinity Square Repertory Company's production of A Man For All Seasons, designer Eugene Lee transformed an open theater space into a special configuration of stage area and audience seating. At the top we see his blueprint for the conversion and at the bottom, the actual production. (From Trinity Square Repertory Co., Providence, R.I., designed by Eugene Lee; photo by William L. Smith.)

Figure 12-2 *A theater experience begins before the performance.* An audience enters a Broadway theater for a production of Hamlet. *The physical arrangement of the theater sets up specific expectations for the spectator. A formal space signals one kind of experience, an informal space a different kind of experience. (Photo—Worldwide Photos.)*

CREATING THE ENVIRONMENT

Once spectators arrive at the theater for a performance, they immediately take in the environment in which the event will take place. The physical environment of a theater creates definite expectations about the event to come, and conditions the experience once it gets underway. The atmosphere of the theater building itself has a great deal to do with the audience's mood in approaching a performance. Spectators have one feeling if they come into a formal setting—a picture-frame stage surrounded by carved, gold inlaid figures, with crystal chandeliers and red plush seats in the auditorium—and quite another if they come into an old warehouse converted into a theater, with bare brick walls, and a stage in the middle of the floor surrounded by folding chairs. If the environment of a theater is consistent with the kind of production to be presented, the total experience will be enhanced; if the environment runs counter to the production, it will be confusing and detract from the overall effect.

For many years people took the physical arrangement of a theater for granted. This was particularly true in the period when all houses were a facsimile of the Broadway theater with its proscenium, or picture-frame stage. In the recent past, though, not only have people been exposed to other types of theaters, they have become more aware of the importance of environment. Many experimental groups have deliberately made awareness of the environment a part of the experience. An extreme example was a production in the early 1970s off-Broadway, *And They Put Handcuffs on the Flowers*—a radical, political play by the Spanish dramatist Arrabal (1932–). In order to get into the theater, spectators had to enter a dark corridor one at a time. They were blindfolded, hit in the pit of the stomach, clutched by the throat, then hurled into the theater space. The idea was to give members of the audience a sense of what it was like to be treated as a prisoner.

A New Theater production of Euripides's *The Bacchae*, called *Dionysus in 69*, by the Performance Group in New York, was considerably less startling, but carried out the same idea of introducing the audience to the performance in a controlled manner. Spectators were not allowed in the theater when they arrived, but were made to line up on the street outside. The procedure is outlined in a book describing the production:

> The audience begins to assemble at around 7:45 p.m. They line up on Wooster Street below Greenwich Village. Sometimes the line goes up the block almost to the corner of Broome. On rainy nights, or during the coldest parts of the winter, the audience waits upstairs over the theater. The theater is a large space, some 50 by 40 and 20 feet high. At 8:15 the performance begins for the audience when the stage manager, Vicki May Strang, makes the following announcement. Inside the performers begin warming up their voices and bodies at 7:45.

Vickie: Ladies and gentlemen! May I have your attention, please. We are going to start letting you in now. You will be admitted to the theater one at a time, and if you're with someone you may be split up. But you can find each other again once you're inside. Take your time to explore the environment. It's very interesting space, and there are all different kinds of places you can sit. We recommend going up high on the towers and platforms, or down underneath them. The password is "Go high or take cover." There is no smoking inside and no cameras. Thank you.

In an interview in the book, Ms. Strang gave her own view of this procedure:

> We let the public in one at a time. People on the queue outside the theater ask me why. I explain that this is a rite of initiation, a chance for each person to confront the environment alone, without comparing notes with friends. People are skeptical. Some few are angry. Many think it's a put-on. I must confess to a perverse pleasure in teasing people on a line. Many will come up and ask anxiously, "Has it already begun?" "Well," I say, "it begins before we let anybody in, but it begins when everybody is in, and really it begins when you go in." True.[1]

By making spectators enter the theater in an unconventional way, and by rearranging the theater space itself, certain contemporary groups deliberately make the spectators conscious of the theater environment. But the feeling we have about the atmosphere of a theater building as we enter it has always been an important element in the experience. In the past, spectators may not have been conscious of it, but they were affected by it nevertheless. Today, with the many varieties of theater experience available to us, the first thing we should become aware of is the environment in which the event takes place. Whether it is large or small, indoors or outdoors, formal or informal, familiar or unfamiliar, will inevitably play a part in our response to the performance.

FOUR BASIC STAGE SPACES

A consideration of environment leads directly to an examination of the various forms and styles of theater buildings, including the basic arrangements of audience seating. Throughout theater history, there have been four basic types of stages, each with its own advantages and disadvantages, each suited to certain types of plays and certain types of productions, and each providing the audience with a somewhat different viewing experience. The four are (1) the proscenium or picture-frame stage, (2) the arena or circle stage, (3) the thrust stage with three-quarters seating, and (4) created and found stage space.

PROSCENIUM STAGE

The type of stage most familiar to us is the proscenium or picture-frame stage. Broadway theaters, which as we noted were models for

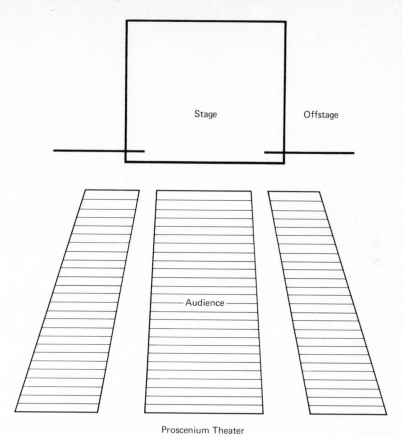

Stage   Offstage

— Audience —

Proscenium Theater

Figure 12-3 **The proscenium theater.** *The audience faces in one direction, toward an enclosed stage encased by a picture-frame opening. Scene changes and performers' entrances and exits are made behind the proscenium opening, out of sight of the audience.*

theaters throughout the country, have proscenium stages. The name *proscenium* comes from the open wall which separates the audience from the stage—in the past it was called an arch but it is actually a rectangle—and which forms an outline for the stage itself. It resembles a large picture frame through which the audience looks at the stage. Prior to the 1950s there was invariably a curtain just behind the proscenium opening; when the curtain rose, it revealed the picture. Another term for this type of stage is *fourth wall,* from the idea that the proscenium opening is an invisible glass wall through which the audience looks at the other three walls of a room.

Because the action takes place largely behind the proscenium

Figure 12-4 A formal proscenium theater. The interior of the Covent Garden
Theatre in London in 1810 was typical of elegant proscenium theaters found
throughout Europe and America. It featured elegant décor, tiers of boxes around
the sides and back of the auditorium, orchestra seats on the main floor, and a
picture-frame stage. (Courtesy of Henry E. Huntington, Library and Art
Gallery.)

opening or frame, the seats in the auditorium all face in the same
direction toward the stage, just as seats in a movie theater face the
screen. The auditorium itself is slanted downward from the back of the
auditorium, or *house* as it is called, to the stage. (The slant of an
auditorium or stage floor is called a *rake* in the theater.) The stage
itself is raised several feet above the auditorium floor to aid visibility.
There is usually a balcony, and sometimes two, protruding about half
way over the main floor. The main floor, incidentally, is called the
orchestra. In certain theaters, as well as concert halls and opera houses
which have the proscenium arrangement, there are horseshoe-shaped
tiers or *boxes*, which ring the auditorium for several floors above the
orchestra floor.

The popularity of the proscenium stage on Broadway and
throughout the United States in the nineteenth and early twentieth
centuries was partly due to its wide acceptance throughout Europe.
Beginning in the seventeenth century, the proscenium theater was
adopted in every European country. Examples of theaters in this style
in the eighteenth century include the Drury Lane and Covent Garden
in London; the Royal Theater in Turin, Italy; the Hotel de Bourgogne
in Paris; the Bolshoi in St. Petersburg, Russia; and the Drottningholm
near Stockholm, Sweden (a theater still preserved in its original state).

And in the nineteenth century they included the Teatro Espagnol in Madrid; the Haymarket in London; the Park Theater and Burton's Chambers Street in New York; the Brug Theater, Vienna, Austria; and the Teatro alla Scala, Milan, Italy.

The stage area of these theaters was usually deep, allowing for elaborate scenery, including scene shifts, with a tall *fly loft* above the stage to hold scenery. The loft had to be twice as high as the proscenium opening so that scenery could be concealed when it was raised or flown. (The term *to fly* comes from the notion that when pieces of scenery are raised out of sight, they fly.) Scenery was usually hung by rope or cable on a series of parallel pipes running from side to side across the stage. By hanging the pieces straight across, one behind the other, a great deal of scenery could be employed.

Several mechanisms for raising and lowering scenery were developed during the period when the proscenium stage itself was being adopted. An Italian, Giacomo Torelli (1608–1678), created a counterweight system in which weights hung on a series of ropes and pulleys balanced the scenery, allowing heavy scenery to be moved easily by a few men. Torelli's system also allowed side pieces, known as *wings,* to move in and out of the stage picture. By attaching both the hanging pieces and the side pieces to a central drum below the stage, Torelli made it possible for a complete stage set to be changed at one time. Those seeing this effect when it was first developed must have thought it was magic, and, indeed, Torelli was called *il gran stregone,* "the great wizard." Sortly after Torelli, a dynasty of scenic artists emerged who carried scene painting to a degree of perfection rarely equaled before or since. Their name was Bibiena, and for over a century, beginning with Ferdinando (1657–1743) and continuing through several generations to Carlo (1728–1787), they dominated the art of scene painting. Their sets usually consisted of vast halls, palaces, or gardens. Towering columns and arches framed spacious corridors or hallways which disappeared in an endless series of vistas as far as the eye could see.

Throughout this period, audiences, as well as scene designers and technicians, became so carried away with spectacle that they began to emphasize it to the exclusion of everything else, including the script and the acting. In Paris, a theater called Salle des Machines, by its very name, "Hall of the Machines," indicated that visual effects were the chief attraction. At times there was nothing on stage but visual display: cloud machines brought angels or deities from on high; rocks opened to reveal wood nymphs; the stage rotated on a turntable to change from a banquet hall to a forest; smoke, fire, twinkling lights, and every imaginable effect appeared as if by magic. Because the

Figure 12-5 Elaborate designs for the proscenium stage. *During the 18th century, the Bibiena family from Italy created scene designs on a grand scale for theaters throughout Europe. They painted backdrops with vistas which seemed to disappear into the infinite distance. This scene is by Giuseppe Galli Bibiena for a theatrical production honoring the Royal Prince of Poland, Prince Elector of Saxony.* (From Giuseppe Galli Bibiena, Architectural and Perspective Designs, Dover Publications, Inc., 1964.)

machinery and the workings of the scene changes can be concealed, the proscenium is the perfect arrangement for spectacle.

The days of such heavy concentration on spectacle have long since passed, but our fascination with it has not. We still find ingenious displays of visual effects in proscenium theaters. The modern musical comedy *My Fair Lady* had a number of impressive scene changes and tableaux. (The term for a scene change which occurs in view of the audience is *a vista*, an Italian phrase meaning "in sight." In view of the important contributions of Italians to the art, it is not surprising that the word is Italian.) One particularly striking change in the Broadway production of *My Fair Lady* took place toward the end of the first act. Eliza Doolittle is in Henry Higgins's study with Higgins and Colonel Pickering, preparing to go to the ball at which she will prove how well she has been transformed from a flower girl to a lady. As they leave the study for the ball, the stage rotates on a turntable and other pieces of scenery fly out of sight. The furniture on *wagons*—small platforms on wheels—moves offstage. Before our eyes the entire library disappears, and in its place we see the outside of a ballroom, shortly to become the ballroom itself. Eighteen chandeliers drop from the flies, while arches and other trappings of elegance move into the scene. In a brief moment, we have been transported from a cluttered room to a spacious, resplendent hall.

To take a more recent example, in the Broadway version of the rock opera *Jesus Christ, Superstar*, the visual effects almost overshadowed everything else. The entire stage was on hydraulic lifts and rose like a ramp to a height of 20 feet. Amidst clouds of smoke and incense, trapezes holding singers, sinners, and saints were lowered and raised from 40 feet above the stage, while huge sculptured figures moved in and out from the sides. At one point a large shell opened revealing Christ standing on a small platform. Invisibly, the platform rose and Christ ascended in the air as his white robe billowed out below him, blown by a wind machine. At the very end Christ hangs on a cross in a triangle at the back of the stage, which slowly moves toward the audience, suspended in space. Clearly, the interest in spectacle is still with us.

In addition to providing the opportunity for spectacle, there are other advantages to the proscenium stage. Realistic scenery as well—a living room, an office, or a kitchen—looks good behind the proscenium frame. Also, the strong central focus provided by the frame rivets the attention of the audience. There are times, too, when members of

Figure 12-6   A beautiful stage picture. *Because the backstage area is hidden from the audience and the stage is enclosed in a frame, elaborate, magical visions are possible in a proscenium theater. This setting is by Will Steven Armstrong for a production of* Ring Round The Moon *at the Williamstown Theatre Festival. (Photo—Williamstown Theatre Festival, Williamstown, Mass.)*

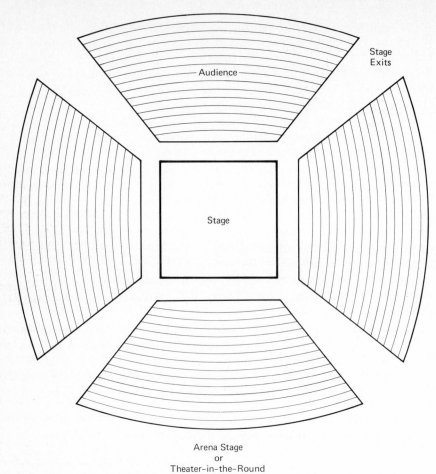

Stage
Exits

Audience

Stage

Arena Stage
or
Theater-in-the-Round

Figure 12-7 **Arena stage.** *The audience sits on four sides or in a circle surrounding the stage. Entrances and exits are made through the aisles or through tunnels underneath the aisles. A feeling of intimacy is achieved because the audience is close to the action and encloses it.*

the audience want the detachment, the distancing, which a proscenium provides.

Besides the temptation for visual pyrotechnics, the drawbacks of the proscenium stage include its tendency to remoteness and to formality. In extreme cases proscenium theaters are decorated in gold and red plush, looking more like temples of art than theaters. In short, as with any theater environment, the proscenium theater offers clear advantages, together with attendant disadvantages.

ARENA STAGE

In the period just after the Second World War, many people in theater wanted to break away from the formality which proscenium theaters tend to create. There was a desire to bring theater closer to everyday life: in acting styles, in the subject matter of the plays, in the manner of presentation, and in the shape of the theater space. This last had to do both with the atmosphere of the building and with the audience-actor relationship. One result of this reaction was to return to the arena stage.

The arena stage (also called circle theater or theater-in-the-round) has a playing space in the center of a square or circle, with seats for spectators around the circle or on the four sides. The arrangement is similar to sports arenas which feature boxing or basketball. The stage may be a raised area, about 2 feet off the main floor with seats rising from the floor, or it may be on the floor itself, with seats raised on levels around it. When seating is close to the stage, there is usually some kind of demarcation indicating the boundaries of the playing area. In the late 1940s and early 1950s arena theaters appeared in cities all over the United States: Houston, Texas; Seattle, Washington; Nashville, Tennessee; and Washington, D.C., to list a few.

There is no question that these theaters offer more intimacy than the ordinary proscenium. By having actors in the center, even in a larger theater, the audience can be closer to the actors. If the same number of people attend an arena as a proscenium event, at least half of them will be nearer the action: someone who would have been on the twelfth row in a proscenium theater will be on the sixth row in an arena theater. Besides the proximity to the stage, there is no frame or barrier to separate actor and audience. Beyond these considerations, in the arrangement of arena seating there is the unconscious communion which comes from people in a circle. This seems basic to human beings, from the embrace of two people, to a circle for children's games, to a larger gathering where people form a human enclosure around a fire or an altar.

There is a further, more practical, reason why there was such a proliferation of arena theaters in the United States at that time—economy. All you need for this kind of theater is a large room. You designate a playing space, arrange rows of seats around the sides, hang lights on pipes above, and you have a theater. There can be no elaborate scenery because it would block the view of large parts of the audience. A few pieces of furniture, with perhaps a lamp or sign hung from the ceiling, are all you need to indicate where the scene takes

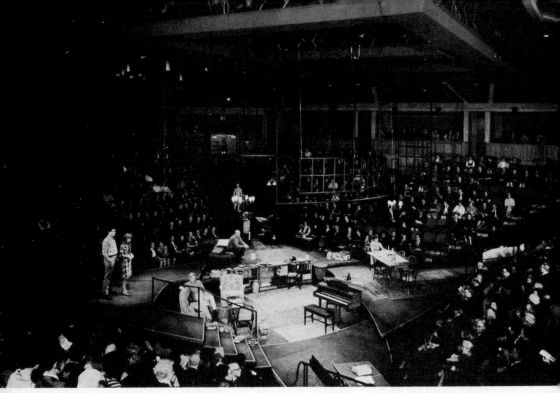

Figure 12-8 A performance in an arena theater. At the Arena Stage in Washington, D. C., the audience surrounds the action. Lighting instruments are visible above and scenery is minimal, but a strong sense of place is suggested and everyone is close to the action. (Photo—Arena Stage, Washington, D. C.)

place. Many low-budget groups found they could build a workable and even attractive theater-in-the-round when a proscenium would have been out of the question.

These two factors—intimacy and economy—no doubt explain why arena theater is one of the oldest stage forms. From as far back as we have records, we know that tribal ceremonies and rituals, in all parts of the world, have been held in some form of circle theater. The war dance of the Apache Indians is a good example, as are two ancient ceremonies which still survive today: the festival plays of Tibet which portray the struggle of Buddhism to replace an earlier religion, and the Otomi ritual in Mexican villages in which men fling themselves on a rope from a 70-foot tower pole and "fly" through the air in a wide arc until they touch the ground.

The Greek theater with which we are familiar evolved from an arena form. Tribes beat down a circle in a field of thrashed grain; an altar was placed in the center, and ceremonies were performed around it, while members of the tribe stood on the edge of the circle. This arrangement was later made more permanent as the ceremonies and festivals became formalized. It is assumed that both religious festivals and Dionysian revels—forerunners of the Greek theater—were held in such theaters.

The arena form has emerged at other times in history. Several of the cycle plays of the medieval period are known to have been performed in the round: in Lincolnshire and Cornwall in England, and in Touraine in France, for example. In Cornwall, the earthen embankments still survive that surrounded the circular playing area where the spectators stood. A plan survives, too, of an arena theater set up in a river bed in Kyoto, Japan, in 1464, for three days of performances before the ruler, known as the *shogun*.[2] The shogun sat at one end of the circle, and the actors entered at the other, while the audience sat in two semicircles around the playing area, completely encircling the actors.

In spite of its long history and its resurgence in recent years, the arena stage has often been eclipsed by other forms. One reason is that its design, while allowing for intimacy, also dictates a certain austerity. It is impossible to have elaborate scenery or much in the way of visual effects. On top of this, the actors must make all their entrances and exits along aisles running through the audience and can some-

Fig. 12-9 *An early arena theater. Dances or ceremonies performed in a circle are typical of many cultures. Here the Apache Indians prepare for war against the Navajos. While spectators surround them, the performers in the center draw power from the tall spear in their midst. (Based on a drawing by George Catlin.)*

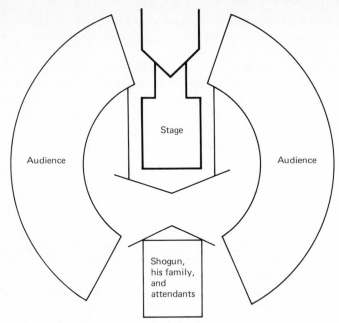

Figure 12-10 *An Oriental arena theater. At Kyōto, Japan, in 1464, a theater was set up in a river bed where an acting troupe performed for three days. The Shōgun, his family, and attendants sat at one end. Other members of the audience surrounded the stage on two sides. (From a drawing in* The Nō Plays of Japan *by Arthur Waley, published by Grove Press, Inc., N.Y.)*

times be seen before and after they are supposed to be on stage. The arena's lack of adaptability in this respect may explain why some of the circle theaters which opened twenty or thirty years ago have since closed. A number survive, however, and continue to do well. One of the best known is the Arena Stage in Washington, D.C., where such plays as *The Great White Hope* and the musical *Raisin* originated. In addition, throughout this country there are a number of musical "tent" theaters in the arena form where musical revivals and concerts are given.

THRUST STAGE

Falling between the proscenium and the arena is a third type of theater: the thrust stage with three-quarter seating. In one form or another it has been the most widely used stage of all. The basic arrangement for this type of theater has the audience sitting on three sides, or in a semicircle, enclosing a stage which protrudes into the center. At the back of the playing area is some form of stage house providing for the entrances and exits of the actors as well as scene changes. The thrust stage combines some of the best features of the other two: the sense of intimacy for the audience, the "wraparound" feeling of the arena, and a focused stage set against a single background.

The thrust stage was developed by the Greeks for their great tragedies and comedies. They took the circle, called the *orchestra*, of the tribal rituals, and placed it at the base of a curving hillside. The slope of the hill formed a natural viewing area for the spectators, and the level circle at the foot formed the stage. At the back of the circle, opposite the hillside, they placed a stage house or *skene*. The skene had formal doors through which characters made their entrances and exits and which formed a background for the action. It also provided a place for the actors to change their costumes. During the time of the Greek playwright Aeschylus, in the first half of the fifth century B.C.,

Figure 12-11 Thrust stage with three-quarter seating. *The stage is surrounded on three sides by the audience. Sometimes seating is a semicircle. Entrances and exits are made from the sides and backstage. Spectators surround the action, but there is still the possibility of scene changes and other stage effects.*

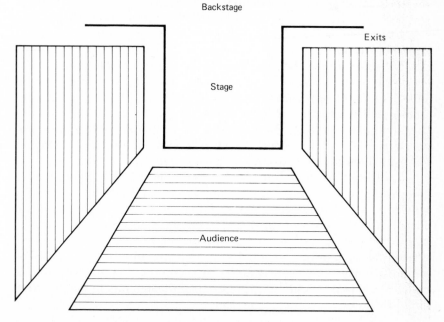

Thrust stage with three-quarter seating

Figure 12-12 Greek amphitheater. This theater at Delphi is typical of ancient Greek theaters which were built on a hillside with seats on three sides surrounding the stage. Eventually stage houses were built behind the playing area. Audiences could look past the stage to mountains or the sea in the distance. (Photo—courtesy of the Greek National Tourist Office.)

the skene may have been a temporary structure, erected each year for the festivals. In the next two or three centuries, however, it was refined to the point where the skene became a permanent stone building, two or three stories in height, with a platform stage in front. At the same time, the wooden benches on the hillsides for the spectators were replaced by stone seats. The largest theaters seated 15,000 or more spectators, and the design was duplicated all over Greece, particularly in the years following the conquests of Alexander the Great (356–323 B.C.). Remnants of these theaters remain throughout that part of the world, in such places as Epidaurus, Priene, Ephesus, Delphi, and Corinth, to name a few.

The Romans took the Greek form and simply built it as a complete structure. Instead of using the natural amphitheater of a hillside, they constructed a free-standing stone building, joining the stage house to the seating area, and making the orchestra a semicircle. In front of the stage house, decorated with arches and statues, they erected a long platform stage. The overall size and the basic arrangement, however, were similar to the Greek model. Counting the Greek and Roman period together, this form of theater was in use for over eight centuries.

Around A.D. 1200, performances of religious plays, which had been held inside churches and cathedrals, were moved outdoors. One popular stage for these outdoor performances was the *platform stage*. A simple platform was set on trestles (it was sometimes called a *trestle stage*), with a curtain at the back which the actors used for entrances and costume changes. The area underneath the stage was closed off and provided, among other things, a space from which devils and other characters could appear, sometimes in a cloud of smoke. In some places the platform was on wheels (a *wagon stage*) and moved from place to place through a town. The audience stood on three sides of the platform, making it an improvised thrust stage. This type of stage was used throughout the medieval period, between the thirteenth and fifteenth centuries.

The next step was a thrust stage which appeared in England in the sixteenth century, just before Shakespeare began writing for the theater. A platform stage was set up at one end of the open courtyard of an inn. The inns of this period were three or four stories high, and the rooms facing the inner courtyard served as boxes from which spectators could watch the performance. On ground level, spectators stood on three sides of the stage, while the fourth side of the courtyard, behind the platform, served as the stage house.

Interestingly enough, an almost identical theater took shape in Spain at the same time. The inns in Spain were called *corrales*, the same name given to the theaters which developed there. In addition to a similarity of theaters in England and Spain, a further coincidence lies in the fact that a talented and prolific dramatist, Lope de Vega (1562–1635), was born within two years of Shakespeare's birth and emerged as his Spanish counterpart.

In England, the formal theaters of Shakespeare's day, such as the Globe and the Fortune, were adaptations of the inn theaters: the audience stood in an open area around a platform stage, and three levels of spectators sat in closed galleries at the back and sides. A roof covered part of the stage, and at the back was an upper level for balcony scenes (as in *Romeo and Juliet*). At the rear of the stage was an area where scenes could be concealed and then "discovered." On each side at the rear was a door used for entrances and exits.

These theaters were fascinating combinations of diverse elements: they were both indoors and outdoors; some spectators stood while others sat; and the audience was composed of almost all levels of society. The physical environment must have been a stimulating one: an actor standing at the front of the thrust stage was in the center of a hemisphere of spectators, ranging on three sides around him as

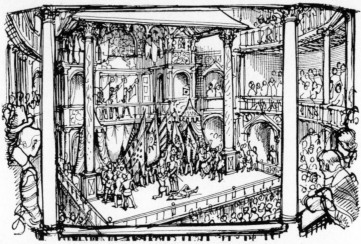

Figure 12-13   An Elizabethan playhouse. *This drawing indicates the kind of stage on which the plays of Shakespeare and his contemporaries were first presented. A platform stage juts into an open courtyard, with spectators standing on three sides. Three levels of enclosed seats rise above the courtyard. There are doors at the rear of the stage for entrances and exits and an upper level for balcony scenes. (Drawing from C. Walter Hodges,* Shakespeare and the Players. *Courtesy of Coward, McCann & Geohegan, Inc., and G. Bell and Sons, Ltd.)*

well as above and below. While these theaters held 2,000 to 3,000 spectators, no person was more than 60 feet or so from the stage, and most were much closer. Being in the midst of so many people, enclosed on all sides but with an open sky above, must have instilled a feeling of great communion among the audience and actors.

Shortly after Shakespeare's day, in the latter part of the seventeenth century, two things occurred in England and Spain, as well as throughout Europe: (1) the theater moved completely indoors, and (2) the stage began a slow but steady retreat behind the proscenium, partly because of being indoors, but more because the style of theater changed. For over two centuries the thrust stage was in eclipse, not to reappear until about 1900, when a few theaters in England began using a version of the thrust stage to produce Shakespeare. The return to the thrust stage resulted from a growing realization that Elizabethan plays could be done best on a stage similar to the one for which they were written. In the United States and Canada, it was not until after the Second World War that the thrust stage came to the fore again. Since then a number of fine theaters of this type have been built. Examples include the Tyrone Guthrie in Minneapolis; the Shakespeare Theater at Stratford, Ontario; the Mark Taper Forum in Los Angeles; and the Long Wharf in New Haven, Connecticut.

The basic stage of traditional Chinese and Japanese drama (including the Noh theater and the Kabuki theater of Japan) is a form of thrust stage: a raised, open platform, frequently covered by a roof, with the audience sitting on two or three sides around the platform stage. Entrances and exits are made from doors or ramps at the rear of the stage.

The obvious advantages of the thrust stage—the intimacy of the three-quarter seating and the close audience-actor relationship, together with the fact that so many of the world's great dramatic works were written for it—give it a permanent place alongside the other major forms.

CREATED OR FOUND SPACE

Previously we discussed Jerzy Grotowski and others in the New Theater movement who challenged traditional concepts in theater.

Figure 12-14 A modern thrust stage. A performance in the New York Shakespeare Festival in Central Park shows the audience surrounding the action on three sides. There is intimacy for the spectators but also a scenic background for the performers. (Photo—George E. Joseph.)

Figure 12-15 Modern Japanese thrust stage. The Japanese Kabuki theater *uses a form of platform stage with spectators sitting on three sides. Musicians sit at the rear in view of the audience and there is a roof over the stage supported by columns. (From the Consulate General of Japan, New York.)*

They wished to reform theater at every level, and since the various elements of theater are inextricably bound together, the search for a more basic kind of theater by New Theater groups included a close look at the physical arrangement of the playing area and its relationship to the audience. The Performance Group, which led spectators one at a time into the production of *Dionysus in 69*, is typical in this regard. It presented its productions in a large garage converted into an open theater space. At various points in the garage, scaffolding and ledges were built for audience seating. The Performance Group, like all New Theater groups, owed a great debt to a Frenchman, Antonin Artaud (1896–1948), one of the first men to examine in depth the questions raised by the New Theater. An actor and director who wrote a series of articles and essays about the theater, Artaud was inconsistent, but brilliant. (He spent several periods of his life in mental institutions.) Many of his ideas were to prove prophetic: notions he put forward in the 1920s and 1930s, considered mad or impossible at the time, have since become common practice among adherents of the New Theater.

Among his proposals was one on the physical theater:

We abolish the stage and auditorium and replace them by a single site, without partition or barrier of any kind, which will become the theater of the action. A direct communication will be re-established between the spectator and the spectacle, between the actor and the spectator, from the fact that the spectator, placed in the middle of the action, is engulfed and physically affected by it. This envelopment results, in part, from the very configuration of the room itself.

Thus, abandoning the architecture of present-day theaters, we shall take some hangar or barn, which we shall have reconstructed according to processes which have culminated in the architecture of certain churches or holy places, and of certain temples in Tibet.

In the interior of this construction special proportions of height and depth will prevail. The hall will be enclosed by four walls, without any kind of ornament, and the public will be seated in the middle of the room, on the ground floor, on mobile chairs

Fig. 12-16 Created theater space. *For a production of* Commune, *the Performance Group transformed a large empty room into a series of playing areas and spaces for audience seating. Spectators enjoyed an unusual vantage point from which to view the action. The environment was especially created to fit the play. (Photo—Frederick Eberstadt.)*

which will allow them to follow the spectacle which will take place all around them. In effect, the absence of a stage in the usual sense of the word will provide for the deployment of the action in the four corners of the room. Particular positions will be reserved for actors and action at the four cardinal points of the room. . . . However, a central position will be reserved which, without serving, properly speaking, as a stage, will permit the bulk of the action to be concentrated and brought to a climax whenever necessary.[3]

Some of Artaud's ideas were put into practice later, when the movement to explore New Theater concepts became widespread. In the generation after Artaud, Jerzy Grotowski included the physical arrangements of stage space in his experiments. Not only Grotowski, but others in the New Theater movement developed theater space in a variety of ways.

Use of Nontheater Buildings

Artaud mentioned a barn or hangar for performances. In recent years virtually every kind of structure has been used: lofts, warehouses, fire stations, basements, churches, breweries, and gymnasiums. We should not confuse New Theater practice with the conversion of unusual spaces to full-scale theaters; this has numerous precedents in the past. Historically, indoor tennis courts, palace ballrooms, and monastery dining halls have been converted into theaters. We are speaking here of using unusual structures as they are, with their original architectural elements intact. Special areas are carved out for acting and viewing, as with the garage of the Performance Group, but they are not to be mistaken for a traditional theater building.

Adaptation of Space to Fit Individual Productions

One practice adopted frequently by New Theater advocates was the use of space to fit the play, rather than making the play fit the space, as is normally the case. Grotowski in particular pursued the notion of a different configuration for each production, one which seems appropriate to the play being done. In Grotwoski's version of the Dr. Faustus story, Faustus gives a banquet. For this production, the theater was filled with two long tables at which spectators sat as if they were guests at a dinner party. The action took place at the heads of the tables and even on the table tops. For Grotowski's production of *The Constant Prince*, a fence was built around the playing area, and the audience sat behind it, looking over the fence, like spectators at a bullfight. In his version of *Kordian* the theater was transformed to resemble the ward of a mental institution, with viewers interspersed among the beds and patients. In the last quarter century there have been similar attempts to deal with theater space throughout Europe and the United States.

Outdoor Settings

One development—which was actually a return to ancient practices in classical Greece and medieval Europe—was theater held out of doors. In 1971, the English director Peter Brook (1925–) created a theater piece called *Orghast* in the ruins of the ancient palace of Darius the Great at Persepolis in the mountains of Persia, known today as Iran. Spectators had to hike up the mountain to reach the site, where they saw performances at night with moonlight and blazing torches for illumination. No doubt it was a ghostly, awe-inspiring setting.

Not long ago, a new town called Nova Jerusalem was built in the wilderness of northeastern Brazil. It is a modern replica of ancient Jerusalem in the Holy Land and includes the temple, Pilate's forum, Herod's palace, and Calvary. In effect, the entire city is a stage set—in this case a very real one. Each year during Holy Week over 500 villagers and professional actors reenact the Passion of Christ. And some 5,000 spectators participate in the drama as well, moving to the scene of action, and walking each night with actors along the road to Calvary.

Street Theater

We mentioned street theater earlier. Generally it is of three types: (1) plays from the standard repertoire presented in the streets, (2) neighborhood theater in which an original play deals with the problems and aspirations of a specific area of a city—Puerto Rican, black, Italian, etc.—and (3) guerilla theater—aggressive, politically oriented theater produced by an activist group in the streets in an attempt to persuade listeners to become more politically involved. Whatever the form, the important point for our purposes is that these productions take place in the streets, not in a theater building.

In the past few years, theater has been presented not only in the streets, but in fields, parks, bus stations, in fact, in almost every imaginable locale. In Hartford, Connecticut, a theater troupe presented a play in the plaza of a large insurance company office building. At national political conventions, beginning with Chicago in 1968 and Miami in 1972, drama by protest groups has become commonplace. In New York City, plays have been presented outside jails and hospitals and in subway stations.

In these productions theater is brought to people who might not

Figure 12-17 An entire village as a stage setting. *In Brazil a town has been built—Nova Jerusalem—which reproduces the well-known landmarks of the original Jerusalem. Each year during Holy Week a large-scale drama is enacted depicting Christ's entry into Jerusalem, his betrayal, his trail, his crucifixion, and his resurrection in the appropriate setting. Hundreds of actors take part and thousands of spectators become the witnesses who were present at the first Passion Week. (From The New York Times. Photo—Marvine Howe.)*

see it otherwise. Also, those watching theater in such unusual settings are challenged to rethink what theater is all about. On the other hand, there are inherent disadvantages to the impromptu productions in the streets or other "found space": the audience must be caught on the run, and there is rarely time for more than a sketch or vignette. Nor are there facilities to present a fully developed work. But then that is often not the purpose of these undertakings in the first place. Some street theater groups, realizing the limitations of the totally informal offering, have begun to acquire more sophisticated equipment and more permanent stage arrangements.

Multifocus Environments

An approach, which sometimes accompanies these unusual arrangements, is *multifocus* theater. In simple terms, this means that not only is there more than one playing area, such as the four corners of the room suggested by Artaud, but something is going on in several of them simultaneously. This is somewhat like a three-ring circus, where the spectator sees an activity in each ring and must choose the one on which to concentrate.

There are several theories behind the idea of multifocus theater, some of them debatable. One is that a multifocus event is more like everyday life; if you stand on a street corner, there is activity all around you—in the four directions of the streets, in the buildings above—not just in one spot. You select which area you will observe, or perhaps you watch several at one time. The argument is that you should have the same choice in the theater. In multifocus productions no single space or activity is supposed to be more important than any other. The spectator either takes in several impressions at once—as in multimedia—and synthesizes them in his or her own mind or selects the one item he or she finds most arresting and concentrates on that. There is no such thing as the "best seat in the house"; all seats are equally good because the activity in all parts of the theater is equally important. Sometimes multifocus is joined with *multimedia*—presentations in which some combination of acting, films, dance, music, slides, and light shows is offered.

One problem with multifocus theater is that we seek in art precisely the selectivity and focus we do not find in everyday life. Besides, even those presentations which claim to be multifocus ultimately have a central point of interest—a three-ring circus, after all, has a center ring. It is difficult for a spectator to maintain interest in a multifocus event for very long. For some types of theater, a multifocus event is interesting, as well as appropriate, but by and large members of the audience want to concentrate their attention on one space and one group of characters at a time.

Taken all in all, whether single-focus or multifocus, indoors or outdoors, the recent innovations in theater milieu have added a further alternative, rich in possibilities, to the settings for theatrical productions. They have also called attention to the importance of environment in the total theater experience.

Historical Precedents

Because created or found space by definition is not permanent, there is not the same tradition of theater buildings for this arrangement as there is for arena, thrust, or proscenium theaters. But there are many historical precedents for performing in outdoor or impromptu settings. No doubt when theater first begins in any culture the playing area and the audience arrangement are improvised. As mentioned before, the first Greek theater is thought to have been an open field, trampled down in the center to provide a playing area around which spectators stood. The medieval theater frequently took place on platform or wagon stages in the streets. When we say, therefore, that street theater is new, we mean new to our day, not that it has never appeared before. Also, the miracle plays of the medieval theater were sometimes presented in town squares, in the fashion of the Passion play at Nova Jerusalem described above.

THE VARIETY IN THEATER ENVIRONMENTS

Simply assigning a theater to a category does not adequately describe the environment. We must take into account a number of other variables in theater architecture as well. Two theaters may be of the same type and still be quite different in size, atmosphere, and setting. The small Sullivan Street Theater in New York, where the off-Broadway musical *The Fantasticks* has set records for its long run, seats less than 200 people. The theater experience in the Sullivan Street will be far different from that in another thrust theater several times larger, such as the Tyrone Guthrie in Minneapolis. Also, one theater may be indoors and another outdoors. Rather than having one type of theater building with only one form of stage, theater audiences today are fortunate in having a full range of environments in which to experience theater.

SUMMARY

1 The atmosphere and environment of theater space play a large part in setting the tone of the event.

2 Experimental theater groups in recent years have deliberately made spectators aware of the environment.

3 Throughout theater history there have been four basic stage and auditorium arrangements.

4 The proscenium theater features the picture-frame stage, in which the audience faces directly toward the stage and looks through the proscenium opening at the "picture." This type of stage has the potential for elaborate scene shifts and visual displays because it generally has a large backstage area and a flyloft. It also creates a distancing effect which works to the advantage of certain types of drama. At the same time the proscenium frame sets up a barrier between the performers and the audience.

5 The arena or circle stage places the playing area in the center with the audience ranged in a circle or square around the outside. It

offers an economical way to produce theater and an opportunity for great intimacy between actors and spectators. It cannot offer full visual displays in terms of scenery and scene changes.

6 The thrust stage with three-quarter seating has a platform stage with seating on three sides. Entrances and exits are made at the rear, and there is an opportunity for a certain amount of scenery. It combines some of the scenic features of the proscenium theater with the intimacy of the arena stage.

7 Created or found space takes several forms: **(a)** use of nontheater buildings, **(b)** adaptation of a given space to fit individual productions, **(c)** use of outdoor settings, **(d)** street theater, and **(e)** multifocus environments.

8 The size and the location (indoors or outdoors, etc.), along with the shape and character of the theater building, affect the environment.

We have examined environmental factors influencing our experience at a theatrical event, including the location of the theater building, its size, its setting, its atmosphere, and its layout. In addition to a general environment in a theater building, there is a specific environment for the performers; within the limits of the stage, or whatever has been designated as a playing area, a visual world is created for the actors and actresses to inhabit. Once a performance begins, the audience is always aware, even if unconsciously, of the scenery and lighting effects on stage.

13
SCENERY AND LIGHTING

The theater experience does not occur in a visual vacuum. Spectators sit in the theater, their eyes open, watching what unfolds before them. Naturally, they focus most keenly on the performers as they speak and move about the stage, but always present are the visual images of scenery and lighting—transformations of colors and shapes which add a significant ingredient to the total mixture of theater. The creation of these effects is the responsibility of the scene designer and the lighting designer. The two may be the same person, but their functions remain distinct.

The scene designer is responsible for the stage set, which can run the gamut from a bare stage with stools or orange crates to the most elaborate, large-scale production. No matter how simple, however,

Figure 13-1 *Scenery and lighting: key visual elements.* Robert U. Taylor's sketch of a stage set for The Royal Hunt of the Sun *emphasizes vertical lines creating strength and importance in the stage picture. This shows the center portion of Mr. Taylor's design which features a vivid visual image supporting the theme and main action of the play. (Courtesy of Robert U. Taylor.)*

every set has a design. Even the absence of scenery constitutes a stage set and can benefit from the ideas of a designer: in the way the furniture is arranged, for example.

Stage lighting, quite simply, includes all forms of illumination on the stage. The lighting designer makes decisions in every area of lighting: the color of the lights, the mixture of colors, the number of lights, the intensity and brightness of the lights, the angles at which the lights strike performers, and the length of time required for the lights to come up or fade out.

Both scene and lighting designers must deal with practical as well as aesthetic considerations. A scene designer must know in which direction a door should open on stage and how high each tread should be on a flight of stairs. A lighting designer must know exactly how many feet above a performer's head a particular light should be placed, and whether it requires a 500-watt or a 750-watt bulb.

As in other elements of theater—characters, dialogue, and structure for example—symbols play a large role in scenery and lighting design. A single item on stage can suggest an entire room: a bookcase, for instance, suggests a professor's office or a library; a stained glass window suspended in midair suggests a church or synagogue. A stage filled with a bright, yellow-orange glow suggests a cheerful sunny day, whereas a single shaft of pale blue light suggests moonlight or an eerie churchyard at night. The ways in which scene and lighting designers deal with the aesthetic and practical requirements of the stage will be clearer when we examine the two fields in detail, beginning with scene design.

"STAGE SETS" IN EVERYDAY LIFE

As with other areas of theater there is an analogue or parallel between scene design and our experiences in everyday life. Every building and room we go into can be regarded as a form of stage set. Interior decorating—the creation of special atmosphere in a home or a public building—is scene designing for everyday life. A good example is the trend in recent years for restaurants to have a foreign motif—French, Italian, Spanish, Olde English—with "scenery" to give the feeling that you are in a different world, when in fact you have just stepped off the street. A church decorated for a wedding is a form of stage set; so is the posh lobby of a hotel, or an apartment with flowers, candlelight, and soft music.

In every case the "designer," the person who has arranged the setting, has selected elements which signal an impression to the viewer. The combination of colors, fabrics, furniture, and styles tells the person entering the space exactly where he or she is. These things are calculated with great care, and a premium is set on an appropriate environment and atmosphere. When we see a library with leather-bound books, attractive wood paneling, comfortable leather chairs, and a beautiful carved wooden desk, we get a sense of stability, tradition, and comfort. A totally different kind of feeling would come from a modern room with everything white and black, with glass-top tables, furniture of chrome and stainless steel, and indirect lighting. From this spare, functional look, we get a "modern" feeling. Interior decorators know that appearance is important, that the visual elements of a room can communicate an overall impression to which an observer responds with a series of feelings, attitudes, and assumptions.

We are accustomed in everyday life to seeing such "stage settings," but as with other elements in theater, there is a difference between interior decorations in real life and set designs for the stage. Robert Edmond Jones (1887–1954), considered by many to be the most outstanding American scene designer of the first half of this century, put it in these terms:

> A good scene should be, not a picture, but an image. Scene-designing is not what most people imagine it is—a branch of interior decorating. There is no more reason for a room on a stage to be a reproduction of an actual room than for an actor who plays the part of Napoleon to be Napoleon or for an actor who plays Death in the old morality play to be dead. Everything that is actual must undergo a strange metamorphosis, a kind of sea-change, before it can become truth in the theater.[1]

While a stage set signals an atmosphere to the viewer, in the same way that rooms in real life do, the scene designer must go a step further. As we have pointed out many times, the theater is not life: it resembles life. It has both the opportunity and the obligation to be more than mere reproduction, as Jones suggests.

AESTHETICS OF SCENE DESIGN

Because scenic elements have such strong symbolic values and are so important to the overall effect of a production, the designer has an obligation to provide scenery consistent with the intent of the play and the director's concept. What must never be forgotten—just as it must never be forgotten when we read a play in book form—is the presence of the actor. Scene design is not a picture; it is an environment: a place for actors to move and have their being. Robert Edmond Jones spoke forcefully on this point when he said: "Players act in a setting, not against it."[2] He went on to explain:

> A stage setting holds a curious kind of suspense. Go, for instance, into an ordinary empty drawing-room as it exists normally. There is no particular suspense about this room. It is just—empty. Now imagine the same drawing-room arranged and decorated for a particular function—a Christmas party for children, let us say. It is not completed as a room, not until the children are in it. And if we wish to visualize for ourselves how important a part the sense of expectancy plays in such a room, let us imagine that there is a storm and the children cannot come. A scene on the stage is filled with the same expectancy. It is like a mixture of chemical elements held in solution. The actor adds the one element that releases the hidden energy of the whole. Meanwhile, wanting the actor, the various elements which go to make up the setting remain suspended, as it were, in an indefinable tension. To create this suspense, this tension, is the essence of the problem of stage designing.[3]

Jones is saying that a stage set, rather than being a complete picture in and of itself, is an environment with one element missing—the actor. Empty, it has a sense of incompleteness. A stage set is like a giant piece of mobile sculpture, motionless until set in motion by the actors. This of course fits with our notion that theater is an experience, an unfolding encounter which moves through time. Were the stage picture complete when we first entered the theater, or when the curtain went up, where would the experience lie? The job of the scene designer is not to create a beautiful shadowbox or three-dimensional painting but to create a stage environment which is practical as well as artistic.

Scene Design Distinguished from Painting

There have been times in the history of theater when scene design was looked on as the painting of a large picture. In our discussion of the proscenium stage we noted the temptation to use the proscenium arch as a frame and put behind it a gigantic picture. The tradition of fine scene painting, begun in Italy in the late seventeenth century, continued throughout Europe in the eighteenth and nineteenth centuries. It was still flourishing in Europe and America in the early part

Figure 13-2 An environment for performers. *Scenic designer Robert Edmond Jones insisted that a stage setting should not be complete in itself, but should provide background and atmosphere: a world for the actors to inhabit. A good example is his design for Desdemona's chamber in Shakespeare's* Othello. *(Photo—Museum of the City of New York, Theatre and Music Collection.)*

of this century, when many famous painters, including Pablo Picasso, Salvadore Dali, and Marc Chagall, attempted scene design. Painters, accustomed to seeing their work stand on its own, are of course interested in the effect of the picture, the visual image itself, aside from activity on the stage. But the static picture, the purely visual impression which is more important than the environment, presents serious problems in the theater.

The distinction between scenery as painting and scenery as part of a total stage production can hardly be overemphasized. Frequently in the theater—particularly in an elaborate production—the audience breaks into applause when the visual image of the set is revealed as the curtain rises. There is nothing wrong with admiring the beauty or excitement of a stage picture. Taken to extremes, however, the emphasis on illustration or a "pretty picture" runs counter to the purpose of scene design. If members of the audience spend their time admiring the beauty of the scenery, they may miss the words of the playwright and the actions of the performers and as a result, they may not grasp the meaning of the play. This suggests how important it is to have a stage setting in tune with the total production.

A stage setting must be consistent with the play for which it is intended, that is, with the mood, style, and meaning of the play. A farce calls for comic, exaggerated scenery, in the manner of a cartoon, perhaps with outrageous colors. A satire calls for a comment in the design, like the twist in the lines of a caricature in a political drawing. A serious play calls for sober, straightforward scenery, even in a nonrealistic piece. Scene design should be neither so beautiful nor so *busy*, that is, so cluttered with detail, that it distracts the spectator's eye from the action onstage. Following Robert Edmond Jones's advice, the scene designer must see to it that the set does not distract from the actors nor call attention to itself. Otherwise, we have an inversion of the values of theater, for the performers and the play must be paramount. Scene design is at its best when it underlines and emphasizes the primary values of the play, not competing with the play or overpowering it, but enhancing and supporting it.

As examples of what is called for in scene design, let us consider two plays by the Spanish playwright Federico Garcia Lorca (1899–1936). His *Blood Wedding* is the story of a young bride-to-be who runs away with a former lover on the day she is to be married. The two young lovers flee to a forest, and in the forest the play becomes expressionistic: allegorical figures of the Moon and a Beggar Woman, representing Death, appear in the forest to echo the fierce emotional struggle taking place within the characters. It would be quite inappropriate to design a realistic, earthbound set for *Blood Wedding*, particularly for the forest portion of the play. The setting must have the same sense of mystery, of the unreal, which rules the passions of the characters. We must see this visually in the images of the forest as well as in the figures of the Moon and the Beggar Woman.

Another play of Lorca's, *The House of Bernarda Alba*, tells of a woman and her five daughters. The woman has grown to hate and distrust men, and so she locks up her house, like a convent, preventing her daughters from going out. From a design point of view it is important to convey the closed-in, cloistered feeling of the house in which the women are held as virtual prisoners. The sense of entrapment must be omnipresent.

Occasionally, scenery runs deliberately counter to the play—as a comment on it. Ionesco's *The Bald Soprano*, a zany Theater of the Absurd piece, might be set is a realistic family living room as an ironic contrast to the content of the play. This, however, is the exception rather than the rule.

Realistic Scenery

The stage designer's role is of special importance in distinguishing between realistic and nonrealistic stage sets. In realistic theater, a setting is called for which looks very much like the same thing in real

Figure 13-3 **Scenery sets the style.** *Scenery should be appropriate to the play for which it is designed. This stage setting of a ship for Aristophanes' The Frogs has the proper comic, satiric tone. The design elements are caricature, cut-outs from a comic book. The audience knows immediately from seeing the set what kind of play to expect. (Courtesy of the University of Iowa. Production directed by Peter D. Arnott, designed by A. S. Gillette, costumes by Margaret S. Hall, lights by David L. Thayer.)*

life. A kitchen resembles a kitchen, a dining room a dining room, and so on. One exponent of realism, David Balasco, a producer-director of the early twentieth century, sometimes reproduced an actual kitchen or a room from a house, including wallpaper and light fixtures, on stage.

These are extremes, however, for even in realism the stage designer selects items to go on stage, and his or her talent and imagination play an important role. The point is to make the room resemble, but not duplicate, its counterpart from real life. In the same way that a playwright does not simply take a tape recorder into the streets and record conversations like a stenographer, the scene designer does not reproduce each detail of a room. A set calls for selectivity and editing. In a realistic setting, it is up to the designer to pick and choose those items, or symbols, that will give the proper

Figure 13-4 *Symbolic scenery in Chinese theater. In this University of Tulsa production of a Chinese play, the boxes on which the performers stand represent a bridge or a mountainside from which the characters view the world below. In Chinese theater, simple elements are accepted for a complete scene or locale. (Photo—courtesy of University of Tulsa. Production directed by Beaumont Bruestle, designed by Harold Barrows.)*

feeling and impression. The significance of these items must be highlighted by eliminating everything irrelevant or distracting. The result should convey to us not only the life-style but the individual characteristics of the persons in the play.

At times the designer may provide only partial settings for realistic plays. We will see a portion of a room—a cutout with only door frames and windows, but no walls, or walls suggested by an outline. The remaining elements will be realistic, but the total set will be fragmentary. In any case, it is through selectivity and emphasis that the designer provides an appropriate setting.

Nonrealistic Scenery

In nonrealistic theater, the designer can give full rein to imagination, and the use of symbol is of special importance. Chinese theater affords a graphic example of the possibilities of symbol in stage design. Throughout the history of Chinese theater, an elaborate set of conventions has been developed in which a single prop or item represents a complete locale or action. An embroidered curtain on a pole stands for a general's tent, an official seal signifies an office, and an incense tripod stands for a palace. A plain table may represent a judge's bench, but when two chairs are placed at each end of the table, it can become a bridge. When actors climb on the table, it can be a mountain; when they jump over it, a wall. A banner with fish on it represents the sea, a man with a riding whip is riding a horse, and two banners with wheels are a chariot. Clearly, the Chinese have developed the art of scenic symbolism to a high level, and interestingly enough the symbols are thoroughly convincing even to Westerners.

Productions in the United States also provide examples of imaginative, nonrealistic scenery. In a previous chapter we mentioned the expressionistic play *The Adding Machine*. In designing the original production of this play, Lee Simonson (1888–1967) used abstract settings, with vertical lines set at odd angles. Like the angle of vision in the play itself, the set was tilted, creating a sense of imbalance and unreality.

For the revival of Sophocles's *Electra*, Ming Cho Lee (1930–), suspended large stone formations on three sides of the stage, suggesting the three doors of the ancient Greek theater, but more important, his design conveyed the solidity, dignity, and rough-hewn quality of the play. In contrast, Boris Aronson (1900–), for the musical *Company,* designed a sharp, sleek set of chrome and Lucite, with straight lines. Actors moved from one area to another in modern, open elevators, symbolic of the chic, antiseptic world of the characters. The set was the epitome of sophisticated, urban living.

When the director and designer decide to change the period or style of a play—to update a Shakespearean play, for instance—they must develop a "concept" to implement the change. As a part of this process, the designer's concept becomes crucial in establishing the new period and style. Modern stage designs for two plays by Shakespeare will illustrate the point. Shakespeare's *A Midsummer Night's Dream* is traditionally played in palace rooms and a forest, as suggested by the script. For Peter Brook's production of the early 1970s, however, designer Sally Jacobs (1932–) fashioned three white, bare walls—like the sides of a white gymnasium. Trapezes were lowered onto the stage at various times for the actors, and in some scenes they actually performed their parts while suspended in midair. The clean, spare look of Ms. Jacob's setting was nontraditional to say the least.

Figure 13-5 A world off balance. The odd angles in Lee Simonson's set for the original Broadway production of The Adding Machine *symbolize the off-center world of the main character, Mr. Zero. In this courtroom scene his life appears to be falling apart; the scenery is an outward manifestation of his inner feelings. (Courtesy of the New York Public Library at Lincoln Center, Theatre Collection. Astor, Lenox and Tilden Foundations. Photo—Vandamm.)*

In the 1972 New York Shakespeare Festival production of *Much Ado about Nothing* the play was set, not in its original time and place, but in the United States at the end of the nineteenth century. The set by Ming Cho Lee made use of band stands, Japanese lanterns, canoes, and the filigree and finery of turn-of-the-century architecture. Once again, the visual image provided the strongest possible clue to the world the director and designer wished us to inhabit: a world in marked contrast to the traditional setting.

The concept developed by a scene designer for a stage setting is closely related to the idea of a central design metaphor.

Central Image or Metaphor in Scene Design

Stage design must not only be consistent with the play; it should have its own integrity. The elements of the design—the lines, the shapes, the colors—should add up to a whole. In many cases, a designer tries to develop a central image or metaphor. For the original production of *The Royal Hunt of the Sun*, a play about Pizarro and the conquest of Peru, Michael Annals set a huge sunburst, resembling a gold medallion, in midair at the back of the stage. Twelve feet in diameter and symbolizing both gold and the sun, the sunburst dominated the stage, providing a vivid focal point for the production.

In *Death of a Salesman*, Jo Mielziner (1901–) created a set combining various elements inherent in the play. On the one hand, there was the real home of Willy Loman: the kitchen with a refrigerator, table, and chairs. At the same time, surrounding the house was a

Figure 13-6 Imaginative design for Sophocles' Electra. *Designer Ming Cho Lee, basing his concept on the three doors of original Greek theater buildings, created a piece of stage sculpture as a setting for Sophocles' play. Simple yet forceful, with a beauty all its own, it is an ideal setting for this ancient tale of revenge and honor reclaimed. (Design by Ming Cho Lee. Photo by Nathan Rabin.)*

Figure 13-7 A single image dominates the stage. The original Broadway production of The Royal Hunt of the Sun *featured a single large gold sunburst in the center of the stage. The setting above for a production at the Virginia Museum Theater uses a similar approach, an inventive design giving visual force and unity to the play. Compare this with Robert U. Taylor's setting for the same play found at the opening of the chapter. (Photo—Virginia Museum Theatre Repertory Company.)*

skyline consisting of apartment houses closing in on Willy's world. When Willy moved from the present to his memory of the past, the lights would shift so the audience could see through transparent walls of his house to the world around him. From the real world, Willy moved as if by magic through the walls of his home into the past, figuratively and literally. The hope and promise of Willy's youth, when his world was full of fresh, growing things, was symbolized by projections of green leaves thrown over the entire set. Once again, the set provided a central metaphor for the play, with the past and the present appearing simultaneously.

Designing the Total Theater Environment

In contemporary theater productions, where found space and overall environment are of paramount importance, the scene designer frequently decides where and how the audience will be placed as well as where the playing areas will be. It goes beyond deciding what will be placed on the stage. For instance, in an open space such as a gym or a warehouse, a designer will build an entire theater, including the seats or stands for the audience and the designated acting areas. In this case, the designer considers the size and shape of the space, the texture and nature of the building materials, the atmosphere of the space, and the needs of the play itself. These conditions apply in the case of multifocus theater as well.

PRACTICAL ASPECTS OF STAGE DESIGN

We have been discussing aesthetic considerations of scenery, but as with everything in theater there is a practical side to scenery as well.

Requirements of the Physical Layout

The playing area must fit into a certain stage space, and more important, it must accommodate actors. In terms of space, a designer cannot plan a gigantic stage setting for a theater where the proscenium opening is only 20 feet wide and the depth of the stage no more than 18 feet. By the same token, to design a small room in the midst of a 40-foot stage would be ludicrous. As for the requirements of the play, the designer must take into account the physical layout of the stage space. If an actor must leave by a door on the right side of the stage, and a few moments later return by a door on the left, the designer must make allowance for the actor to cross over behind the scenery; otherwise he cannot make his entrance. If an actor needs to change costumes quickly offstage, the scene designer must make certain that there is room offstage for the change. If there is to be a sword fight, the actors must have space in which to make their turns, to advance and retreat.

Any type of physical movement requires a certain amount of space, and the scene designer must allow for this in his *ground plan*. The ground plan is the blueprint, or floor plan, outlining the various levels on the stage and indicating the placement of all scenery, furniture, doors, windows, etc. Working in conjunction with the director, the designer is chiefly responsible for a workable ground plan.

The way doors open and close, the way a sofa is set, the angle at which steps lead to a second floor—all are the responsibility of the designer and are important to both the actor and the play. Performers must be able to execute steps easily and to sit in such a way that the audience can see them clearly, and they must have the space to interact with other performers naturally and convincingly. If an actress opens a door on stage and is immediately blocked from the view of the audience, this is obviously an error on the part of the scene designer.

Figure 13-8 Design model and finished set. *Designers usually prepare a sketch or model of the stage set to indicate to the director and those building the scenery how the finished product will look. At the top we see Ming Cho Lee's model for a production of Ibsen's* Peer Gynt *by the New York Shakespeare Festival, and below, the actual set during a performance. (Photo of Ming Cho Lee model by Nathan Rabin. Production photo—Nathan Rabin.)*

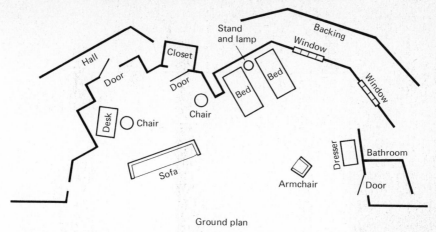

Ground plan

Figure 13-9 Ground plan. *In order to aid the director, performers, and stage technicians, the designer draws a ground plan or blueprint of the stage showing the exact locations of furniture, walls, windows, doors, and other scenic elements.*

To designate areas of the stage the scene designer uses terminology peculiar to the theater. *Stage right* means the right side of the stage as seen from the actor's right, and *stage left*, from the actor's left. In other words, when the audience looks at the stage, the side to its left is stage right, and vice versa. Also, the area of the stage nearest the audience is known as *downstage* and the area farthest away from the audience is *upstage*. These designations, downstage and upstage, come from the time in the eighteenth and nineteenth centuries when the stage was *raked*, that is, the stage sloped downward from back to front. As a result of this downward slope, the performer farthest away from the audience was higher, or *up*, and could be seen better. This is the origin of the expression "she upstaged everyone." The term has come to mean that one actor grabs the spotlight from everyone else and calls attention to himself or herself by any means whatever. At first, however, it meant that one performer was in a better position than the others because he or she was standing farther back on the raked stage and hence was higher.

Materials of the Scene Designer

In creating a stage set, the designer begins with the stage floor itself. Sometimes the stage floor is a turntable, meaning that a circle set into the floor can turn mechanically to bring one set into view as another disappears. At times trapdoors are set in the floor through which

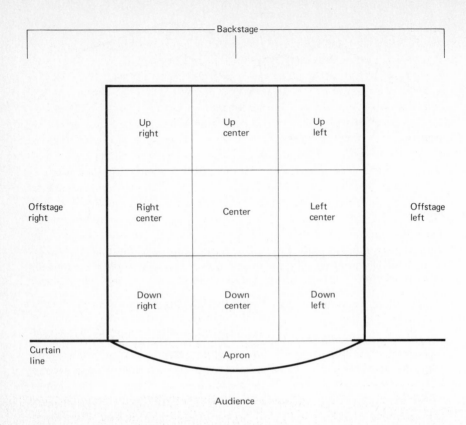

Figure 13-10 Stage areas. *Various parts of the stage are given specific designations. Near the audience is downstage; away from the audience is upstage. Right and left are from the performers' point of view, not the audience's. Everything out of sight from the audience is offstage. Using this scheme, everyone working in the theater can carefully pinpoint stage areas.*

actors can enter or leave the stage. For some productions, tracks or slots are set in the stage floor and set pieces or *wagons* are brought on stage in the tracks and stopped at the proper point. A wagon in this case is a low platform set on wheels. Wagon stages are brought on stage mechanically or by stagehands hidden behind them. This type of scene change is frequently used in musical comedy.

From floor level, ramps and platforms can be built to any height desired. To create walls or divisions of other kinds, the most common element is the *flat*, so named because it is a single flat unit. It is usually about 4 feet wide by 8 feet high and consists of canvas stretched on wood. The side facing the audience can be painted to look like a solid wall. Used in conjunction with other flats, it can be made to look like a complete room. The scene designer's art comes into play at this point, creating the illusion—with flats and other units—of virtually any type of room or architecture required. Other vertical units are *cutouts*—small pieces made like canvas flats or cut out of plywood. Again, they can be painted to create the illusion of a solid piece of architecture. Instead of scenery coming from the sides, it can be dropped from the fly loft—*to fly,* it will be recalled, is the term used when scenery is raised into the fly loft out of the view of the audience.

A very special type of scenery is a *scrim*. The scrim is a gauze or cloth screen which can be painted like a regular flat. The wide mesh of the cloth, however, allows light to pass through. When light shines on a scrim from in front—that is, from the audience's point of view—it is reflected off the painted surface and the scrim appears to be a solid

Figure 13-11 Projections: effective scenic device. *Supplementing regular scenery are projections on a screen, or perhaps over most of the stage area, allowing for rapid changes of locale, panoramic views, or unusual abstract designs. A central screen for projections is employed in this production of Brecht's* The Good Woman of Setzuan. *(Photo—courtesy of University of Texas. Production directed by Francis Hodge, setting by John Rothgeb, costumes by Paul Reinhardt, lighting by H. Neil Whiting.)*

wall. When light comes from behind, however, the scrim becomes transparent and the spectators can see performers and scenery behind the scrim. The scrim is particularly effective in scenes where ghosts are called for or when an eerie effect is desired. Scrims are likewise useful in memory plays or plays with flashbacks: the spectators see the scene in the present in front of the scrim, and then as lights in the front fade and those behind come up, they see through this gauzelike scrim a scene with a cloudy, translucent quality, indicating a memory or a scene in the past.

A development which has taken hold with great force in recent years is *screen projection*. A picture or drawing is projected on a screen either from in front—as in an ordinary movie house—or from behind the screen. The advantage of the latter is that the actors will not be in the beam of the light, so there will be no shadows or silhouettes. Obviously there are many advantages to projections: pictures can change with the rapidity of the cinema, and there is an opportunity to present vast scenes on stage in a way which would hardly be possible except with tremendously elaborate scene painting.

Projections, along with the other items discussed above, indicate the technical resources available to the scene designer.

THE OBJECTIVES OF SET DESIGN

In fulfilling its practical and aesthetic functions, good set design should accomplish the following:

1 Establish the locale of the play. Tell us where the actors are—in a saloon, a bedroom, or a courtroom.

2 Create playing areas for the actors: the places where they fight, love, or merely sit to talk. In a play like *Julius Caesar*, for instance, there must be room for Brutus and Mark Antony to address the multitudes and for the crowds themselves to circulate on stage.

3 Suggest the kinds of people who inhabit the space. Are they neat and formal? Are they lazy and sloppy? Are they kings, queens, and other royalty; or are they a suburban family?

4 Set the style of the play. Is it realistic, or fantastic? If comic, for example, the design of the scenery might be exaggerated, perhaps to the point of caricature. If the play is highly imaginative, the scenery should reflect this immediately.

5 Provide a central image or metaphor.

6 Develop individual images, including small details or isolated set pieces, to contribute to the whole.

When a designer has performed well, we sense that the space is correct for the play and that the set visually underlines the intent of the play. Obviously, the visual element of a production is an essential, ever-present component of any theater experience, filling the eye with images and ideas to add to the total experience. Together with the text and the activities of the performers, the visual aspects of a theater event contribute to a central impression—a unified world of sight, sound, and movement.

STAGE LIGHTING

Lighting, the last design element incorporated in theater production from a historical point of view, is the most modern in terms of equipment and technique. For the first 2,000 years of its recorded

Figure 13-12 A proper setting for King Lear. *Ming Cho Lee's model of a set for Shakespeare's* King Lear *incorporates the elements of good scene design. A unified concept is filled with interesting details. The wheel overhead relates to the tragic "wheel of fortune" mentioned in the play. The texture of the materials is rough-hewn, conveying a feeling of strength and closeness to nature. (Design by Ming Cho Lee. Photo—Nathan Rabin.)*

history, theater was held mostly outdoors during the day: a primary reason being, no doubt, the need for illumination. Sunlight, after all, is an excellent source of illumination.

Since sophisticated lighting was unavailable, playwrights used imagination—the handiest tool available—to suggest nighttime or shifts in lighting. Actors brought on torches, or a candle, as Lady Macbeth does, to indicate night. Playwrights also used language: when Shakespeare has Lorenzo in *The Merchant of Venice* say "How sweet the moonlight sleeps upon this bank," it is not just a pretty line of poetry; it also serves to remind us that it is nighttime. The same is true of the eloquent passage when Romeo tells Juliet he must leave because dawn is breaking:

> Look, love, what envious streaks
> Do lace the severing clouds in yonder East:
> Night's candles are burnt out, and jocund day
> Stands tiptoe on the misty mountain tops.

Around A.D. 1600, theater began to move indoors. Candles and oil lamps were used for illumination until 1803, when a theater in London installed gas lights. Though lighting became more manageable during the eighteenth and nineteenth centuries, it was always limited in its effectiveness. In addition, the open flames of the lighting systems posed a constant threat of fire. Through the years there were several tragic and costly fires in theaters, both in Europe and in America.

In 1879 Thomas Edison invented the incandescent lamp (the electric light bulb) and the era of imaginative lighting for the theater began. Not only are incandescent lamps safe, but they can be controlled. The brightness or intensity can be increased or decreased by an electrical *dimmer*. The same lighting instrument will produce the bright lights of noonday or the dim lights of dusk. Besides, by putting a colored film, or *gel* (from the word "gelatin"), over the light, color can be controlled. The resulting flexibility is a remarkable tool in achieving stage effects.

Aesthetic Function of Light

Adolphe Appia (1862–1928), a Swiss scene designer, was one of the first to see the vast aesthetic or artistic possibilities of light in the theater. He wrote: "Light is to the production what music is to the score: the expressive element in opposition to the literal signs; and, like music, light can express only what belongs to the 'inner essence of all vision's vision.'" Norman Bel Geddes (1893–1958), an imaginative American designer and follower of Appia, put it in these words: "Good lighting adds space, depth, mood, mystery, parody, contrast, change of emotion, intimacy, fear."

In symbolic terms lighting can establish the following:

1 Time and place. By color, shade, and intensity, lighting can suggest the time of day, giving us the pale light of dawn, the bright light of midday, the vivid colors of sunset, or the muted light of evening. Lighting can also indicate the season of the year, with winter or summer lights, and it can suggest place, by showing indoor or outdoor light.

2 Mood. A happy, carefree play calls for bright, warm colors: yellows, oranges, and pinks. A more somber piece will lean toward blues, blue-greens, and muted tones.

3 Style. In a realistic play, the lighting will simulate the effect of ordinary sources—table lamps and outside sunlight. In a nonrealistic production, the designer can be more imaginative: shafts of light can cut through the dark, sculpturing actors on stage; a glowing red light can envelop a scene of damnation; a ghostly green light can cast a spell over a nightmare scene. By its tone and texture, lighting can indicate immediately the style of a production.

4 Rhythm. Since light changes occur on a time continuum, they establish a rhythm running through the production. Abrupt, staccato changes with stark blackouts will convey one rhythm, whereas languid, slow fades and gradual cross fades will convey another. Lighting changes are coordinated with scene changes for timing. The importance of this is recognized by directors and designers, who take great care to assure the proper changes—"choreographing" shifts in light and scenery like dancer's movements.

5 Reinforcement of a central image. Lighting, like scenery, costume, and all other elements, must be consistent with the overall style and mood of the production. The wrong lighting can distort, or even destroy, the total effect of a play. At the same time lighting, because it is the least obtrusive of the visual elements of theater, while being at the same time the most flexible, can aid enormously in creating the theater experience.

Gordon Craig (1872–1966), an innovative British designer, spoke of "painting with light." The lighting designer can indeed paint with light, but far more can be done; on the deepest sensual and symbolic level, the lighting designer can convey something of the feeling, and even the substance, of the play.

PRACTICAL ASPECTS OF LIGHTING

We have pointed out that each visual element in theater has a practical as well as an aesthetic function. On the practical side, lighting's chief role is *illumination.* We must be able, first and foremost, to see the actors' faces and their actions on stage. Occasionally, lighting designers, carried away with the atmospheric possibilities of light, will make a scene so dark we can hardly see what is happening on stage. Mood is important, of course, but obviously seeing the performers is even more so. At times the script calls for the lights to dim—in a suspense play, for instance, when the lights in a haunted house go out. But these are exceptions. Ordinarily, unless you can see the actors, the lighting designer has not carried out his or her assignment.

Another practical factor is *focus*, which has aesthetic aspects as well. Focus in lighting directs our attention to one part of the stage—generally where the important action is occurring—and away from other areas. Lights should illuminate the playing area, not the scenery or some area offstage. Most stage scenery is not painted to withstand the harsh glare of direct light and will not be effective when too brightly lit. Also, if scenery is lit to the exclusion of everything else, spectators will focus on the scenery rather than the performers. So the first object of focus is to aim the light in the right place. In this regard, designers must be careful to avoid *spill*, that is, allowing light from one area to fall into an adjacent area.

As an example of a positive benefit of focus: on a split stage, with half the action on one side of the stage and half on the other, the lights can direct our attention from side to side, as they go down in one area and come up in another.

Type of Stage Lights

Basically, lights are of three types:

1 *Spotlights*, which throw a sharp, concentrated beam. (A mobile spotlight, with which an operator can follow a performer across the stage, is called a *follow spot.*)

2 *Area lights*, or *floodlights*, which cover a small area with general light.

3 *Strip* or *border lights*, a row of lights which bathe a section of stage or scenery in light.

In earlier days, *footlights*—a row of lights across the front of the stage—were popular. Because the light source was from below, however, footlights had the disadvantage of casting ghostly shadows

Figure 13-13 Dramatic stage lighting. *The visual image of the main character in a production of Ionesco's* Exit the King *illustrates the striking sculptured effect created by imaginative lighting. Light beams from above and behind are combined with strong cross lighting to cast deep shadows on the face and the folds of the robe. (Photo—Van Williams.)*

on the faces of the actors, and they served as a kind of barrier between actors and audience. With the development of more powerful, versatile lights, footlights were eliminated.

Today, most lighting hits the stage from above, coming from instruments in front of the stage and from the sides. The vertical angle of light beams is close to 45 degrees to approximate the average angle of sunlight. Generally, too, light on an area of the stage comes from several sources: from at least two lights above a proscenium stage, and from at least four above an arena stage. The lights converge from different sides to avoid the harsh shadows on the face which result when light hits only one side of the face. Once performers are properly illuminated by lights from the front and above, other lighting is added: *down lighting* from directly overhead, and *back lighting* from behind, to give further dimension and depth to the figures on stage.

As for color, it too is mixed so that the strong tones of one shade do not dominate, giving an unnatural appearance. The lights beamed from one side are *warm* (amber, straw, gold) and from the other side, *cool* (blue, blue-green, lavender). Warms and cools together produce depth and texture, as well as naturalness. The exception to mixing angles and colors of light would be a scene calling for special effects; we expect stark shadows and strange colors, for example, when Hamlet confronts the ghost of his father.

The general lighting for a production of *Hamlet* would stand in marked contrast to that for another type of play. To emphasize the eerie, tragic quality of *Hamlet*, with its murders and graveyard scene, the lighting would be generally cool rather than warm. As for angles, if the production took place on a proscenium stage, there would be down lighting and back lighting to give a sculptured, occasionally unreal quality to the characters. By contrast, a performance of a musical like *Godspell* would be lit mostly by warm lights, coming from all sides of the stage, to reinforce the joyous, open feeling of the play.

Lighting Controls

We spoke of the advances of lighting: in technical terms, it is easily the most highly developed aspect of theater. Lighting instruments can be hung all over the theater and beamed at every part of the stage, and these many instruments can be controlled by one person sitting at an electronic panel, or switchboard. Lighting changes, or *cues* as they are called, can be arranged ahead of time. Sometimes, in a complicated production (a musical, say, or a Shakespearean play) there will be from 75 to 150 light cues. A cue can range from a *blackout* (where all the lights are shut off at once), to a *fade* (the lights dim slowly, from brighter to darker), to a *cross fade* (one set of lights comes down while another comes up). Moreover, with today's modern equipment, the changes can be timed automatically so that a cross fade in lights will take exactly the number of seconds called for; guesswork is eliminated.

Cues can be prearranged by computer and stored on cards or in a memory bank on a magnetic tape. During a performance, the operator at the console pushes a button and the entire change occurs automatically. As an illustration, Strindberg's *A Dream Play* has innumerable scene changes—after the manner of a dream—in which one scene fades into another before our eyes. At one point in the play, a young woman, called the Daughter, sits at an organ in a church. In Strindberg's words, "The stage darkens as the Daughter rises and approaches the Lawyer. By means of lighting the organ is changed to the wall of a grotto. The sea seeps in between basalt pillars with a harmony of waves and wind." At the light cue for this change, a

Figure 13-14 Lighting controlled by computer. *Today lighting is perhaps the most technologically advanced of the theater arts. Here a young woman sits at a console and controls lighting changes—fades, shifts in color, brightness—by pushing buttons which activate changes stored in a computer memory bank. In this manner lighting changes can be made subtly and with great precision. (Photo—Kliegl Bros. Lighting.)*

button is pushed and all the lights creating the majesty of the church fade, as the lights creating the grotto come up. All this takes place at the touch of a button.

SCENERY AND LIGHTING ENHANCE THE TOTAL EXPERIENCE

The practical aspects of lighting and scenery are means to an end: implementing visually the artistic and aesthetic aspects of a production. The colors, shapes, and lines of scenic and lighting effects interact with other elements of theater and contribute to the overall experience. In terms of performers, a stage set provides the environment in which they live, move, and interact with others. With the proper setting and lighting they are rooted in a visual reality and their words and actions are perceived by members of the audience against an appropriate background, and in a meaningful framework.

Scenery and lighting underscore the structure of a play. As examples, a closed-in setting will reinforce the structure of a climactic play; and a series of fluid lighting changes will establish the rhythm of an episodic play. Scenery and lighting are bound up with another element—point of view; and their relationship to realism and nonrealism has been described in some detail. In terms of comic or serious drama, scenery and lighting are crucial as well. Cleverness, lightness, and warmth in the visual elements of theater establish a comic feeling, whereas somberness, solidity, and darker colors underline a serious approach.

SUMMARY

1 Scenery and lighting provide a background and environment for the performers in a stage area.

2 We encounter forms of scene design in everyday life: in the carefully planned decor of a restaurant, for instance, or a hotel lobby.

3 Scene design for the stage differs from interior decorating in that it creates an environment and an atmosphere which is not filled until the performers occupy it. A good stage set creates a space of suspended animation. A stage set should not be too pretty or too busy; otherwise it will distract our attention from the performers and the action of the play.

4 Scenery can be realistic or nonrealistic; in either instance, it should suggest the time, location, and atmosphere of the play. It should also be consistent with the spirit and point of view of the play, indicating a happy comedy on the one hand or a serious tragedy on the other.

5 In practical terms the scene designer must deal with the limits of the stage space and the offstage area. Ramps must not be inclined too steeply and platforms must provide adequate playing area for the performers. In short, the stage designer must know the practical considerations of stage usage and stage carpentry, as well as the materials available, in order to achieve desired effects.

6 Ideally, the scene designer develops a visual metaphor in the design, consistent with the meaning of the play and the interpretation of the director.

7 Lighting, historically the last of the stage elements to come fully into play, is today the most mechanically sophisticated of all. Once the electric incandescent lamp was introduced, it was possible to achieve almost total control of the color, intensity, and timing of lights.

8 The colors and angles of light create an atmosphere: warm colors indicate brightness and cheerfulness; cold colors indicate the opposite. The lighting designer uses light in order to influence in a subtle way the manner in which we view characters and the action.

9 Changes in light are important to the flow of the action in a production. Quick changes create a fast pace; leisurely changes create a more measured pace. In short, lighting changes affect the rhythm of a production.

10 As for practical considerations, lighting must illuminate the performers' faces as well as the general stage area. It must also focus our attention on the part of the stage being used at a particular moment.

11 Like scenery, lighting can suggest time, place, mood, and style and can even underscore meaning.

A theater event is cumulative: performers' actions are added to their words, visual elements are added to the ideas of the playwright, and so forth. The visual elements are cumulative as well, with the costumes of the actors and actresses added to the images created by scenery and lighting. In the following chapter we will focus on stage costumes, which help complete the stage picture.

14
STAGE COSTUMES

Of the various visual elements in theater, the most personal are costumes and masks because they are worn by performers themselves. Visually, the performer and the costume are perceived as one; they merge into a single image on stage. At the same time, costumes have value in their own right, adding color, shape, texture, and symbolism to the overall effect. Because of their close identity with performers, as well as their strong visual impact, costumes are important to the spectator's perception of a theater event and contribute to the total theater experience.

Figure 14-1 Costumes suit the characters and the play. In her costume designs for the musical Pippin, *Patricia Zipprodt captured the flamboyance and theatricality of the characters. Notice the details of the outfits: the hats and mask, the use of fabric, the cut of the cloth, the shoes and boots. (Photo— Martha Swope.)*

COSTUMES IN EVERYDAY LIFE

Aside from theater, most people think of costumes in terms of a pageant with historical figures such as Queen Elizabeth or George Washington, or a masquerade ball with bizarre outfits. As with other aspects of theater, however, costumes play a significant role in daily life. People wear clothes not only for comfort but for the information they wish to signal others about themselves. If we look around us, we are surrounded by the costumes of daily life: the formal, subdued uniform of a policeman, the sparkling outfit of a drum majorette at a football game, sports gear such as hockey or baseball uniforms, the cap and gown for graduation, a priest's cassock, and brightly colored bathing suits at the shore.

We spoke earlier of the power of symbols, and nowhere is this more manifest than in clothes and personal adornments. Primitive people put on animal skins to give themselves characteristics of the animal—ferocity or courage. Feathers and elaborate headdresses were worn to accentuate height; bracelets and belts with charms were worn as sources of power. Today we still wear clothes to symbolize different qualities in society. A young person might wear informal clothes as a statement of independence from his or her parents. Parents, on the other hand, might wear conventional clothes in order not to stand out in a crowd or be criticized by friends. How one appears to one's peers or to those in an outside group, is a paramount issue with many people, and this is most readily apparent in styles of dress.

Frequently we judge others by their appearance, particularly when we first meet them. If we see a man in a dark blue pin-stripe suit with a tie and vest, we assume he is middle or upper-middle class; we judge him to be conservative, and probably a banker or a lawyer. Beyond that, we make assumptions about his politics, family life, social attitudes, and, in fact, his whole psychological profile.

A good example of a symbolic outfit is a judge's robe. The black color of the robe suggests seriousness and dignity; also, the robe is draped from the shoulders straight to the ground, covering the whole person, thereby wrapping the person in the importance and presumed impartiality of the office. In our minds, the robe of a judge invests the wearer with authority and wisdom, and when we see someone in the judicial robe, we automatically accept that image. Though individual judges may be foolish or corrupt, it is considered important in our society for the *institution* of the judiciary to be just and incorrupt, and a judge's robe is an important factor in reinforcing that concept.

Clothes have always signaled a number of things regarding the wearer, including the following:

1   Position and status
2   Sex
3   Occupation
4   Relative flamboyance or modesty
5   Degree of independence or regimentation
6   Whether one is dressed for work or leisure, for a routine event or a special occasion

The moment we see the clothes people are wearing, we receive a great many messages and impressions about them; we instantaneously relate those messages to past experience and to our preconceptions, and we form judgments, including value judgments. Even if we have never laid eyes on someone, we feel we know a great deal when we first see the clothes the person wears.

COSTUMES FOR THE STAGE

In the theater, clothes send us signals similar to those in everyday life, but as with other elements of theater, there are significant differences between the costumes of everyday life and those in the theater. Stage costumes communicate the same information as ordinary clothes with regard to sex, position, and occupation, but on stage this information is magnified because every element in theater is in the spotlight. Beyond that, stage costumes provide further insights for the audience.

Costumes indicate the period of the play. Is it historical—seventeenth-century Spanish or ancient Egyptian—or is it modern? Sometimes the costume designer and the director decide to shift the period of a play. For example, *Hamlet* might be performed in modern dress. There have been productions in which Hamlet was in a tuxedo and Gertrude in a long evening dress. Obviously such a shift comes as a shock to the audience, and it is up to the costume designer to assist the audience in adjusting to it.

For most historical plays, costume designers have a range of choices. For a production of Shakespeare's *Julius Caesar*, for instance, the costumes could indicate the ancient Roman period when Caesar actually ruled. In this case the costumes would include togas and Roman soldiers' helmets. Or, the costumes for *Julius Caesar* could feature Elizabethan dress. We know that in Shakespeare's day, the costumes were heightened versions of English clothes at that time, regardless of the period in which the play was set. As a third choice, the designer could create costumes for an entirely different period, including the modern. Whatever the choice, the historical period should be clearly indicated in the costumes.

Figure 14-2 Costumes provide beauty and information. *The elegant costumes for the original production of the musical* My Fair Lady *are lovely to look at, but also tell us that we are among people of wealth and position. We know this because of the formal dress of both women and men. (Photo—Museum of the City of New York, Theatre and Music Collection.)*

Along with indicating period, costumes can distinguish the major characters from the minor ones. Frequently the costume designer will point to the major characters in a play by dressing them in distinctive colors—in sharp contrast to other characters. Consider, for example, Shaw's *Saint Joan*, a play about Joan of Arc. Obviously, Joan should stand out from the soldiers surrounding her. Therefore, her costume might be bright blue while theirs are steel gray. Her costume signals her importance. In another play of Shaw's, *Caesar and Cleopatra*, Cleopatra should stand out from her servants and soldiers. Though dressed in an Egyptian costume, she should be in brighter colors and wear a far more elegant outfit.

Costumes underline important group divisions. In *Romeo and Juliet*, the Montagues wear costumes of one color, and the Capulets, another. In a modern counterpart of *Romeo and Juliet*, the musical *West Side Story*, the two gangs of young men are dressed in contrasting colors: the Jets in various shades of pink, purple, and lavender, and the Sharks in shades of green, yellow, and lemon. Costumes also indicate age. This is particularly helpful when an older actor is playing a young person, or vice versa. The young person can wear padding or a beard to change appearance, for example.

Costumes inform us about the style of the play. For a Restoration comedy, the costumes would be quite elegant, with lace at the men's collars and cuffs, and fancy gowns for the women. For a tragedy the clothes would be somber and dignified; seeing them, the audience would know immediately that the play itself was somber and its tone likely to be serious.

Symbolic or Exaggerated Costumes

In many plays, special costumes, denoting abstract ideas or fantastic creatures, are called for. Here the costume designer must develop an outfit which carries with it the imaginative and symbolic qualities required. How does one clothe the witches in *Macbeth* or the ghost of Banquo, for instance? A way must be found to symbolize the qualities they represent. To illustrate how costumes can suggest ideas or characteristics, a costume of animal skins can symbolize bestiality, and a costume of feathers can indicate a birdlike quality, while a costume made of a metallic material can suggest a hard and mechanical quality.

In *Peer Gynt* by Ibsen, the main character, Peer, meets a supernatural being in the mountains. It is called the Boyg and is a symbolic presence urging Peer to compromise in life and go "roundabout." A costume designer might fashion for the Boyg a soft, round outfit with no sharp outlines or edges—a large blob like a sack of potatoes—to indicate its indecisive, amorphous quality.

A modern play which calls for exaggerated as well as symbolic costumes is *The Balcony*, by the French playwright Genet. The play is set in a house of prostitution where ordinary men act out their fantasies: one pretends to be a general, another a bishop, and a third a judge. They dress in exaggerated costumes, looking almost like caricatures of the originals, with platform shoes, shoulder pads wider than their own shoulders, and high head pieces. The women who serve them also dress fantastically. The woman serving the general is dressed as a horse, and the costume designer has the task of making a costume for her which will bring out her attractiveness as a person, but still give her a tail and mane like that of a horse.

Figure 14-3 Exaggerated costumes. *In Genet's* The Balcony, *ordinary men pretend to be mighty figures. To emphasize their assumed importance they wear oversized costumes with large shoulder pads and platform shoes. In this scene we see men impersonating a bishop, a general, and a judge. (Design by Patricia Zipprodt. Photo—Martha Swope.)*

Costumes and the Total Production

It is incumbent upon the costume designer to be consistent with the rest of the production. If the director has developed a central metaphor for the play, then the costume designer must provide costumes which fit into the general scheme: in style, tone, period, as well as every other respect. To take an obvious example, it would be inappropriate for costumes to be symbolic, when the rest of the production is realistic. On the other hand, when properly created, a costume can tell us a great deal about the play itself, in addition to what it tells us about the character.

For the Broadway musical *Pippin*, costume designer Patricia Zipprodt (1925–) combined elements of medieval costumes—such as armored breastplates—with clown outfits, burlesque costumes, and *commedia dell'arte* costumes, including the traditional half masks. The play is a vaudeville version of a medieval story, filled with magic and theatricality, and Ms. Zipprodt's costumes made a forceful visual statement of that concept. She pulled the various elements of the musical together into a single pictorial image. The costumes were

Figures 14-4a and 14-4b Costume design: plan and execution. *Like scene designers, costume designers prepare sketches to show what finished costumes will look like. Below, Patricia Zipprodt's sketch for a chorus girl in* Pippin *is shown next to the actual outfit worn by the actress at the right. Note particularly the headpiece which is a frame for the face from the front and a mask from the back. (Design by Patricia Zipprodt. Photo—Martha Swope.)*

individually exciting, but they also suggested the period of the story and the style of the presentation. They announced to the spectators what kind of theater experience they were likely to have.

PRACTICAL REQUIREMENTS OF COSTUMES

Virtually every aspect of theater has practical as well as aesthetic requirements, and costume design is no exception. No matter how attractive or how symbolic, stage costumes must work for the actors. A long, flowing gown may look beautiful, but if it is too long and the actress wearing it trips every time she walks down a flight of steps, the designer has overlooked an important practical consideration. If actors are required to duel or engage in hand-to-hand combat, their costumes must stand up to this wear and tear, and their arms and legs must have freedom of movement and not be bound by the costume. If actors are to dance, they must be able to turn, leap, and move freely.

Quick costume changes are frequently called for in the theater. In the Broadway musical *Gypsy*, when an emerging young star sang "Let Me Entertain You," she was required to go offstage between choruses and reappear a few brief seconds later in another costume. The actress went through three or four dazzling costume changes in seconds, to the astonishment of the audience. The costumes had to be made so that the actress, with the help of dressers offstage, could rapidly get out of one outfit and into another. Tear-away seams and special fasteners were used so that one costume could be ripped off and another quickly put on.

Unlike scenery which stays in place until it is moved, a costume is constantly in motion; it moves as the actor moves. This provides an opportunity for the designer to develop grace and rhythm in the way a costume looks as it moves across the stage, but it carries with it a great responsibility to make the costume workable and appropriate.

THE COSTUME DESIGNER

The person putting into effect the ideas we have been discussing is the costume designer. Every production requires someone who takes responsibility for the costumes. When costumes are rented, the designer chooses the style, the period, the color, and the design of the rented costumes. When costumes are *built*—that is, cut and sewn from scratch—the costume designer sketches the way the costumes

Figure 14-5 Costumes: practical as well as imaginative. *Costume design must allow for the physical requirements of the role and individual characteristics of the performer. In this sketch the designer has shown performers from the musical* Pippin *in motion, indicating that they will be able to dance and move freely, at the same time that they present an attractive visual effect. (Design by Patricia Zipprodt.)*

will look. Obviously, this requires both training and talent.

The costume designer should begin with a thorough knowledge of the play: its subject matter, period, style, and point of view. The costume designer must also have an intimate knowledge of the individual characters in the play. The designer must know each character's personality, idiosyncrasies, relative importance to the play, relationship to other characters, and symbolic value. The designer must be aware, too, of the physical demands of each role: what is called for in terms of sitting, moving from level to level, dancing, falling down, fighting, etc. Finally, the designer must become thoroughly acquainted with the characteristics of the performers themselves in order to create costumes accommodating their physiques and movement patterns.

Resources of the Costume Designer

Among the elements with which the designer works, one of prime importance is the cut or line of the clothes. Do the lines of an outfit flow, or are they sharp and jagged? Do the clothes follow the lines of the body, or is there some element of exaggeration, such as shoulder pads for men or a bustle at the back of a woman's dress? The outline or silhouette of a costume has always been significant. There is a strong visual contrast, for instance, between the line of an Egyptian female garment flowing smoothly from shoulder to the floor, and the Empire gowns of the early nineteenth century in France which featured a horizontal line high above the waist, just below the breasts, with a line flowing from below the bosom to the feet. The silhouettes of these two styles stand in marked contrast to a third design: the female dress in the United States in the early 1930s, a short outfit with a prominent belt or sash cutting horizontally across the hips.

A second important resource for costume designers is color. Earlier we suggested that the leading characters can be dressed in a color which contrasts with the colors worn by other characters and that the characters from one family can be dressed in a different color from those in a rival family. Color also suggests mood: bright, warm colors for a happy mood, and dark, somber colors for a more serious mood. Beyond these applications, however, color can indicate changes in character and changes in mood. Near the beginning of Eugene O'Neill's *Mourning Becomes Electra*, General Manon, who has recently returned from the Civil War, dies, and his wife and daughter wear dark mourning clothes. Lavinia, the daughter, knows that her mother had something to do with her father's death, and she and her brother

Figures 14-6a, 14-6b, and 14-6c   The importance of line in costume design.
*Three outfits suggest the variety of effects achieved by altering the outline or
silhouette of a costume. The Egyptian dress has no horizontal lines but falls
straight from the shoulders to the floor. The Empire style—popular in Europe in
the early 19th century—is broken by a strong horizontal line just below the
bosom, and the flapper dress from the 1920s has a much lower horizontal line
across the hips. Not only various outlines but different fabrics and colors
determine the appearance of costumes.*

conspire to murder the mother. Once they have done so, Lavinia feels a great sense of release. She adopts characteristics of her mother, and as an important symbol of this transformation she puts on brightly colored clothes in the same colors her mother had worn before.

Fabric is still another tool of the costume designer. Burlap or other roughly textured cloth suggests people of the earth or of modest means. Silks and satins, on the other hand, suggest elegance, refinement, and perhaps even royalty. Ornamentation and accessories can be utilized, too. Fringe, lace, ruffles, feathers, belts, beads—these can add to the attractiveness and individuality of a costume. Also, walking sticks, parasols, purses, and other items carried or worn by people can give distinction and definition to an outfit.

Using the combined resources of line, color, fabric, and accessories, the costume designer arrives at individual outfits which tell us a great deal about the characters who wear them and convey important visual signals about the style and meaning of the play as a whole.

MAKEUP

Related to costume is *makeup*—the application of cosmetics (paints, powders, and rouges) to the face and body. Makeup used to be more popular in the theater than it is today. In the modern theater, actors in a small theater playing a realistic part will simply go without makeup of any consequence. But makeup has a long and important history in the theater. Sometimes it is a necessity, a good example being makeup to highlight facial features which would not otherwise be visible in a large theater. Even in a smaller theater, bright lights tend to wash out cheekbones, eyebrows, etc. Use of makeup is often essential where the age of the character is involved. Suppose that a nineteen-year-old performer is playing the part of a forty-two-year-old character. Through the use of makeup—putting a little gray in the hair or simulating wrinkles—the appropriate age can be suggested. Another situation calling for makeup to indicate age is a play in which the characters grow older during the course of the action. In the musical *I Do, I Do*, based on the play *The Fourposter*, a husband and wife are shown in scenes covering many years in their married life, from the time when they are first married until they are quite old. In order to convey the passing years and their advancing ages, the actress and actor playing the wife and husband must use makeup extensively. For fantastic or other nonrealistic creatures makeup is a necessity too.

Oriental theater frequently relies on heavy makeup. For instance, the Japanese Kabuki, a highly stylized type of theater, employs

Figure 14-7   Makeup: prominent in Oriental theater. *Makeup can be used to make facial features stand out at a distance in the theater or under the glare of bright lights. It can also create a kind of mask on the face. This is frequently the case in Oriental theater as illustrated by this warrior in a Japanese drama. (Photo—courtesy of the Consulate General of Japan.)*

completely nonrealistic makeup. The main characters must apply a base of white covering the entire face, over which bold patterns of red, blue, black, and brown are painted. The colors and patterns are symbolic of the character. In Chinese theater, too, the colors of makeup are symbolic: all white means treachery; black means tough integrity; red means loyalty; green indicates demons; yellow stands for hidden cunning; and so forth.

A contemporary American company, The Everyman Players of Pineville, Kentucky, employs makeup with startling results. For their religious pieces, they create faces on the actors which resemble the fragmented look of stained glass windows.

Douglas Turner Ward (1930–), a black playwright, wrote *Days of Absence* to be performed by black actors playing in whiteface. The implications of this effect are many, not the least being the reversal of

Figure 14-8 **White face in a black play.** *In Douglas Turner Ward's* Days of Absence, *the black performers wore white makeup. In this case the makeup provides a strong satirical comment on society and underlines the theme of the play. (Photo—Bert Andrews.)*

the old minstrel performances in which white actors wore blackface. Ward is not the first to put black actors in whiteface; Genet had part of the cast of his play *The Blacks* wear white masks.

When makeup is used, the face becomes almost like a canvas for a painting. The regular features of the face are heightened or exaggerated. At other times symbolic aspects of the human face are emphasized. In either case, makeup serves as an additional tool for the performer in creating an image of the character.

MASKS

Masks seem to be as old as theater, having been used in ancient Greek theater and in the drama developed by primitive tribes. In one sense, the mask is an extension of the actor—a face on top of a face. There are several ways to look at masks: they remind us, first of all, that we are in the theater, that the act going on before our eyes is not real in a literal sense, but is rather a symbolic or an artistic presentation. For another thing, masks allow the face to be frozen in one expression: a look of horror, perhaps, which we see throughout a production.

Masks can also make the face larger than life, and they can create stereotypes, similar to stock characters in which one particular feature—e.g., cunning, haughtiness—is emphasized to the exclusion of everything else.

There are other symbolic possibilities with the use of masks. In his play *The Great God Brown*, Eugene O'Neill calls for the actors to hold masks in front of their faces. When the masks are in place, the characters present a facade to the public, withholding their true characters. When the masks are down, the characters reveal how they feel inside. In *Motel*, a short play and part of a trilogy called *America Hurrah!* by Jean-Claude van Itallie, the actors—a man, a woman, and a woman motel keeper—wear enlarged papier-mâché heads and arms, giving the appearance of huge, somewhat grotesque dolls. The play deals with violence and loss of humanity in American life, and their impersonal, masklike figures underline the theme.

COORDINATION WITH THE WHOLE

Costumes, makeup, and masks must be integrated with other aspects of a production. First, they have a close relationship with performers and the parts they play. Each is highly personal in nature, being

Figure 14-9 Masks: ancient theatrical device. Masks have been used in theater almost from the beginning. They can change the appearance of a performer, make the face and head larger than life, and freeze the face into a fixed expression. The highly artistic masks shown here—depicting birdlike creatures—were created for the Royal Shakespeare Company's production of Anthony and Cleopatra. *(Photo—Max Waldman.)*

literally attached to a performer and moving when the performer moves. They exist only as a part of the performers. In fact, they are so much a part of the performers that we sometimes lose sight of them as separate entities. Actors and actresses would have great difficulty in creating a part without the proper costume, and in some cases without makeup and a mask as well. They help the performer define his or her role.

On another level, costumes, makeup, and masks are essential in carrying out a point of view in a production. Masks, for instance, are clearly nonrealistic and signal to the audience that the character wearing the mask and the play itself are likely to be nonrealistic too. Costumes suggest whether a play is a comedy or a serious play, a wild farce or a stark tragedy. To be effective in this respect, they must also be coordinated with scenery and lighting. The wrong kind of lighting can wash out or discolor costumes and makeup. It would be self-defeating, too, if scenery were in one mood or style and the costumes in a different one. Ideally, these elements should support and reinforce one another, and spectators should be aware of how essential it is for them to work together. Visually, if something looks out of place in a production, lack of coordination among these elements might be the reason.

Quite clearly, costumes, makeup, and masks are an important part of the theater experience.

SUMMARY

1 The clothes we wear in daily life are a form of costume. They indicate station in life, occupation, and a sense of formality or informality.

2 On the stage, costumes similarly convey information about the people wearing them; more than that, they are consciously chosen and are designed to provide the audience with important information.

3 Costumes can tell us the period and style of the play, the relative importance of various characters, and the group or family to which a character belongs. Costumes can also suggest whether a play is serious or comic, realistic or nonrealistic.

4 Costumes can convey symbolic or abstract qualities; they can also suggest ideas, ghosts, and animals.

5 Like other elements of a production, costumes must be consistent with the overall concept; they must fit its mood, style, and approach.

6 Costumes have practical as well as aesthetic requirements. They should be made so that performers can move and sit easily in them and can perform whatever physical tasks are required of them.

7 The person responsible for designing and selecting the costumes—as well as supervising their construction—is the *costume designer*, who uses line, color, and fabric to achieve the goals of good costume design.

8 Makeup is the application of greasepaint, powders, or rouges to the face or body. In some cases, it highlights ordinary human features—cheekbones, chin and jaws, etc. In other cases, makeup is used to indicate a symbolic quality: colors and shapes are distorted or exaggerated, and the face becomes a living painting.

9 Masks are used in theater for the purpose of heightening human features or creating a symbolic image. Through the device of a mask an expression can be frozen, and masks are effective in indicating the facade people wear as well as in creating a strong visual image of a character.

10 Costumes, makeup, and masks must be coordinated with all elements of theater—scenery and lighting, as well as point of view—to create an integrated whole.

In this section we have examined the physical environment and the visual elements of theater, exploring the contributions they make to the total theater experience. Up to this time we have covered the essential ingredients of theater separately, but we have also stressed that these ingredients must work together. At various points we have seen how two or more elements join together; eventually, however, all elements coalesce to form a single, unified experience. The people responsible for bringing this about and the ways in which spectators bring the elements together in their minds' eyes will be the subject of the final section.

POINT OF VIEW

DRAMATIC STRUCTURE

PART SIX

BRINGING THE ELEMENTS TOGETHER

ENVIRONMENT

PERFORMERS   AUDIENCE

15

THE DIRECTOR

For the most part, theater is not seen by spectators as fragmented but as a single experience. Though made of many parts, a theater event should form a complete picture. This is not a simple matter. Theater is one of the most complex of the arts, involving not one or two elements, but many simultaneously: script, performance, costumes, scenery, lighting, and point of view. These diverse elements—a mixture of the tangible and intangible—must be brought together into an organic whole.

We have suggested that those working in the theater have a responsibility to one another to create a single vision as they prepare a

Figure 15-1 The director in rehearsal. *The director must pull all of the elements of theater together on stage. He or she is particularly responsible for the performers' interpretations of their roles. Here we see director Nikos Psacharopoulos exhorting a group of actors in rehearsal at the Williamstown Theatre Festival. (Photo—The Williamstown Theatre Festival, Williamstown, Mass.)*

production. The playwright must incorporate a definite structure in the script and infuse it with a clear point of view; the performers' interpretations of their roles must be consistent with the playwright's viewpoint; the costume designer must work closely with individual actors and actresses and with scene and lighting designers; and the scene designer must coordinate colors and shapes with the costume designer and understand the point of view of the script.

Even though they work together, however, these artists must of necessity work on segments of the production rather than the entire enterprise. The performers, for instance, are much too busy working on their roles or their interactions with other performers to worry much about scenery. Also, a performer who appears only in the first act of a three-act play has no control over what happens in the second and third acts. The same is true of designers and others. The one person who does have an overall perspective—and the awesome responsibility of attempting to bring the many elements of theater together—is the *director*.

A HISTORICAL PERSPECTIVE

Certain theater historians are fond of saying that the director did not exist in the theater prior to 1874, when a German nobleman, the Duke of Saxe-Meiningen, began supervising every element of his theatrical productions—rehearsals, scenic elements, and other aspects—coordinating them into an integrated whole. Beginning with Saxe-Meiningen, the director emerged as a full-fledged, indispensable member of the theatrical team, taking his place alongside the playwright, the performers, and the designers.

The title may have been new, but the *function* of the director had always been present in one way or another. We know, for example, that the Greek playwright Aeschylus directed his own plays and that the chorus for Greek plays rehearsed for many weeks under the supervision of a leader prior to a performance. At various points in theater history, the leading actor or playwright of a company served as a director, though without the name. Molière, for instance, was not only the playwright of his company and the chief actor, but he functioned as the director also. We know from his short play *The Impromptu of Versailles* that he had definite ideas about the way actors should perform; no doubt the same advice he offered in that play was frequently given to his actors in rehearsal. In England from the seventeenth through the nineteenth centuries there was a long line of actor-managers who gave strong leadership to individual theater companies and who performed many of the functions of the directors even though they were not actually called by that name. Among the most famous were Thomas Betterton (1635–1710), David Garrick (1717–1779), Charles Kemble (1775–1854), William Charles Macready (1793–1873), and Henry Irving (1838–1905).

Nevertheless, the term *director* did not come into common usage until the end of the nineteenth century. It is significant perhaps that the emergence of the director as a separate creative person coincides with important changes which began to take place in society during the nineteenth century. First, there was a breakdown in established social, religious, and political concepts which came with Freud, Darwin, and Marx. Second came a marked increase in communication. With the advent of the telegraph, the telephone, photography, motion pictures, and finally television, various cultures which had remained remote or unknown to one another were suddenly quite aware of each other. The effect of these two changes was to alter the monolithic, ordered view of the world which societies had maintained before.

Prior to these developments, consistency of style in theater was easier to achieve. Within a given society there was common ground among writers, performers, and spectators. For example, the comedies of the English writers Wycherley and Congreve, written during the Restoration period at the end of the eighteenth century, were aimed at a specific audience—the elite, upper class, which relished gossip, acid remarks, and well-turned phrases. The code of behavior of the society was well understood by actors and audience alike, and questions of style in a production hardly arose because a common approach to style was already present in the fabric of society. The way a man took a pinch of snuff, a maid flirted with a nobleman, or a lady flung open her fan was so clearly delineated in daily behavior that the actors had only to refine and perfect the action for the stage. The director's task was not so much to impose a style on a production as to prevent the performers from overacting and to see that they spoke their lines properly and that the cast worked as a cohesive unit. Today, however, because style, unity, and a cohesive view of society are so illusive, the director's task is more important.

THE DIRECTOR'S TASK

The director's work on a production is one of the last elements of which the audience becomes aware. Performers are on stage and are immediately visible to spectators, as are scenery and costumes, and the words of the playwright are heard throughout the performance, but the director's work consists of interpreting and blending these elements and takes place largely behind the scenes. It is therefore much less readily apparent to the audience. Except for the playwright, however, the director is the first person to become involved in the creative process of a production, and the choices he or she makes at every stage along the way largely determine whether the ultimate experience will be satisfactory for the spectators or not.

Frequently the director chooses the script to be produced. Generally it is a play which the director is attracted to or feels a special affinity for. If the director does not actually choose the script but is asked to direct it by a playwright or a producer, he or she must still have an understanding and appreciation of the material. This attraction and basic understanding on the part of the director for the script is an important first step in launching a production. Once the script is chosen, the actual work on the production begins.

Director and Playwright

If the play is new and has never been tested in production, the director may see problems in the script which must be corrected before rehearsals begin. The director will have a series of meetings with the playwright to iron out the difficulties ahead of time. The director may feel, for example, that the leading character is not clearly defined or is underwritten, or that a clash of personalities between two characters never reaches a climax. If the playwright agrees with the director's assessment, steps will be taken to correct the manuscript. Generally there is considerable give and take between the director and playwright in these preliminary sessions, as well as during the rehearsal period. Ideally, there should be a spirit of cooperation, compromise, and mutual respect in this relationship.

Concept

Once the script—whether well established or original—is selected, the director must begin to formulate the all-important *concept* of the production. The concept comes from a controlling idea, vision, point of view, or metaphor, which will result in a cohesive production and present the spectator with a unified artistic experience.

To indicate what is involved for the director with an established play, let us take the case of Shakespeare's *Troilus and Cressida*. The play was written in the Elizabethan period, but is set at the time of the Trojan War, when the ancient Greeks were fighting the Trojans. In presenting the play today, a director has several choices as to the period in which to set the production. This is similar to the problem discussed with regard to costume, but here it will affect everything—not only costumes and scenery, but interpretation of the script, actor behavior, etc. One director might choose to stick to the period indicated in the script, and place it in Troy, with both Trojans and Greeks wearing armor, tunics, and other appropriate garments. Another might set the play in the time when Shakespeare wrote it, and in this case the director and the designers would devise court and military costumes reflecting Shakespeare's day.

Another option for the director would be to modernize the play. There have been a number of modern productions of *Troilus and Cressida* in recent years. Shakespeare's words are retained, but since many of the play's antiwar sentiments and statements about the corruption of love in the face of war are quite relevant today, the play is transferred to the present by means of costumes, settings, and behavior. For example, in 1956 Tyrone Guthrie, a British director, presented a version which was set in the period just prior to 1914 in England, that is, just before World War I. The play was shifted to English drawing rooms and other localities conveying the clear impression of England in the early twentieth century. The uniforms were those of English soldiers of the period, and the women wore dresses typical of that era. The set had grand pianos, the men drank cocktails, and the women used cigarette holders: all intended to portray a sophisticated, urban environment.

When such a transposition in period is made, the director must see to it that every element fits: the way the actors move, the way the set looks including details of walls and doors, the appearance of costumes and other ornamentations worn by the actors. In short, the total production—in details and overall mood—must reflect the chosen time and place.

This kind of transposition has been carried out frequently with Greek plays, Elizabethan plays, French plays of the seventeenth century, and other dramatic classics. The important consideration is that the director develop an overall concept. If a certain age or a certain nationality in the play is going to be stressed—if the scene is going to be shifted from France to America or the time shifted from the eighteenth century to the present—the director must make certain that this is done thoroughly and consistently.

Rather than placing the play in a historical period, the director's concept might involve another approach. A director might decide, for instance, to develop a play around a theme or a production concept. A play with a narrator and episodic scenes might be conceived in circus terms, with the narrator serving as a ringmaster and scenes from the play taking place in circus rings. To carry this further, the performers might dress in clown outfits or other costumes of the circus.

Just as there is an obligation for a director to develop a concept, there is also a great danger. The best concept is one that remains true to the spirit and meaning of the script. If the director can translate that spirit and meaning into stage terms in an inspired way, he or she will have created an exciting theater experience. The temptation for a director is to develop a concept that displays the director's originality but distorts or violates the integrity of the script. The circus idea described above might appear to be theatrical and inventive, but would be quite wrong for certain plays because it would distract the audience's attention from quieter moments or deeper meanings at the heart of the script. This would be the case, for example, with most realistic plays. A directorial concept which is flashy on the surface may very well call too much attention to itself and rob the spectators of the full, honest experience to which they are entitled.

The director should find a middle ground and develop an imaginative concept which will pull the many elements of the production into a coherent whole without doing violence to the spirit of the play or the work of the performers.

A Central Image or Metaphor

Closely related to the notion of a directorial concept is the idea of a central image or metaphor for a theatrical production. Some directors use this as a means of tying the production elements together. The circus concept mentioned above could serve as a production metaphor. When such an image is chosen, it must be carried out throughout the play. Let us assume that for a production of *Hamlet* the director has an image of a vast net or spider web in which Hamlet is caught. The motif of a net or spider web could be carried out on several levels: in the design; in the ways in which the actors relate to one another; and in a host of details relating to the central image. There might be a huge rope net hanging over the entire stage, for instance. Actors could play string games with their fingers. It might even be possible for certain characters to wear rope belts. In short, the metaphor of Hamlet being caught in a net would be emphasized and reinforced on every level: tangible and intangible. It is the responsibility of the director not only to develop the central image but to see that it is executed properly.

Casting

Having picked the play and developed a concept, the director then *casts* the play. *Casting* means picking the actors for the individual roles in a production. Obviously the word comes from casting a mold,

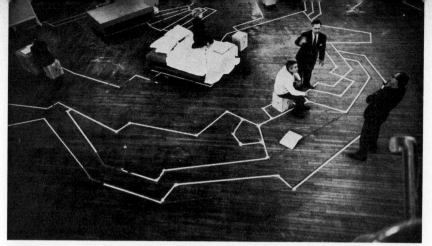

Figure 15-2   The director at work. *Director Elia Kazan, standing in the center, rehearses a scene from Arthur Miller's* After the Fall, *while the author looks on from the right. Actor Jason Robards is sitting next to Kazan and actress Barbara Loden is on the bed. The taped white lines on the stage floor are used during rehearsals to indicate where steps and levels will be when the set is completed. (Courtesy of Magnum. Photo—Inge Morath.)*

and in the theater it means fitting the actor to the part. In the modern theater, performers frequently *audition* for parts in a play and the director casts from those actors who audition. In an audition, actors and actresses read scenes from a play or perform portions of the script to give the director an indication of the way they talk, move, and handle themselves on stage. From this the director determines whether a performer is right for a given part or not.

Historically, casting was rarely done by audition because theatrical companies were more permanent. In Shakespeare's time and in Molière's, certain actors always played certain parts in a theatrical troupe. One actor played heroic parts, while another always played the clown. Under these conditions, when a play was selected, it was a matter of assigning roles to the actors who were on hand; auditioning would occur only when a new member was chosen for the company.

Appropriateness is a key element in casting. If the character depicted in a script is phlegmatic or lazy, the director seeks an actor who is able to look and act in that fashion. By the same token, for the part of a virile, masculine man, it would be inappropriate to cast an effeminite or frightened-looking man. Occasionally—particularly for comic or satiric purposes—the director will cast *against type*, meaning that a short person is deliberately chosen for the part of a tall one, or a sinister-looking actor is chosen for an angelic part. This is a deliberate comment on the play, and its purpose should be clear to the audience.

Rehearsals

Once the play is cast, the director supervises all rehearsals. He or she listens to the performers as they go through their lines and begin to move about the stage. Different directors work in different ways in the early stages of rehearsal: some directors *block* the play in advance, giving precise instructions to the actors. (By *blocking*, you recall, we mean establishing the places where actors move and position themselves on the stage.) Other directors let the actors find their relationships, their movements, and their vocal interpretations on their own. And of course there are directors who do a bit of both. It is worth pointing out that in recent years directors have tended to move toward the less structured approach, to direct far less in terms of specific instructions or commands than was the case throughout the whole of the nineteenth and the early part of the twentieth century. In former times it was customary for directors to give actors precise commands: "Move three paces to the right, and then turn to face the audience. Now speak the next line in a stage whisper." Today this approach is less common.

During the rehearsal period, the director must make certain that the actors are realizing the intention of the playwright, that they make sense of the script and bring out its meaning. Also, the director must ensure that the performers are working well together and must help them overcome any personal problems they have, such as insecurity about a role or fear of failure.

The Audience's Eye

During rehearsals the director acts as the eye of the audience. Prior to public performances, the director is the only one who sees the production from the spectator's point of view. For this reason the director must assist the performers in showing the audience exactly what they intend to show. If one performer hides another at an important moment, if a crucial gesture is not visible, if an actor makes an awkward movement, if an actress cannot be heard when she delivers an emotional speech, the director points it out. Also, the director underscores the meaning of specific scenes through visual composition and stage pictures, that is, through the physical arrangement of performers on stage. The spatial relationships of performers convey information about characters. As an example, important characters are frequently placed on a level above other characters: on a platform or step, for instance. Another spatial device is to place an important character alone in one area of the stage while grouping other characters in another area. This causes the eye to give special

Figure 15-3 The stage picture. *The director is responsible for the performers' blocking—their movements and positions on stage—and for the visual picture they present. Here the heroine of the play* Anastasia *is given a place of prominence in the center of the stage. Other performers are focused on her and are placed at lower levels or in clusters around her. (Photo—The Williamstown Theatre Festival, Williamstown, Mass.)*

attention to the character standing alone. If two characters are opposed to each other, they should be placed in positions of physical confrontation on stage.

Certain areas on stage assume special significance: a fireplace, with its sense of warmth, can become an area to which a character returns for warmth and reassurance. A door opening on a garden can serve as a place where characters go when they want to renew their spirits or to escape from a hemmed-in feeling. By guiding performers to make the best use of stage space, the director assists them in communicating important visual images to the audience—images consistent with the overall meaning of the play.

Balance, Proportion, and Pace

The director gives shape and structure to a play in two spheres or dimensions: in space, in the way just described, and in time. Since a production occurs through time, it is important for the director to see that the movement, the pace, and the rhythm of the play are correct. If the play moves too quickly, if we miss words and do not understand what is going on, it is the director's fault. The director must determine whether there is too short or too long a time between speeches or whether an actor moves too slowly across the stage. The director must attempt to control the pace and rhythm within a scene—the dynamics and the manner in which the actors move from moment to moment—and the rhythm between scenes.

One of the most common faults of directors is not to establish a clear rhythm in a production. An audience at a performance is impatient, almost unconsciously, to see what is coming next, and if expectations are frustrated too long, the audience will become unhappy. The director must see to it that the movement from moment to moment and scene to scene has a thrust and a drive moving through the play, thus maintaining our interest. Variety is important too. If the play moves ahead at only one pace, whether slow or fast, the audience will be fatigued simply by the monotony of that pace.

The rhythm within scenes and between scenes becomes an important aspect of a production. This rhythm enters our psyche as we watch a performance and thus contributes to our overall response. Of course, it must be borne in mind that the responsibilities of the director for pace, proportion, and overall effect ultimately rest with the performers. Once the performance begins, the actors and actresses are on stage and the director is not. Unlike the cinema in which the pace and rhythm can be determined in the editing room, in theater there is great elasticity and variety; so much depends on the mood of the actors. The director must instill and implant in the performers such a strong sense of inner rhythm in rehearsals that they have an internal clock which tells them how they should play. And, of course, audience reaction will vary from night to night and alter the pace as well. The director's work is done prior to the performance and behind the scenes. But if it is done well, the director will leave such a clear stamp on the work that it will shine through in the final performance.

Physical Production

At the same time that rehearsals with performers are going forward, the director is also working with designers on the physical production. At the outset—once the director's concept is established—the director confers with the costume, scene, and lighting designers to give shape and substance to the concept in visual terms. As suggested previously, designers attempt to provide images and impressions which will carry out the style and ideas of the production.

During the preproduction and rehearsal period the director meets with designers to make certain that the work in their areas is on schedule and keeping pace with the rehearsals. Obviously the preparation of these elements must begin long before the actual performance, just as rehearsals for the actors must, so that everything will be ready before the performance itself takes place. Any number of problems can arise with the physical elements of a production: the appropriate props are not available, a costume does not allow an actress enough freedom of movement, scene changes are too slow. Early planning will allow time to solve these problems.

Technical Rehearsal

Just prior to public performances a *technical rehearsal* is held. The actors and actresses are on stage in their costumes with the scenery and lighting for the first time, and there is a *run-through* of the show from beginning to end, with all props, costumes, and scene changes. The stagehands move scenery, the crew handle props, and the lighting technicians control the dimming and raising of lights: they must coordinate their work with that of the performers. Let us say that one scene ends in a garden, and the next scene opens in a library. Once the performers leave the garden set, the lighting fades, the scenery is removed, and the garden furniture is taken off the stage. Following that, the scenery for the library must be flown in or brought in on wagons and adjusted by the stagehands; the books and other props are put in place. Then, the performers for the new scene in the library take their places as the lighting comes up.

Extensive rehearsals are required to ensure that the lighting comes up at just the moment when the scenery is prepared and the actors are in place. Any mishap on the part of the stage crew, lighting crew, prop crew, or actors would affect the illusion and destroy the aesthetic effect of the scene change. The importance of the technical rehearsal is therefore considerable.

Tryout or First Public Performance

Once the technical rehearsal is completed and the problems which occurred are solved, the next step arrives: a performance in front of an audience. We have stressed from the beginning the importance of actor-audience interaction and the fact that no play is complete until it is actually performed for an audience. It is crucial, therefore, for a production to be tried out before a group of spectators. What has gone before, in terms of script, rehearsals, and visual elements, must now meet the test of combining harmoniously in front of an audience. For this purpose there is a period of *tryouts*—also called *previews* or public rehearsals—when the director and the performers discover which parts of the play are successful and which are not. Frequently, the director and performers find that one part of the play is moving too slowly; they know this because the audience becomes restless and begins to cough or stir. Sometimes, in a comedy, there is a great deal of laughter where little was expected, and the performers and the director must adjust to this.

The tryout is an important period, and these early audiences become genuine collaborators in the shaping of the play. (In the days when Broadway was the chief forum for new plays in the United States, tryouts were held in other cities—Philadelphia, New Haven, or Boston—before the play was exposed to critics in New York. When plays did not have that opportunity, they held a series of previews.) After several performances in front of an audience, the directors and actors get the "feel" of the audience and know whether the play is ready or not.

Director's Power and Responsibility

Clearly, the director has great power, and one of the great dangers is that the director will use this power to overstresss certain elements to the exclusion or detriment of other elements. A second danger lies in the possibility that the director will develop an inconsistent or incongruous scheme. As suggested previously, the director might go overboard with a production concept. For instance, a director might decide to make *Macbeth* into a cowboy play, with Duncan as a sheriff and Macbeth as a deputy who wishes to kill the sheriff in order to take the job himself. In this version, Lady Macbeth would be the deputy's wife whom he had met in a Western saloon. *Macbeth* could be done this way, but it would be ludicrous, carrying reinterpretation too far. It would be an attempt to rewrite the play and make the director's work more important than Shakespeare's.

Any artistic event must have a unity not encountered in real life. We expect the parts to be brought together so that the total effect will enlighten us, move us, or amuse us. All the parts must fit and be consistent with one another; there must be no jarring notes unless they are intentional. This is the director's responsibility. When the director has a strong point of view—one which is correct for the play—the experience for the audience is likely to be meaningful and exciting. By the same token, if the director gets too carried away with one idea or lets the scene designer create a design which overpowers the performers and buries the production in a mountain of scenic effects, then the experience will be neither satisfactory nor complete. The director must have a keen sense of proportion so that various elements work together rather than against one another. It is this juggling act, this weaving together of the tangible and the intangible, the spiritual and the physical, the symbolic and the literal, which must take place in the chemistry of theater, and it is the director who has the final responsibility to see that it occurs.

THE PRODUCER OR MANAGER

The director is responsible for bringing the artistic elements of a production together, but no production would ever be performed for the public without a technical and business component. Here, too, the coordination of elements is crucial, and the person chiefly responsible is the producer or manager. The producer in a commercial venture raises the money to finance the production; picks the play; hires the director, the playwright, the actors, the designers, and the stage-hands; and rents the theater. The producer must have the artistic sensibility to pick the right script and hire the right director if a production is to succeed. Aside from raising capital and having the final say in hiring and firing, the producer oversees all financial and business operations in a production. In a nonprofit theater the person

Figure 15-4 **The director's job: bringing elements together.** *The director coordinates every element in a production. Peter Hunt, seated in the center, directs a production of* Threepenny Opera *at the Williamstown Theatre Festival. He is flanked by those whose work he must bring together: designer John Conklin on his right, musical director Herb Kaplan on his left, and the large cast behind him. In addition, there is a sizeable technical staff backstage. (Photo— The Williamstown Theatre Festival, Williamstown, Mass.)*

having these same responsibilities is called the manager. In terms of day-to-day operations, the duties of the producer and manager are roughly equivalent.

The producer or manager is responsible for the maintenance of the theater building, including the dressing rooms, the public facilities, and the lobby. The producer or manager is also responsible for the budget, making certain that the production stays within established limits. This includes salaries for the director, designers, actors, and stage crews, and expenditures for scenery, costumes, and music. Again, an artistic element enters the picture; important decisions as to whether a certain costume needs to be replaced or whether scenery needs to be altered affect costs. The producer or manager must find additional sources of money, or determine that changes are important enough artistically to take sums from another place. In other words, the producer or manager must work very closely with the director and the designers in balancing artistic and financial needs.

The producer or manager is also responsible for publicity. The audience would never get to the theater if it did not know when and where a play was being presented. The producer or manager must advertise a production and decide whether such advertisements should be placed in daily newspapers, on radio, on television, in student newspapers, in magazines, or elsewhere.

A host of other problems come under the supervision of the producer or manager: tickets must be ordered, the box office maintained, and plans made ahead of time for the way in which tickets are sold. The securing of ushers, the printing of programs, the maintenance of the auditorium—(usually called the *front* of the house)—are also the responsibility of the producer or manager.

Once again, plans must be made well in advance. In the case of many theater organizations, an entire season—the plays to be produced, the personnel who will be in charge, and requirements in terms of supplies—is planned a year ahead of time. It should be clear that coordination and cooperation are as important in this area as they are for the director and the production itself.

COMPLETING THE PICTURE

A theater presentation can be compared to a mosaic consisting of many bright-colored pieces of stone fitting together to form a complete picture. The playwright puts the words and ideas together, the producer or manager puts the business side of a production together, and the director puts the artistic elements together. Those elements in theater which exist as separate pieces in the mosaic must be arranged into a pattern and become parts of an artistic whole, thereby providing a complete theater experience.

SUMMARY

1 The term *director* did not come into general use until the end of the nineteenth century. Certain functions of the director, however—organizing the production, instilling discipline in the performers, setting a tone for the production—have been carried out since the beginning of theater by someone in authority.

2 The director's duties became more crucial in the twentieth century. Because of the fragmentation of society and the many styles and cultures existing side by side, it became necessary for someone to impose a point of view and a single vision on individual productions.

3 The director has many responsibilities:
   a Selecting the script
   b Working with the writer on a new play
   c Developing an interpretation for an established play
   d Evolving a concept or an approach to the script
   e Holding auditions and casting the roles
   f Conducting rehearsals, guaranteeing that stage action communicates the meaning of the play
   g Working with performers to develop their individual roles
   h Developing the visual side of the production in conjunction with the designers
   i Supervising the technical and tryout rehearsals
   j Establishing the proper pace and rhythm in the movements of the scenes and the dynamics of the production as a whole

4 Because the director has such wide-ranging power and responsibilities, he or she can distort a production and create an imbalance in elements or an improper emphasis. The director is responsible for a sense of proportion and order in the production.

5 The producer or manager of a production is responsible for the business aspects: maintaining the theater, arranging publicity, handling finances, and managing ticket sales, budgets, ushers, etc.

The director attempts to put elements together on stage, and at the same time we in the audience observe and hear these elements and put them together in our minds. The ways in which we in the audience receive and put together the multiplicity of images and impressions at a theatrical event will be discussed in the next chapter.

16

THE TOTAL EXPERIENCE

Theater is a remarkable convergence of human and artistic endeavors. This is underscored by the many elements that must come together to produce a theater event: the writing of a play and the planning of a production, which may take weeks, months, perhaps even years; the rehearsal period; the designing and building of scenery and costumes; the technical coordination of light changes, scene shifts, and performers' activities; the adjustments made to the responses of preview audiences. All these contribute to the moment when members of the audience see the performance itself.

Figure 16-1 The total experience. A production of Antigone *at the Studio Arena Theatre, Buffalo, New York, shows the many elements of theater brought together—stage environment, set, lights, performers, and audience. (Courtesy of Studio Arena Theatre, Buffalo, N. Y. Photo—Greenberg May Productions, Inc.)*

The excitement which comes to a group of performers working together or to a crew working backstage on scenery or lights is difficult to describe adequately, as is any human endeavor in which a group joins forces to achieve a goal. An athletic team, for example, which has trained together for weeks has its moment of triumph on the playing field. Any group which works for a common purpose—to win an election, to accomplish some scientific breakthrough, or to organize a neighborhood to make it better—has this same sense of group achievement. Each member knows the task could not be achieved alone.

In the arts, theater is a supreme example of this phenomenon, because, with the possible exception of opera, it is the most complex of the arts. It passes through many hands, and the contribution of each party is essential to its success. When the people creating a theater event work effectively together, they share with one another the deep satisfaction of having collaborated in a difficult but eminently rewarding task. And when the work is performed on stage, the audience senses this achievement, and joins in the collaboration with its response to the work.

RISKS AND OPPORTUNITIES

The danger in theater is that the number of people involved increases the chance of failure. Any one link in this creative chain can affect the outcome. The opportunity for a mistake is much greater than in the case of a painting in which one artist works with a canvas and paints. A stagehand can destroy an entire scene by a miscue; so can a lighting technician. A performer can forget his or her lines, negating much of the work that has gone into this moment. Any one person can interrupt or short-circuit the final effect.

Furthermore, because so many creative people are involved there is always the possibility that divergent points of view will be at war with one another. The director and the playwright may not see eye to eye on the interpretation of the script. A creative actor is yet another vital force who may be at odds with either the playwright or the director or both. When we add the ideas of the scene designer, the lighting designer, and the costume designer, and perhaps others involved—a musical composer, for example—we can see the possibilities for conflicts.

The risk we run when we go to the theater is that the inconsistencies arising from these conflicts will mar the outcome, namely that the level of the performances will not be up to the grandeur of the text or that the play will not measure up to the performances. Generally, though, this is not the case because everyone working on a production is doing his or her best to make it successful. The great opportunity in theater is that many people working together can produce results that no one person working alone ever could. The audience, too, has a chance to share in this unique collaborative effort.

Fortunately we do not need to encounter the ideal each time we go to the theater for the experience to be meaningful. A production can fall short of perfection and still be exciting. In a production of *King Lear*, for example, if the performance of the actor playing the Fool is not quite as strong as that of the other performers, it need not destroy the overall effect. And if a member of the audience does not understand every subtlety and nuance in the text, it will not lessen the basic impact of the production. As long as those who create a theater event present the audience with a reasonably clear and cohesive vision on stage, they will have done their part. They will have provided the basis for a genuine theater experience. The rest is up to the audience.

INTEGRATING THE ELEMENTS

The ultimate integration of a theater event takes place in each spectator's mind. No matter how closely the people who produce a theater event work together, and no matter how well the director coordinates the various elements, individual audience members must eventually bring the parts together. So many elements make up a theater production that we might wonder how a spectator can combine them. The answer lies in our ability to take many kinds of information and bring them together to form a complete picture. Our everyday activities suggest that human beings have a great capacity to absorb data and stimuli and to integrate them into a single experience.

A good example is what happens when someone drives an automobile. The person at the wheel is aware, first of all, of the parts of the car itself: the steering wheel, the accelerator, and the brakes. He or she concentrates on the road, anticipating turns in the highway or stoplights ahead. There are also other cars and pedestrians to consider; the driver is aware of automobiles to the left and right, and glances in the rear-view mirror to see what is behind. In addition, the driver might be listening to the radio or to the conversation of other passengers in the car. While dealing with these mechanical or personal details, the driver might also be daydreaming: thinking of some past event or imagining a future one.

This same ability to absorb and deal simultaneously with an abundance of activities and thoughts can be brought to bear on every kind of undertaking. It applies to emotional and intellectual as well as physical tasks; without it we would not be able to survive.

In terms of theater, our powers of assimilation make it possible to form a cohesive whole out of the fragments we see before us on stage: we watch individual performers in action and tune in to their personalities; we observe the costumes, scenery, and lighting effects; we note the progress of the action as characters confront one another; we hear the words of the playwright; and we associate ideas and emotions in the play with our own experiences.

Along the way we relate each present moment with the past. Two kinds of memories contribute to this process. First, we have a lifetime of personal memories—experiences which an event on stage might trigger in our mind—linking our individual past with what is happening on stage. Second, we have the memory of what has just occurred in the play itself. When we attend the theater our attention is sharply focused on the stage; we have come for the express purpose of seeing one event, and everything centers our attention on that event. The lights converge on the playing area, and the audience becomes abnormally quiet in order to hear what is being said. The ability of spectators to pick up clues is heightened as they become keenly aware of what every character does or says. If the audience sees someone hide a gun in a desk drawer in the first act, and a character goes to the drawer in the third, the audience knows the gun is about to be used.

Not only do we connect the past with what is happening at each moment in a performance; we also anticipate the future. People have immense curiosity about what lies ahead; they are fascinated by prophecy and predictions of future events, in everything from religion to horse racing. Again, this is a human activity which comes into play in the theater. We ask ourselves: How will Electra react when she finds that the brother she thought was dead is actually alive? What will Blanche DuBois do when Stanley Kowalski shows her the bus ticket that will send her out of town to oblivion? We constantly speculate on the fate of characters and look forward—with both fear and excitement—to their encounters with one another.

Each moment in the theater forms a miniexperience of its own, resulting from a series of collisions or intersections on many levels: the past meets the present; the present meets the future; performers interact with their roles; ideas combine with emotions; sights fuse with sounds; and so forth. If the playwright, director, performers, and designers have worked together to present a single vision, these impressions and collisions do not result in a fragmented experience;

rather, because of the audience's ability to integrate a number of stimuli, they can be pulled together to form a rich, multilayered experience. In order for spectators to get the most out of this experience, however, they must do two things: (1) be aware of the separate elements in a production, knowing what each contributes to the whole, and (2) combine and integrate the elements into a full, complete picture.

Observing Individual Elements as Parts of a Whole

In different sections of this book we have spoken of the separate elements which contribute to the overall theater experience. By using the extraordinary powers of perception described above, spectators can focus on specific areas in a production without losing sight of the total effect. They can also relate individual elements to one another. If members of the audience learn to use these powers to the fullest, their enjoyment and understanding of theater events will be enhanced.

We can concentrate for a time on acting, for instance, and ask ourselves if a particular performer is giving the proper interpretation to the role. Perhaps an actor is being too realistic in a nonrealistic role, or an actress is calling attention to herself and overplaying her part, thereby destroying the character's credibility. We can ask, too, how well the performers are playing with one another. Do they look at each other when they speak, and do they listen to fellow actors and respond?

As we watch a play unfold, we can also take a moment to observe the visual elements. Do the costumes suit the play? Does the scenery make a statement of its own consistent with the theme and concept? Is the setting symbolic, and if so, what does it symbolize? Do the colors in the scenery convey a particular mood or feeling?

Though the elements of structure and viewpoint are not as visible as acting or scenery, it is also possible to pause during a performance and consider them as well. As events occur on stage, we can determine what structure is being developed and whether it is maintained. If the play is climactic in structure, we can ask if the events in the play are plausible and follow one another logically. If the play is absurdist, we can judge whether the actions, though illogical and seemingly crazy, nevertheless present a pattern which makes us aware of a method in the madness or of an underlying theme.

In looking at separate elements of theater in this fashion, we need not fear that we will lose sight of the whole. If we set our minds to it, our power to absorb and integrate data can pull the experience together for us. The more we become aware of distinct elements, the more we can fit them into the overall picture. In watching a nonrealistic comedy, for instance, we can observe how the acting underlines and points up the humor of the script; we can note how the costumes assist the performers in creating comic characters—perhaps with an exaggeration of style—and, at the same time, observe how the costumes present a visual image of their own, appropriately bright and lighthearted; we can observe, too, how lighting reinforces the comic spirit of the costumes and the performers. In short, we can see how the various aspects fuse and combine, how they heighten, underscore, and collaborate with one another to create the final experience.

Combining Elements in a Scene from King Lear

To illustrate the process of integration in the minds of spectators, let us analyze what occurs when we watch the scene in *King Lear* in which Lear is on the heath in the midst of a storm. You will remember that Lear has divided his kingdom between his two wicked daughters, Goneril and Regan, but they have both thrown him out of their houses. Lear is now without shelter, and he is suffering the indignity and humiliation of having been treacherously deceived by two of his daughters. He has lost everything—as a king and as a person. Against this background, he wanders onto a barren heath just as a terrible storm begins. He is accompanied by his clown, the Fool. They are joined shortly by Kent, a faithful follower of Lear's whom Lear does not recognize. As the storm gathers strength, the group approaches a hut where they meet Edgar, disguised as a madman. The heavens unleash wind, thunder, and rain while these four men huddle together to curse their fate and to seek comfort from one another. If we imagine that we are watching the scene on stage, we can discern separate elements—at the same time that we bring them together to form a single experience.

First, we are aware of the physical presence of the actors: the man playing Lear is older and possibly larger in stature than the others, his voice full and resonant; the Fool is played by an actor quick on his feet and quick with his tongue; the actor playing Edgar wears rags and has splotches of dirt on his face and body; Kent is a stolid, straightforward man, eager to help his beloved king but unable to do so.

It is cold, the rain beats down, and the wind blows unceasingly. We know this because both the sounds of the words and the ideas they express tell us so. Also, we watch the actors shiver and seek shelter. We might also hear the sound effects of a howling wind and falling rains, and through the use of lighting effects, see flashes of lightning in a darkened sky.

Beyond this we observe a number of symbols. The storm on the heath is an outward, physical occurrence which mirrors the inward, emotional storm in Lear's mind. Because of what he has gone through with his daughters, he is afraid he is losing his mind; he says to himself at one point that he should think no more of his daughters, for "that way madness lies." The theme of insanity is underscored not only by the storm but by Edgar's pretending to be crazy: a man feigning madness stands alongside one who fears he actually is becoming insane. A parallel to this is the relationship of the Fool to Lear: Lear, the king, is more of a fool than the Fool. In a sense these two men are exchanging places, the Fool becoming the wise man, and Lear the fool.

A strong visual image reinforces Lear's personal situation. In the opening scenes, we have seen Lear clothed in robes of royal splendor. But during the storm, these outward trappings of kingship are stripped from him, and he stands amid the storm in tattered clothes. He

Figure 16-2 ***King Lear on the heath.*** *When Lear is caught in a storm on the heath the play operates on many levels simultaneously. The words of the script, the sounds of the storm, the presence of the performers, the torn costumes they wear: These combine to show us a man stripped bare—losing his sanity and worldly possessions in the midst of an emotional storm. Afterwards he begins a slow march back to spiritual regeneration. (Photo—The Tyrone Guthrie Theater, Minneapolis, Minn.)*

becomes the epitome of what he describes as "unaccommodated man": "a poor, bare, forked animal." Again, an outward image reflects an inner one: Lear's body is being stripped of outer garments in the same way that his soul is being laid bare on the inside.

Closely related to these themes is the notion of appearance and reality—an idea which runs through the whole play but comes into sharp focus in this scene. Lear is beginning the slow, painful process of discovering which daughter truly loves him. In the beginning, he banished his third daughter, Cordelia, because she refused to flatter him as he wished her to. To Lear she *appeared* to be an ungrateful, unloving daughter, while her sisters appeared to be the opposite. But events proved the reverse to be true; Cordelia is the daughter who truly loves him. Also, two of the men with Lear—Kent and Edgar—are in disguise; they are not the men they appear to be. This pattern suggests that people disguise themselves and that the truth is often hidden; we must look beyond appearances to discover who people really are and whom we can trust.

Other elements can be added to the picture of forces coming together in this scene from *King Lear*. To the physical and intellectual elements on stage, we join our own thoughts and memories. As we watch the scene, for instance, we might recall a time when we were caught in a storm or stranded in the cold. We might also remember being deceived by someone we trusted. Or, we might have an image of an old person who reminds us of Lear.

If we watch this scene in performance, we are aware of these diverse elements operating on several levels, and simultaneously we can put them together. They do go together: the sounds of the words go with the visual images, the symbolic meaning parallels the physical reality of the performers. If we keep these various elements in balance and relate them to one another, the scene becomes a rich, integrated experience; the elements fuse into a single impression of an old man and his friends forced out of doors in a storm, suffering both human and natural humiliations.

WHAT DOES THEATER "MEAN"?

The overall effect of a scene or an entire play raises the question of what a play "means." In a discussion of a play we might hear someone ask: "But what does it mean?" The reply frequently is a catch phrase or a brief summary: "The meaning of this play is that love conquers all," or "he who hesitates is lost," or "all's well that ends well." Someone might say, for instance, that the meaning of

Shakespeare's *Othello* is that people should not be too hasty to believe gossip and should trust those they love. Certainly one can conclude that *Othello* contains ideas which could be interpreted this way. But is this really what *Othello* means? Isn't this a far too simplistic and perhaps even erroneous idea of what *Othello* is about? Can we ever summarize the meaning of a play in one sentence?

Two Kinds of Meaning

There are two ways to look at meaning when we are discussing drama. Some plays specifically underscore a meaning in the text. They seem almost to have been written to point toward a moral or to teach a lesson. The title of Lillian Hellman's *The Little Foxes* comes from the Song of Solomon in the Bible; the verse reads, "Take us the foxes, the little foxes that spoil the vines, for our vines have tender grapes." The idea of the quotation is that the foxes are evil because they spoil the vines and ravage and destroy the grapes. The title, therefore, introduces a theme of plunder and exploitation, and this theme is carried out in the action. At the close of the play the theme is summed up by a young woman, Alexandra, who has come to realize what has been happening in her family. Recognizing that her mother is one of the greediest and most cunning of the foxes, she confronts her with this newfound knowledge. Alexandra says to her mother: "Addie said there were people who ate the earth and other people who stood around and watched them do it. And just now Uncle Ben said the same thing. . . . Well, tell him for me, Mama, I'm not going to stand around and watch you do it. Tell him I'll be fighting as hard as he'll be fighting some place where people don't just stand around and watch."

In a case like *The Little Foxes* the author has invited us to find a "meaning" in the play which can be put in a few straightforward sentences. Most plays, however, do not contain such direct statements of their meaning. Their substance resides rather in their total effect on the spectator. Even the relatively few plays, like *The Little Foxes*, which have clearcut themes are far more complex than a few sentences suggest.

In the final analysis, a theater event does not *mean*; it *is*—its existence is its meaning. The writer Gertrude Stein once said, "A rose is a rose is a rose." On the face of it, this seems to be a simple, repetitive statement; a reiteration of the obvious. As far as art is concerned, though, there is a great truth hidden in Ms. Stein's words. She is telling us that a rose is itself, not something else. In any other form it ceases to have its own existence and thus loses its unique quality. A poetic description, an oil painting, or a color photograph of a rose might have a certain beauty and give us a notion of a rose, but none of these can take the place of the real thing. A picture or a description can never duplicate the experience of seeing a real rose in a garden or in a vase of flowers. Only in its presence can we see the texture of the petals and smell the fragrance of the rose. If our direct experience of a rose is irreplaceable, how much more irreplaceable is our experience of a complex art like theater. The theater experience is the sum total of all the impressions we receive from a production.

Meaning in the Fusion of Elements

The scene we cited from *King Lear* provides an example of how meaning is found in the fusion of many elements in theater. A more recent example is the 1974 production of *Equus*, a play by British playwright Peter Shaffer (1926–). Several themes are made explicit in the text of the play. It is the story of a seventeen-year-old boy who is brought to a psychiatrist because the boy has blinded six horses and no one knows why. In working with him, the psychiatrist discovers that through a series of circumstances, the boy has come to look on horses as a kind of god. The boy feels there is a spiritual presence in his horse god—the Latin word *equus* means "horse." He has developed a ritual in which he rides at midnight into the fields bareback on a horse, and at the end of his ride, he falls down on his knees to worship his horse god. When a friendly young woman offers to make love to the boy one night in the stable where they work, he finds that he cannot. One reason is that he fears the horses have seen him with the young woman and are accusing him. And so he takes a metal spike and puts out the horses' eyes.

In treating the case, the psychiatrist becomes fascinated with the boy's intense passion in his worship of his "god." The doctor feels that in spite of the young man's serious mental problems and his behavior toward the horses, his patient has something that the doctor himself lacks. In the doctor's words: "That boy has known a passion more ferocious than I have felt in any second in my life. And let me tell you something: I envy it." One theme of the play—stated quite clearly in lines like that just quoted—is that modern society, in its compulsion for conformity and normality, has lost a sense of passion and worship. The doctor feels that if he cures his patient, the boy might become "normal," but lose the important flame inside him in the process. As the doctor puts it: "The normal is the good smile in a child's eyes—all right. It is also the dead stare in a million adults." The risk the doctor runs in curing the boy is that he will then become dull and ordinary, without emotion; the doctor argues that "passion can be destroyed by a doctor. It cannot be created."

A major theme of the play therefore, is the loss in the modern world of certain primitive feelings—deep passion and worship—which are important to human beings. To understand the play, it is important to understand this theme, but there is more to the play than this. To begin with, there are other themes. For instance, the doctor has problems of his own—he leads an unusually sterile existence—and one question is whether his view of normality is the correct one. Is the dilemma he faces the same dilemma everyone in the contemporary world faces, or is he, too, an extreme? But beyond a grasp of the intellectual concepts of the play we must experience its impact in production. In the same way that there are other elements in *King Lear,* there are visual and aural aspects to the presentation of *Equus* which are indispensable to its full meaning.

The production of *Equus* which appeared in New York in 1974 was directed by John Dexter, who had also directed the original production in London the previous year for the National Theater of Great Britain. In the production concept, Dexter, along with the designers and the composer, fashioned a nonrealistic, ritualistic approach to parts of the story. The stage itself was a square platform set in the middle of a circle. Overhead, exposed spotlights hung on bare pipes, and at the back of the stage, tiers of bleacher seats were set in a semicircle for spectators; this turned the proscenium theater into a modified arena. The square platform at the center had railings on three sides with small benches set against them. By invoking the audience's imagination, the central platform became by turns: a doctor's office, the boy's home, a movie theater, and the stable where the boy worked—all without a change of scenery.

The horses were played by men who wore brown trousers and shirts and large headpieces shaped in the outline of a horse's head. These headpieces, made of alternating bands of silver and leather strips, resembled a piece of sculpture. They were not intended to duplicate a horse's head, but to form a wire outline of a horse's head. The men playing the horses were not attempting to *be* horses—in the way two people inside a costume form a stage horse—but merely to *suggest* horses. The men did not walk on all fours, but stood upright, and on their feet they wore 4-inch wire stilts, to the bottom of which were attached regular horseshoes. These small stilts gave the men height above the boy, and the horseshoes, when struck on the hollow stage floor, provided a clomping sound like horses' hooves pounding the earth.

Figure 16-3 A moment of theater. *The interaction of actor with mask, of actor with another actor, of both actors with the setting and with the script creates a vivid moment of theater. This is from* Equus *by Peter Shaffer, directed by John Dexter. The boy is played by Peter Firth. (Photo—Van Williams)*

The sound of the clomps on the floor formed part of an orchestration of sounds used in the production. In his notes to the play, author Peter Shaffer speaks of an "Equus Noise" which announces or illustrates the presence of the God Equus. Shaffer says he is thinking of "a choric effect, made by all the actors sitting round upstage, and composed of humming, thumping, and stamping—though never of neighing or whinnying." Once more, the production offers a stimulus to the audience's imagination rather than a literal effect.

The same approach is used for the enactment of several key scenes in the play. The presentation of the boy's rides in the fields at night consists of the boy sitting astride the back of one of the horse-men in the center of the platform. To the sounds of the Equus Noise, actors rotate the platform on a turntable in a circle. The boy pretends to be riding, but actually he and his horse are standing still in the middle of the platform. Thus, without moving from one spot they give us the effect of racing wildly through the night.

With so many striking visual images on stage, as well as the incantatory effect of the sounds accompanying the actions, it is impossible to attribute the full meaning of the play to its intellectual concepts. The meaning is as much in the ritual midnight ride as it is in the words of the text. At one point in the play, the boy's mother tells the psychiatrist that when the cavalry of European armies first invaded the Americas, the Indians thought that the horse and rider were one creature—a kind of god. It was only when men fell off their horses that the natives realized that horse and rider were separate. We know when we see a theatrical production—whether *Equus, King Lear*, or any other play—that several elements combine to produce the overall effect. We can be aware of those separate elements, just as we are aware of a separate horse and rider, but in a meaningful theater experience these elements come together. They form a fusion or synthesis which becomes as indivisible as horse and rider were for the

Figure 16-4   *The production encompasses meaning.* *As shown in this dramatic setting for* Equus, *the meaning of a play is more than words. It is the language, plus the movements of the performers, plus the visual images of the scenery, lights, and costumes, plus the dynamics of the play's structure. But truly it is more than any of these—it is the sum of all of them together. The boy, the horses, the setting only begin to suggest the totality of meaning, which is as much emotional as it is intellectual. (Photo—Van Williams.)*

Indians when they saw them for the first time. In this fusion or synthesis we find the final "meaning" of a theatrical experience.

DIFFERENT PURPOSES, DIFFERENT EXPERIENCES

Each theater event has its own meaning and impact, but in today's theater these vary widely from one event to another. The elements we have examined in the various sections of this book can be combined in so many different ways that the results offer a variety of experiences. The same play might be performed in one instance in an outdoor theater with realistic acting, and in another instance in a small, indoor theater with nonrealistic acting. Conversely, the same space might serve two quite different productions: a bare stage with no scenery can be the setting for a stark tragedy or an intimate musical comedy. The combination of the play itself with the way it is presented will determine the final outcome.

As we have noted before, in a given historical period, the kinds of plays presented and the ways in which they were produced were frequently limited within a society. In most of Western Europe in the Middle Ages, plays were chiefly limited to miracle and morality plays. In specific localities, productions were carried out on the same kind of stage with the same production elements year after year. During the past one hundred years, however, there have been marked changes in society and in the theater, with an acceleration of these changes in the past quarter century. In the post-World War II period, we began to see a rapid shift in moral and social mores. Long-held beliefs and customs—in dress, in attitudes toward women, minority groups, and the family—were challenged and changed.

This breaking down of traditional attitudes and customs, along with the introduction of new ideas, was reflected in the theater. No longer was the proscenium stage the chief architectural form for presentations. There was a proliferation of arena and thrust stages, and the use of found space was introduced. No longer, either, were the episodic and climactic forms of structure the only ones considered by playwrights and directors; the Absurd form emerged, as did multifocus, unstructured forms. In the spring of 1974 there was a craze in colleges across the United States called "streaking," in which students ran naked across the campus. This had its counterpart in the theater because by the early seventies, nudity—as well as profanity—was widely accepted on the stage in many parts of the country.

The result of these changes was a multiplicity of theater offerings. It is probably safe to say that never in any culture, at any period in history, has there been the diversity of theater events available to the public that is available today to audiences in metropolitan centers throughout the Western world. This same diversity also reaches into selected areas outside the major cities. The variety of theater productions makes it incumbent on spectators to be keenly aware of the separate elements we have discussed—audiences, performers, dramatic characters, structure, point of view, environment, and visual elements—and to recognize what each contributes to the whole and to understand how these elements work together.

Not only do conditions vary widely in today's theater, but the intentions of writers, directors, and producers vary too. Audience members should keep in mind when they attend the theater that different productions are presented for different purposes. Some plays, such as farces like *Charley's Aunt* or comedies like *The Odd Couple*, are intended to entertain us and make us laugh. The intention of serious dramas, on the other hand, like *King Oedipus* or *Long Day's Journey into Night*, is to make us feel deeply about the human condition and to identify with the people who are suffering. Some plays are presented for the express purpose of giving us information about a person or an event, while others are little concerned with facts; their purpose is to have us lose ourselves in the experience and let sounds and images wash over us without regard for literal truth. Some plays show us horror and violence, not to celebrate or exploit horror and violence, but to make us hate them so much that we will rebel against them and do everything in our power to prevent them in the future. This kind of theater hopes to shock us into recognition and awareness. Other types of theater—such as melodrama—show us horror and violence mainly for the thrill of it. Still other plays attempt to inspire us or raise our spirits.

Then, too, there are productions with combined aims: plays which entertain us but also raise serious questions, or plays which make us laugh and weep at the same time—a phenomenon we discussed in examining tragicomedy.

In the end, we come to the fact that while there are common denominators in theater—the actor-audience encounter being chief among them—each theater experience is unique. It has its own combination of elements and its own particular aim or intention. In turn, audience members have their individual responses to each event. With so much variety in contemporary theater we cannot expect every production to be equally satisfying to every spectator. What we can look forward to are many kinds of experiences in the theater, some of which bring us a sense of fun and some of which arouse in us thoughts and emotions we never knew were there.

The Future

What of the future? Given the many facets of theater, what can we expect in the years ahead? For one thing, we can expect the variety to continue, with plays of all kinds, presented under different conditions. But we might also find a consolidation of the forces that have been let loose in the theater in the past few decades. The production of *Equus* is just such a coming together. On the one hand, it is an old-fashioned detective story combined with a psychiatric case study, and both of these have long been staples of the theater. But these in turn are joined with the ritualistic and symbolic techniques developed by Grotowski and others. The joining of the old with the new, of free-form techniques with more traditional ones, can give the theater new strength. The vitality and energy unleashed in the breaking down of restrictive attitudes and forms, if integrated with time-honored truths about the human condition, can add further to the rich mixture already available in the contemporary theater.

When we go to the theater, we become part of a group with a common bond: an audience sharing an experience. In the exchange between performers and audience, we take part in a direct, human encounter. And from the stage, we hear the dark cry of the soul, we listen to the joyous laughter of the human spirit, and we witness the tragedies and triumphs of the human heart. As long as men and women wish to join together in a communion of the spirit or share with one another their anguish and suffering, the theater experience provides them with a unique way to do it.

SUMMARY

1 Theater is a gamble. The many steps leading to a production, and the great number of people involved in bringing it about, increase the chances for error along the way. Fortunately, we do not need perfection in a theater event for it to be meaningful; a small miscalculation or mistake will not necessarily mar the overall effect.

2 Human beings have an enormous capacity to absorb and integrate data. In the theater this allows us to take the images and stimuli we receive and merge them into a single experience. The ultimate integration of a theater event takes place in each spectator's mind.

3 While watching a theater event, we should be aware of the separate elements of a production, and what each contributes to the whole. We must also note how they relate to one another and synthesize them in our minds.

4 The scene on the heath in *King Lear* illustrates the many

Figure 16-5 Come to the theater. *These performers in the musical* Pippin *seem to be inviting us to come to the theater. It is an appropriate invitation, for the audience must be present for theater to take place. It is the exchange between performer and spectator, their direct communication, which gives theater its unique quality.*

levels on which signals are sent to us in a theater production and also how the elements are interrelated and can be combined to form a whole.

    5 "Meaning" in the theater is sometimes understood to consist of the ideas expressed in the text. Some plays stress this aspect of meaning by emphasizing lines which present the author's position, but in the final analysis, meaning is the sum total of the theater experience. It includes the emotional and sensory data as well as the intellectual content. Any attempt to summarize the meaning of a play in a few words, or to reduce it to a formula, robs it of its full meaning.

    6 The 1974 production in New York of *Equus* combined ritualistic and symbolic elements with the words of the text in a way that illustrates how meaning must be understood in the context of the total event.

7 Each theater event forms a complete experience, but in today's theater, experiences can vary widely. Different kinds of theater buildings and environments, many performance styles, and variety in the plays themselves ensure a diversity of theater productions.

8 In the contemporary theater, plays are produced for different purposes and with different intentions: to move us, to involve us, to amuse us, to entertain us, to inform us, to shock us, to raise our awareness, to inspire us. Audiences should be aware of the variety of experiences available in the modern theater.

9 Because of its complexity, and because it is so people-centered, theater affords audience members a particularly rare experience—especially when the elements of a production come together successfully.

Above   Upstage or away from the audience. An actor crossing *above* a table keeps it between himself and the front of the stage.

Acting area   One of several areas into which the stage space is divided in order to facilitate blocking and the planning of stage movement.

Ad lib   To improvise lines of a speech, especially in response to an emergency such as an actor's forgetting his lines.

Aesthetic distance   Physical or psychological separation or detachment of the audience from the dramatic action, regarded as necessary to maintain the artistic illusion in most kinds of theater.

Amphitheater   A large oval, circular, or semicircular outdoor theater with rising tiers of seats around an open playing area; also, an exceptionally large indoor auditorium.

Antagonist   The chief opponent of the protagonist in a drama. In some cases there may be several antagonists.

Apron The stage space in front of the curtain line or proscenium; also called the *forestage*.

Arena A type of stage which is surrounded by the audience on all four sides; also known as *theater-in-the-round*.

At rise An expression used to indicate what is happening on stage at the moment when the curtain first rises or the lights come up at the beginning of the play.

Backdrop A large drapery or painted canvas which provides the rear or upstage masking of a set.

Backstage The stage area behind the front curtain; also, the areas beyond the setting, including wings and dressing rooms.

Basic situation The specific problem or maladjustment from which the play arises; for example, Romeo and Juliet come from families with a strong rivalry and antipathy.

Batten A pipe or long pole suspended horizontally above the stage, upon which scenery, drapery, or lights may be hung.

Beam projector A lighting instrument without a lens which uses a parabolic reflector to project a narrow, nonadjustable beam of light.

Below Opposite of *above*; toward the front of the stage.

Blackout To plunge the stage into total darkness by switching off the lights; also the condition produced by this operation.

Blocking The arrangement of the actors' movements on stage with respect to each other and the stage space.

Book (1) The spoken (as opposed to sung) portion of the text of a musical play. (2) To schedule engagements for artists or productions.

Border A strip of drapery or painted canvas hung from a batten to mask the area above the stage; also, a row of lights hung from a batten.

Box set An interior setting using flats to form the back and side walls and often the ceiling of a room.

Business Obvious and detailed physical movement of actors to reveal character, aid action, or establish mood (e.g., pouring drinks at a bar, opening a gun case).

Catharsis A Greek word, usually translated as purgation, which Aristotle used in his definition of tragedy. It refers to the vicarious cleansing of certain emotions in the audience through their representation on stage.

Catwalk A narrow metal platform suspended above the stage to permit ready access to lights and scenery hung from the grid.

Center stage A stage position in the middle acting area of the stage or the middle section extended upstage and downstage.

Chorus In ancient Greek drama, a group of performers who sang and danced, sometimes participating in the action but usually simply commenting on it. Also, a number of performers in a musical play who sing and dance as a group rather than individually.

Complication The introduction in a play of a new force which creates a new balance of power and makes a delay in reaching the climax necessary and progressive. It is one way of creating conflict and precipitating a crisis.

Conflict Tension between two or more characters that leads to crises or a climax. The basic conflict is the fundamental struggle or imbalance underlying the play as a whole. May also be a conflict of ideologies, actions, etc.

Counterweight A device for balancing the weight of scenery in a system which allows scenery to be raised above the stage by means of ropes and pulleys.

Crew The backstage team assisting in mounting a production.

Cross A movement by a performer across the stage in a given direction.

Cue Any prearranged signal, such as the last words in a speech, a piece of business, or any action or lighting change that indicates to an actor or stage manager that it is time to proceed to the next line or action.

Cue sheet A prompt book marked with cues, or a list of cues for the use of technicians, especially the stage manager.

Curtain (1) The rise or fall of the physical curtain, which separates a play into structural parts. (2) The last bit of action preceding the fall of the curtain.

Cyclorama A large curved drop used to mask the rear and sides of the stage, painted a neutral color or blue to represent sky or open space. It may also be a permanent stage fixture made of plaster or similar durable material.

Denouement The moment when final suspense is satisfied and "the knot is untied." The term is from the French and was used to refer to the working out of the resolution in a well-made play.

Deus ex machina Literally "the god from the machine," a resolution device in classic Greek drama. A term used to indicate the intervention of supernatural forces—usually at the last moment—to save the action from its logical conclusion. Denotes in modern drama an arbitrary and coincidental solution.

Dimmer A device which permits lighting intensities to be changed smoothly and at varying rates.

Dim out To turn out the lights with a dimmer, the process usually being cued to a predetermined number of seconds or counts.

Director In American usage, the person who is responsible for the overall unity of the production by coordinating the efforts of the contributing artists. The director is in charge of rehearsals and supervises the actors in the preparation of their parts. The American director is the equivalent of the British producer and the French *metteur-en-scène*.

Downstage The front of the stage toward the audience.

Drop A large piece of fabric, generally painted canvas, hung from a batten to the stage floor, usually to serve as backing.

Ensemble playing Acting which stresses the total artistic unity of the performance rather than the individual performances of specific actors.

Entrance The manner and effectiveness with which an actor comes into a scene as well as the actual coming on stage; also, the way it is prepared for by the playwright.

Epilogue A speech addressed to the audience after the conclusion of the play and spoken by one of the actors.

Exit An actor's leaving the stage, as well as the preparation for his leaving.

Exposition The imparting of information necessary for an understanding of the story, not covered by the action on stage. Events or knowledge from the past, or occurring outside the play, which must be introduced for the audience to understand the characters or plot. Exposition is always a problem in drama because relating or conveying information is static. The dramatist must find ways to make expositional scenes dynamic.

Flat A single piece of scenery, usually of standard size and made of canvas stretched over a wooden frame, used with other similar units to create a set.

Flood A lighting instrument without lenses which is used for general or large-area lighting.

Fly loft or flies The space above the stage where scenery may be lifted out of sight by means of ropes and pulleys when it is not needed.

Follow spot A large powerful spotlight with a sharp focus and narrow beam which is used to follow principal performers as they move about the stage.

Footlights A row of lights in the floor along the edge of the stage or apron; once a principal source of stage light, but now only rarely used.

Forestage See *Apron.*

Freeze To remain motionless on stage; especially for laughs.

Fresnel (fruh-NEL) A type of spotlight used over relatively short distances with a soft beam edge which allows the light to blend easily with light from other sources; also the type of lens used in such spotlights.

Front of the house The portion of the theater reserved for the audience, as opposed to the stage and backstage areas; sometimes simply referred to as "the house."

Gauze See *Scrim.*

Gel A thin, flexible color medium used in lighting instruments to give color to a light beam. Properly speaking, the word applies only to such material made of gelatin, but it is often applied to similar sheets made of plastic.

Grid A metal framework above the stage from which lights and scenery are suspended.

Hand props Small props carried on or off stage by actors during the performance.

Inner stage An area at the rear of the stage which can be cut off from the rest by means of curtains or scenery and revealed for special scenes.

Irony A condition the reverse of what we have expected; or an expression whose intended implication is the opposite of its literal sense. A device particularly suited to theater and found in virtually all drama.

Kill To eliminate or suppress, as to remove unwanted light or to ruin an effect through improper execution (e.g., to kill a laugh).

Left stage The left side of the stage from the point of view of an actor facing the audience.

Mask (1) To cut off from the view of the audience by means of scenery the backstage areas or technical equipment, as to mask a row of lighting instruments. (2) A face covering in the image of the character portrayed, sometimes covering the entire head.

Masking Scenery or drapes used to hide or cover.

Mise-en-scène The arrangement of all the elements in the stage picture, either at a given moment or dynamically throughout the performance.

Multiple setting A form of stage setting, common in the Middle Ages, in which several locations are represented at the same time; also called *simultaneous setting*. Used also in various forms of contemporary theater.

Objective Stanislavski's term for that which is urgently desired and sought by a character, the desired goal which propels a character to action.

Obstacle That which delays or prevents the achieving of a goal by a character. An obstacle creates complication and conflict.

Offstage The areas of the stage, usually in the wings, which are not in view of the audience.

Onstage The area of the stage which is in view of the audience.

Open To turn or face more toward the audience.

Orchestra The ground floor seating in an auditorium.

Pace The rate at which a performance is played; also, to play a scene or an entire play in order to determine its proper speed.

Period A term describing any representation on stage of a former age, as *period costume, period play.*

Platform A raised surface on the stage floor serving as an elevation for parts of the stage action and allowing for a multiplicity of stage levels.

Platform stage An elevated stage which does not make use of a proscenium.

Plot As distinct from story, the patterned arrangements of events and characters for a drama. The incidents are selected and arranged for maximum dramatic impact. The *plot* may begin long after the beginning of the *story* (and refer to information regarding the past in flashbacks or exposition).

Point of attack The moment in the story when the play actually begins. The dramatist chooses a point in time along the continuum of events which he or she judges will best start the action and propel it forward.

Preparation The previous arranging of circumstances, pointing of character, and placing of properties in a production so that the ensuing actions will seem reasonable; also, the actions taken by a performer getting ready for a performance.

Producer The person responsible for raising the money for a production and who is ultimately responsible for the business side of the production. In British usage, a producer is the equivalent of an American director.

Prologue An introductory speech delivered to the audience by one of the actors before the play begins.

Prompt To furnish an actor with missed or forgotten lines or cues during a performance.

Prompt book The script of a play indicating performers' movements, light cues, sound cues, etc.

Props Properties; objects used by actors on stage or necessary to complete the set.

Proscenium The arch or frame surrounding the stage opening in a box or picture stage.

Protagonist The principal character in a play, the one whom the drama is about.

Rake To position scenery on a slant or angle other than parallel or perpendicular to the curtain line; also an upward slope of the stage floor away from the audience.

Raked stage A stage which slopes upward away from the audience toward the back of the set.

Regional theater (1) Theater whose subject matter is specific to a particular geographic region. (2) Theaters situated outside major theatrical centers.

Rehearsal The preparation by the actors for the performance of a play through repetition and practice.

Revolving stage A large turntable on which scenery is placed in such a way that, as it moves, one set is brought into view while another one turns out of sight.

Repertory or repertoire A kind of acting company which at any given time has a number of plays which it can perform alternately; also, a collection of plays.

Reversal A sudden switch or reversal of circumstances or knowledge which leads to a result contrary to expectations. Called peripeteia or peripety in Greek drama.

Right stage The right side of the stage from the point of view of an actor facing the audience.

Scene (1) A stage setting. (2) The structural units into which the play or acts of the play are divided. (3) The location of the play's action.

Scrim A thin, open-weave fabric which is nearly transparent when lit from behind and opaque when lit from the front.

Script The written or printed text, consisting of dialogue, stage directions, character descriptions, and the like, of a play or other theatrical representation.

Set The scenery, taken as whole, for a scene or an entire production.

Set piece A piece of scenery which stands independently in the scene.

Slapstick A type of comedy or comic business which relies on ridiculous physical activity—often violent in nature—for its humor.

Spill Light from stage lighting instruments which falls outside of the areas for which it is intended, such as light that falls on the audience.

Spine In the Stanislavski method, the dominant desire or motivation of a character which underlies his or her action in the play; usually thought of as an action and expressed as a verb.

SRO Standing room only. A notice that all seats to a performance have been sold and only standees can be accommodated.

Stage door An outside entrance to the dressing rooms and stage areas which is used by performers and technicians.

Stage convention An understanding established through custom or usage that certain devices will be accepted or assigned specific meaning or significance on an arbitrary basis, that is, without requiring that they be natural or realistic.

Stage house   The stage floor and all the space above it up to the grid.

Stanislavski method   A set of techniques and theories about the problems of acting which promotes a naturalistic style stressing "inner truth" as opposed to conventional theatricality.

Strike   To remove from on stage pieces of scenery or props or to take down the entire set after the final performance.

Subtext   Referring to the meaning and movement of the play below the surface; that which is implied and never stated. Often more important than surface activity.

Summer stock   Theater companies which operate outside of major theatrical centers during the summer months (usually June through August) and have an intensive production schedule, often doing a different play every week.

Teaser   A short horizontal curtain just beyond the proscenium used to mask the fly loft and effectively lowering the height of the proscenium.

Technical   Referring to functions necessary to the production of a play other than those of the actors and the director, such as functions of the stage crew, carpenters, and lighting crew.

Theme   The central thought of the play. The idea or ideas with which the play deals and which it expounds.

Tragic flaw   That factor in a character which is his chief weakness and where he is most vulnerable; often intensifies in time of stress. An abused and often incorrectly applied theory from Greek drama.

Trap   An opening in the stage floor, normally covered, which can be used for special effects, such as having scenery or actors rise from below, or permitting the construction of a staircase which ostensibly leads to a lower floor or cellar.

Unities   A term referring to the preference that a play occur within one day (unity of time), in one place (unity of place), and with no action irrelevant to the plot (unity of action). *Note:* contrary to accepted opinion, Aristotle insisted only upon unity of action. Certain neoclassic critics of the Renaissance insisted on all three.

Unity   A requirement of art; an element often setting art apart from life. In drama, refers to unity of action achieved in a play's structure and story; the integrity and wholeness of a production which combine plot, character, and dialogue within a frame of time and space to present a congruous, complete picture.

Upstage   At or toward the back of the stage, away from the front edge of the stage. (The word dates from the time when the stage sloped upward from the footlights.)

Wagon stage   Low platform mounted on wheels or casters by means of which scenery is moved on and off stage.

Wings   Left and right offstage areas; also, narrow standing pieces of scenery or legs more or less parallel to the proscenium which form the sides of a setting.

Work lights   Lights arranged for the convenience of stage technicians, situated either in backstage areas and shaded or over the stage area for use while the curtain is down.

MAJOR THEATRICAL
FORMS AND
MOVEMENTS

Absurdism See *Theater of the Absurd*.

Allegory The representation of an abstract theme or themes through the symbolic use of character, action, and other concrete elements of a play. In its most direct form—as for example, the medieval morality play—allegory uses the device of personification to present characters representing abstract qualities such as virtues and vices in an action which spells out a moral or intellectual lesson. Less direct forms of allegory may use a relatively realistic story as a guise for a hidden theme. For example, Arthur Miller's *The Crucible* can be regarded as an allegory of the McCarthy congressional investigation in the United States after World War II.

Avant-garde A term applied to plays of an experimental or unorthodox nature which attempt to go beyond standard usage in either form or content. It is applied collectively to a large group of late nineteenth- and twentieth-century plays and includes such diverse movements as expressionism, surrealism, and absurdism.

Burlesque A ludicrous imitation of a dramatic form or a specific play. Closely related to satire, it usually lacks the moral or intellectual purposes of reform typical of the latter, being content to mock the excesses of other works. Famous examples of burlesque include Beaumont's *The Knight of the Burning Pestle* and, more recently, such burlesques of the movies as *Dames at Sea.* In America the term has come to be associated with a form of variety show which stresses sex.

Comedy As one of the oldest enduring categories of Western drama, comedy has gathered under its heading a large number of different subclassifications. Although the range of comedy is broad, generally it can be said to be a play that is light in tone, is concerned with issues tending not to be serious, has a happy ending, and is designed to amuse and provoke laughter. Historically, comedy has gone through many changes. Aristophanic or Old Comedy was farcical, satiric, and nonrealistic. Roman New Comedy, however, was more influential in the development of comedy during the Renaissance. Ben Jonson built his "comedies of humours" on Roman models. In Jonson's plays, ridicule is directed at characters who are dominated to the point of obsession by a single trait, or humour. The comedy of manners became popular in the late seventeenth century with the advent of Moliere and the writers of the English Restoration. It tends to favor a cultivated or sophisticated milieu, witty dialogue, and characters whose concern with social polish is charming, ludicrous, or both. The twentieth century has seen an expansion in the territory covered by comedy as well as a blurring of its boundaries. In the final decades of the nineteenth century George Bernard Shaw used it for the serious discussion of ideas, while Chekhov wrote plays variously interpreted as sentimental and tragicomic. Since then the horizon of the comic has been expanded by playwrights such as Pirandello and Ionesco, whose comic vision is more serious, thoughtful, and disturbing than that found in most traditional comedies.

Commedia dell'arte A form of comic theater which originated in Italy in the sixteenth century in which dialogue was improvised around a loose scenario calling for a set of stock characters, each with a distinctive costume and traditional name. The best known of these characters are probably the *zannis*, buffoons who usually took the roles of servants and who had at their disposal a large number of slapstick routines, called *lazzis*, which ranged from simple grimaces to acrobatic stunts.

Documentary See *Theater of Fact.*

Domestic Drama Also known as bourgeois drama, domestic drama deals with problems of members of the middle and lower classes, particularly problems of the family and home. Conflicts with society, struggles within a family, dashed hopes and renewed determination are frequently characteristics of domestic drama. It attempts to depict on stage the life-style of ordinary people—in language, in dress, in behavior. Domestic drama first came to the fore during the eighteenth century in Europe and Great Britain when the merchant and working classes were emerging. Because general audiences could so readily identify with the people and problems of domestic drama, it continued to gain in popularity during the nineteenth and twentieth centuries and remains a major form today.

Environmental theater A term used by Richard Schechner and others to refer to a branch of the New Theater movement. Among its aims are the elimination of the distinction between audience space and actor space, a more flexible approach to the interactions between actors and audience, and the substitution of a multiple focus for the traditional single focus.

Epic theater A form of presentation which has come to be associated with the name of Bertolt Brecht, its chief advocate and theorist. It is aimed at the intellect rather than the emotions, seeking to present evidence regarding social questions in such a way that they may be objectively considered and an intelligent conclusion reached. Brecht felt that emotional involvement by the audience defeated this aim, and he used various devices designed to produce an emotional "alienation" of the audience from the action on stage. His plays are episodic, with narrative songs separating the segments and large posters or signs announcing the various scenes.

Existentialism A set of philosophical ideas whose principal modern advocate is Jean-Paul Sartre. The term *existentialist* is also applied to plays by Sartre and others which illustrate these views. Sartre's central thesis is that there are no longer any fixed standards or values by which one can live and that each individual must create his or her own code of conduct regardless of the conventions imposed by society. Only in this way can one truly "exist" as a responsible, creative human being; otherwise one is merely a robot or automaton. Sartre's plays typically involve people who are faced with decisions forcing them into an awareness of the choice between living on their own terms or ceasing to exist as individuals.

Expressionism A movement which developed and flourished in Germany during the period immediately preceding and following World War I. Expressionism in the drama was characterized by the attempt to dramatize subjective states through the use of distortion, striking and often grotesque images, and lyric, unrealistic dialogue. It was revolutionary in content as well as in form, portraying the institutions of society, particularly the bourgeois family, as grotesque, oppressive, and materialistic. The expressionist hero was usually a rebel against this mechanistic vision of society. Dramatic conflict tended to be replaced by the development of themes by means of visual images. The movement had great influence because it forcefully demonstrated that dramatic imagination need not be limited to either theatrical conventions or the faithful reproduction of reality. In the United States, expressionism influenced Elmer Rice's *The Adding Machine* and many of O'Neill's early plays. The basic aim of expressionism was to give external expression to inner feelings and ideas; theatrical techniques which adopt this method are frequently referred to as *expressionistic.*

Farce One of the major genres of drama, sometimes regarded as a subclassification of comedy. Farce has few, if any, intellectual pretensions. It aims to entertain, to provoke laughter. Its humor is the result primarily of physical activity and visual effects and it relies less on language and wit than do so-called higher forms of comedy. Violence, rapid movement, and accelerating pace are characteristic of farce. In bedroom farce it is the institution of marriage that is the object of the fun, but medicine, law, and business also provide material for farce.

Happenings A form of theatrical event which was developed out of the experimentation of certain American abstract artists in the 1960s. Happenings are nonliterary, replacing the script with a scenario which provides for chance occurrences. They are performed (often only once) in such places as parks and street corners, with little attempt being made to segregate the action from the audience. Emphasizing the free association of sound and movement, they avoid logical action and rational meaning.

Heroic Drama A form of serious drama, written in verse or elevated prose, which features noble or heroic characters caught in extreme situations or undertaking unusual adventures. In spite of the hardships to which its leading figures are subjected, heroic drama—unlike tragedy—assumes a basically optimistic world view. It either has a happy ending or, in cases where the hero or heroine dies, a triumphant one in which the death is not regarded tragically. Plays from all periods, and from the Orient as well as the West, fall in this category. During the late seventeenth century in England, plays of this type were referred to specifically as "heroic tragedies."

History play In the broadest sense, a play set in a historical milieu which deals with historical personages, but the term is usually applied only to plays which deal with vital issues of public welfare and are nationalistic in tone. The form originated in Elizabethan England, which produced more history plays than any comparable place and time. Based on a religious concept of history, they were influenced by the structure of the morality play. Shakespeare was the major writer of Elizabethan history plays. His style has influenced many later history plays, notably those by the Swedish playwright Strindberg.

Impressionism A style of painting developed in the late nineteenth century which stressed the immediate impressions created by objects—particularly those resulting from the effects of light—and which tended to ignore details. As such its influence on the theater was primarily in the area of scenic design, but the term *impressionistic* is sometimes applied to plays like Chekhov's which rely on a series of impressions and use indirect techniques.

Kabuki The most eclectic and theatrical of the major forms of Japanese theater. It is a more popular form than the aristocratic *Noh* drama and uses live actors, unlike the puppet theater, or *Bunraku*. Nevertheless, it has borrowed freely from both of these forms, particularly the Bunraku.

Roles of both sexes are performed by men in a highly theatrical, nonrealistic style. Kabuki combines music, dance, and dramatic scenes with an emphasis on color and movement. The plays are long and episodic, composed of a series of loosely connected dramatic scenes which are often performed separately.

Masque A lavish and spectacular form of private theatrical entertainment which developed in Renaissance Italy and spread rapidly to the courts of France and England. Usually intended for a single performance, the masque combined poetry, music, elaborate costumes, and spectacular effects of stage machinery. It was a social event which had members of the court acting as both spectators and performers. Loosely constructed, masques were usually written around allegorical or mythological themes.

Medieval drama There is only meager evidence of theatrical activity in Europe between the sixth and tenth centuries, but by the end of the fifteenth century a number of different types of drama had developed. The first of these, known as *liturgical drama*, was sung or chanted in Latin as part of a church service. Plays on religious themes were also written in the vernacular and performed outside of the church. The *mystery plays* (also called *cycle plays*) were based on events taken from the Old and New Testaments. Many such plays were organized into historical cycles which told the story of mankind from the Creation to Doomsday. The entire performance was quite long, sometimes requiring as much as five days to perform. They were produced as a community effort, with a different craft guild usually being responsible for an individual segment. Other forms of religious drama were the *miracle play*—which dealt with events in the life of a saint—and the *morality play*. The morality play was a didactic and allegorical treatment of moral and religious questions, the most famous example being *Everyman*. The medieval period also produced several types of secular plays. Other than the *folk plays*, which dealt with legendary heroes like Robin Hood, most were farcical and fairly short.

Melodrama Historically, a distinct form of drama popular throughout the nineteenth century which emphasized action and spectacular effects and employed music to heighten the dramatic mood. Melodrama employed stock characters and clearly defined villains and heroes. More generally, the term is applied to any dramatic play which presents an unambiguous confrontation between good and evil. Characterization is often shallow and stereotypical, and because the moral conflict is externalized, action and violence are prominent in melodrama, usually culminating in a happy ending meant to demonstrate the eventual triumph of good.

Mime A performance in which the action or story is conveyed through the use of movements and gestures without words. It depends on the performer's ability to suggest or create his or her surroundings through physical reactions to them and the expressiveness of the entire body.

Musical theater A broad category which includes opera, operetta, musical comedy, and other musical plays (the term *lyric theater* is sometimes used to distinguish it from pure dance). It includes any dramatic entertainment in which music and lyrics (and sometimes dance) form an integral and necessary part. The various types of musical theater often overlap and are best distinguished in terms of their separate historical origins, the quality of the music, and the range and type of skills demanded of the performers. Opera is usually defined as a work in which all parts are sung to musical accompaniment. Such works are part of a separate and much older tradition than the modern musical, which is of relatively recent American origin. The term *musical comedy* no longer is adequate to describe all of musical dramas commonly seen on and off Broadway, but they clearly belong together as part of a tradition that can easily be distinguished from both opera and operetta.

Naturalism   See *Realism and naturalism.*

New Theater   (1) A generic term covering innovations made in theater practice since about 1960 by such groups as Grotowski's Polish Laboratory Theater, the Open Theater, and the Living Theater. Perhaps the most important statement of the theoretical aims of the movement is to be found in Jerzy Grotowski's *Towards a Poor Theatre.* Despite differences between the groups, they are alike in their demands that theater be a serious, even spiritual, experience for actors and audience. They seek to eliminate all that is inessential or frivolous in theater. They generally tend to emphasize the importance of ritual, an intimate bond between actors and audience, and the intense dedication of a closely knit group of actors, working together over a long period of time. (2) Sometimes used interchangeably with the term *new stagecraft* in the first half of this century. Both expressions referred to a movement, primarily affecting the visual aspects of theater, which was pioneered largely by Gordon Craig and included such adherents as Robert Edmond Jones, Norman Bel Geddes, and Lee Simonson. The emphasis was on the creative and evocative use of light, color, and form rather than strict realistic representation. Many of their innovations have become standard practice in the theater today.

Noh   (also spelled Nō)   A rigidly traditional form of Japanese drama which dates back in its present form to the fourteenth century. Noh plays are short dramas combining music, dance, and lyric with a highly stylized and ritualistic presentation. Virtually every aspect of the production— including costumes, masks, and a highly symbolic setting—is prescribed by tradition.

Pantomime   Originally a Roman entertainment in which a narrative was sung by a chorus while the story was acted out by dancers. Now used loosely to cover any form of presentation which relies on dance, gesture, and physical movement. (See *Mime.*)

Play of ideas   A play whose principal focus is on the serious treatment of social, moral, or philosophical ideas. The term *problem play* is used to designate those dramas, best exemplified in the work of Ibsen and Shaw, in which several sides of a question are both dramatized and discussed. It is sometimes distinguished from the *pièce à thèse,* or thesis play, which makes a more one-sided presentation and employs a character who sums up the "lesson" of the play and serves as the author's voice.

Poor Theater A term coined by Jerzy Grotowski to describe his ideal of theater stripped to its barest essentials. The lavish sets, lights, and costumes usually associated with the theater, he feels, merely reflect base materialistic values and must be eliminated. If theater is to become rich spiritually and aesthetically, it must first be "poor" in everything that can distract from the actor's relationship with the audience.

Realism and naturalism In its broadest sense, realism is simply the attempt to portray truthfully and directly the facts of contemporary life. In practice, however, the playwright's vision of reality is never completely objective. The difference between the realistic and naturalistic writers stems from the difference in their attitudes toward the nature of man and society. While both schools tend to be concerned with social change, the realists are more optimistic regarding man's ability to learn and to change. The naturalists, viewing human beings as selfish and basically amoral products of heredity and environment, prefer to portray the brutalized lower classes in whom such forces can be most clearly shown, while the realists are more apt to set their plays in the reasonable atmosphere of middle-class drawing rooms. On another level, naturalism is simply a more exact and detailed form of realism.

Restoration drama English drama after the restoration of the monarchy, from 1660 to 1700. Presented for an audience of aristocrats who gathered about the court of Charles II, drama of this period consisted largely of heroic tragedies in the neoclassical style and comedies of manners which reflected a cynical view of human nature.

Romanticism A literary and dramatic movement of the nineteenth century which developed as a reaction to the confining strictures of neo-classicism. Imitating the loose, episodic structure of Shakespeare's plays, the Romantics sought to free the writer from all rules and looked to the unfettered inspiration of artistic genius as the source of all creativity. They laid more stress on mood and atmosphere than on content, but one of their favorite themes was the gulf between human beings' spiritual aspirations and their physical limitations.

Satire Dramatic satire uses the techniques of comedy, such as wit, irony, and exaggeration, to attack and expose folly and vice. Satire can attack specific public figures, as does the political satire *Macbird*, or it can point its barbs at more general traits which can be found in many of us. Thus Molière's *Tartuffe* ridicules religious hypocrisy, Shaw's *Arms and the Man* exposes the romantic glorification of war, and Wilde's *The Importance of Being Earnest* attacks the English upper classes.

Street Theater A generic term which includes a number of groups who perform in the open and attempt to relate to the needs of a specific community or neighborhood. Many such groups sprang up in the 1960s, partly as a response to social unrest and partly because there was a need for a theater which could express the specific concerns of minority and ethnic neighborhoods.

Surrealism A movement attacking formalism in the arts which developed in

Europe after the First World War. Seeking a deeper and more profound reality than that presented to the rational, conscious mind, the surrealists replaced realistic action with the strange logic of the dream and cultivated such techniques as automatic writing and free association of ideas. Although few plays written by the surrealists are highly regarded, the movement has had a great influence on later avant-garde theater—notably the Theater of the Absurd and the Theater of Cruelty.

Symbolism Closely linked to symbolist poetry, symbolist drama was a movement of the late nineteenth and early twentieth centuries which sought to replace realistic representation of life with the expression of an inner truth. Hoping to restore the religious and spiritual significance of theater, symbolism used myth, legend, and symbols in an attempt to reach beyond everyday reality. The plays of Maurice Maeterlinck are among the best known symbolist dramas.

Theater of Cruelty Anton Artaud's visionary concept of a theater based on magic and ritual which would liberate deep, violent, and erotic impulses. He wished to reveal what he saw as the cruelty which exists beneath all human action—the pervasiveness of evil and violent sexuality. To do this, he advocated radical changes in the use of theatrical space, the integration of audience and actors, and the full utilization of the affective power of light, color, movement, and language. Although Artaud had little success implementing his theories himself, he had considerable influence on other writers and directors, particularly Peter Brook, Jean-Louis Barrault, and Jerzy Grotowski.

Theater of Fact A term which encompasses a number of different types of documentary drama which have developed during the twentieth century. Methods of presentation differ: the Living Newspaper Drama of the 1930s used signs and slide projections to deal with broad social problems; other documentary dramas use a more realistic approach. Contemporary Theater of Fact, as represented by such plays as *The Deputy* and *The Investigation* tries to portray actual events with the appearance of authenticity.

Theater of the Absurd A phrase first used by Martin Esslin to describe certain playwrights of the 1950s and 1960s who expressed a similar point of view regarding the absurdity of the human condition. Their plays are dramatizations of the author's inner sense of the absurdity and futility of existence. Rational language is debased and replaced by clichés and trite or irrelevant remarks. Repetitious or meaningless activity is substituted for logical action. Realistic, psychological motivation is replaced by automatic behavior which is often absurdly inappropriate to the situation. Although the subject matter is serious, the tone of these plays is usually comic and ironic. Among the best known absurdists are Beckett, Ionesco, and Albee.

Theatricalism A style of production and playwriting which emphasizes theatricality for its own sake. Less a coherent movement than a quality found in the work of many artists rebelling against realism, it frankly admits the artifice of the stage and borrows freely from the circus, the music hall, and similar entertainments.

Tragedy One of the most fundamental dramatic forms in the Western tradition, tragedy involves a serious action of universal significance and has important moral and philosophical implications. Following Aristotle, most critics agree that the tragic hero should be an essentially admirable person whose downfall elicits our sympathy while leaving us with a feeling that there has in some way been a triumph of the moral and cosmic order which transcends the fate of any individual. The disastrous outcome of a tragedy should be seen as the inevitable result of the character and his situation, including forces beyond his control. Traditionally tragedy was about the lives and fortunes of kings and nobles, and there has been a great deal of debate about whether it is possible to have a modern tragedy—a tragedy about ordinary people. The answers to this question are as varied as the critics who address themselves to it, but most seem to agree that though such plays may be tragedies, they are of a somewhat different order.

Tragicomedy During the Renaissance the word was used for plays having tragic themes and noble characters, yet which ended happily. Modern tragicomedy combines serious and comic elements. Many plays of this type involve a comic or ironic treatment of a serious theme. Tragicomedy is in fact increasingly the form chosen by "serious" playwrights. Sometimes comic behavior and situations have serious or tragic consequences—as in Durrenmatt's *The Visit*. At times the ending is indeterminate or ambivalent—as in Beckett's *Waiting for Godot*. In most cases a quality of despair or hopelessness is introduced because human beings are seen as incapable of rising above their circumstances or their own nature; the fact that the situation is also ridiculous serves to make their plight that much more horrible.

Well-made play A type of play popular in the nineteenth and early twentieth centuries which combined apparent plausibility of incident and surface realism with a tightly constructed and contrived plot. Well-made plays typically revolved about the question of social respectability, and the plot often hinged on the manipulation of a piece of incriminating evidence which threatened to destroy the facade of respectability. Although the well-made play is less popular now, many of its techniques continue to be used by modern playwrights.

APPENDIX III
HISTORICAL OUTLINE

THE ANCIENT WORLD

THEATRICAL	SOCIAL/POLITICAL/CULTURAL

EGYPT

	ca. * 3100 B.C.	Old Kingdom (ca. 3100– 2185 B.C.)
Ritual drama	ca. 2750 B.C.	
Abydos Passion Play	ca. 2500 B.C.	
(ca. 2500–550 B.C.)	2133 B.C.	Middle Kingdom (2133– 1786 B.C.)
	1580 B.C.	New Kingdom (ca. 1580– 1085 B.C.)

*ca. means circa, or approximately the date at which the event took place.

GREECE

THEATRICAL		SOCIAL/POLITICAL/CULTURAL
	ca. 800 B.C.	Homer
Play contests begun in Athens	534 B.C.	
Thespis "first actor" fl.*	ca. 530 B.C.	
	ca. 520 B.C.	Pythagoras fl.
	510 B.C.	Democracy in Athens
	499 B.C.	Persian Wars (499–478 B.C.)
	ca. 460 B.C.	Periclean Athens—"Golden Age" (ca. 460–429 B.C.)
Oresteia, Aeschylus (525–456 B.C.)	458 B.C.	Socrates (469–399 B.C.)
Oedipus the King, Sophocles (496–406 B.C.)	ca. 430 B.C.	Peloponnesian War (431–404 B.C.)
The Trojan Women, Euripides (480–406 B.C.)	415 B.C.	Plato (429–348 B.C.)
Lysistrata, Aristophanes (448–380 B.C.)	411 B.C.	
Poetics (ca. 335–323 B.C.), Aristotle (384–322 B.C.)	335 B.C.	Alexander the Great (356–323 B.C.) occupies Greece
Theater of Dionysus completed	ca. 325 B.C.	
Greek theaters built throughout Mediterranean area (ca. 320–ca. 100 B.C.)	ca. 320 B.C.	Hellenistic culture spreads throughout Eastern Mediterranean
Menander (343–291 B.C.) writer of "New Comedy"		

ROME

THEATRICAL		SOCIAL/POLITICAL/CULTURAL
	264 B.C.	First Punic War (264–241 B.C.) Greek influence on Roman culture.
Roman farce comedy begins		
	218 B.C.	Second Punic War (218–201 B.C.)
Menaechmi (ca. 205–184 B.C.) Plautus (ca. 254–184 B.C.)	205 B.C.	

*fl. means flourished at that time.

THEATRICAL		SOCIAL/POLITICAL/CULTURAL
Phormio, Terence	161 B.C.	
(ca. 190−159 B.C.)	147 B.C.	Rome annexes Macedonia
First permanent theater in Rome	55 B.C.	Golden Age of Roman literature: Catullus, Cicero, Vergil, Ovid (83 B.C.− 14 A.D.)
	44 B.C.	Assassination of Julius Caesar
Seneca (ca. 4 B.C.−65 A.D.) writes tragedies	27 B.C.	Emperor Augustus Caesar begins reign until 14 A.D.
Roman theater and amphitheaters built in 1st and 2d centuries	ca. 30 A.D.	Crucifixion of Jesus
	161 A.D.	Marcus Aurelius rules until 180 A.D.
Theater for 1st through 4th centuries is mostly mime, pantomime, and spectacle	250 A.D.	Persecution of Christians builds for next fifty years
	324 A.D.	Emperor Constantine rules until 337
Strong church opposition to theater		St. Augustine (354−430) St. Jerome (ca. 340−420)
	410	Sack of Rome
	476	Collapse of Western Roman Empire

For almost a thousand years—from the first through the tenth centuries—there was little formal theater in Western civilization. We must skip from Rome at the beginning of the Christian era to the Middle Ages to find significant information concerning theater.

MIDDLE AGES

THEATRICAL		SOCIAL/POLITICAL/CULTURAL
Quem Quaeritis trope (introduction of choral dialogue into church service)	ca. 925	
Hrosvitha, a nun, writes Christian comedies based on Terence	ca. 970	
(Liturgical drama in Latin, 10th century and later)	1066	Normans conquer England
	1095	First Crusade (until 1096)
Play of Adam, oldest known scriptural drama in the vernacular	ca. 1140	(Earliest manufacture of paper in Europe)

THEATRICAL		SOCIAL/POLITICAL/CULTURAL
(Drama moves out of the church)	1215	Magna Carta
Festival of Corpus Christi established	1264	Roger Bacon (1214–94) Thomas Aquinas (d. 1274)
The Play of the Bower, beginning of secular drama in France	ca. 1276	Giotto (ca. 1266–1337), Italian painter
	ca. 1310	*The Divine Comedy*, Dante Alighieri (1265–1321)
	1338	Hundred Years' War between England and France (until 1456) Petrarch (1304–74)
Second Shepherd's Play, one of a series of "cycle" plays based on scriptures	ca. 1375	Chaucer (ca. 1340–1400)
	1431	Joan of Arc burned at the stake
	ca. 1450	Guttenberg, invention of movable type
	1453	Byzantium falls to the Turks

RENAISSANCE TO 1700

THEATRICAL		SOCIAL/POLITICAL/CULTURAL
	1455	Wars of Roses in England (until 1485)
Pierre Pathelin, one of many popular farces in France	ca. 1464	
	1469	Spain united under Isabella and Ferdinand
(Plays in Latin, modeled on Roman drama written in the academies of Italy)	1478	Lorenzo de'Medici controls Florence (until 1492) Inquisition established in Spain
(First professional acting companies in Spain; beginnings of secular drama)	ca. 1480	*Birth of Venus*, Botticelli (1446–1510), Italy
	1492	Expulsion of the Jews from Spain; Columbus discovers America; conquest of Granada
(Growth of professional acting troupes)		
	1494	The Italian Wars weaken Italy politically but spread her

THEATRICAL		SOCIAL/POLITICAL/CULTURAL
Everyman, morality play	1500	cultural influence
	1504	*David*, Michelangelo (1474– 1564), Italy
	1505	*Mona Lisa*, Leonardo da Vinci (1452–1519), Italy
I Suppositi, Lodovico Ariosto (1474–1533), Italian vernacular comedy based on Plautus and Terence	1509	Henry VIII of England (r. 1509–47)
(Interest in classical drama in schools and universities in England)		
Mandragola, Niccolo Machiavelli (1469–1527), Italy	ca. 1512	Sistine Chapel ceiling, Michelangelo (1508–12)
Sofonisba, Giangiorgio Trissino (1478–1550), Italian tragedy based on classic models	1513	*The Prince*, Machiavelli, Italy
	1515	Francis I of France (r. 1515–47)
	1516	*Utopia*, Thomas Moore (1428– 1535), England
	1517	Martin Luther (1483–1546) posts theses, Germany
Confrèrie de la Passion given theatrical monopoly in Paris	1518	
	1519	Cortes conquers Aztecs for Spain
	1530	Pizarro takes Peru
	1532	*Pantagruel*, François Rabelais (1494–1553), France
	1534	Act of Supremacy begins English Reformation
Ralph Roister Doister, English, "school drama"	1540	
Serlio's *Architettura* describes scene design and stage effects	1545	
Lope de Rueda (ca. 1510–65), first important popular dramatist in Spain		
Gammer Gurton's Needle, English, "school drama"	ca. 1552	
	1556	Philip II of Spain (r. 1556–98)
	1558	Elizabeth I of England (r. 1558– 1603)

THEATRICAL		SOCIAL/POLITICAL/CULTURAL
Gorboduc, Sackville and Norton, first English tragedy; drama at the Inns of Court	1561	
	1564	St. Peter's Cathedral (begun 1546)
	1567	Netherlands revolt against Spain
	1572	St. Bartholomew's Day Massacre in France, Protestants murdered
The Theater and the Black-friars, first permanent theaters in England	1576	
Coral de la Cruz, first perma-nent theater in Spain	1579	El Greco (1541–1614), Spain
	1580	*Essays,* Michel Eyquem de Montaigne (1533–92), France
Teatro Olimpico, first perma-ment theater in Italy (*Commedia dell'Arte,* improvised popular theater in Italy)	1584	(Italy divided politically and largely under foreign rule)
The Spanish Tragedy, Thomas Kyd (1558–94), England	ca. 1587	
	1588	Defeat of the Spanish Armada
Alexandre Hardy (ca. 1572–1632) first professional French playwright		
Doctor Faustus, Christopher Marlowe (1564–93), England	1589	Henry IV (r. 1589–1610) unites France
	1593	*The Faerie Queene,* Edmund Spencer (ca. 1552–99), England
	1598	Edict of Nantes ends Religious Wars in France
Hamlet, William Shakespeare (1564–1616), England	ca. 1600	
	1603	James I of England (r. 1603–25)
Volpone, Ben Jonson (1572–1637), England	1606	
	1607	Jamestown, Virginia, founded
	1611	King James Bible, England
The Duchess of Malfi, John Webster (ca. 1580–1630), England	1613	

The Sheep Well, Lope de Vega   ca. 1614
(1562–1635), Spain
The Cave of Salamanca, Miguel
de Cervantes (1547–1616),
Spain

     1616   *Don Quixote*, Cervantes, Spain

Teatro Farnese in Italy, first   1618
surviving proscenium arch
theater

Inigo Jones (1573–1652), court   1620   *Novum Organum*, Francis Bacon
masques in England, Jacobean   (1561–1626), England
playwrights: Beaumont, Fletcher,
Webster, Shirley, and Ford

(Italian *commedia* popular in   1624   Administration of Richelieu
France.)   consolidates power of the
         king in France (until 1642)

     1625   Charles I of England (r. 1625–49)
     1629   Charles dissolves English
         Parliament

'Tis Pity She's a Whore, John   ca. 1633
Ford (1586–ca. 1639),
England

The Cid, Pierre Corneille   1636
(1606–84), France
Life is a Dream, Calderón de la
Barca (1600–81), Spain

     1637   French Academy founded:
         Discourse on Method, René
         Descartes (1596–1650)

The Opinions of the French   1638   Galileo Galilei (1564–1642),
Academy on The Cid establish   Italy
the rule of neoclassicism in
France

Theaters in England closed by   1642   English Civil War (until 1646)
Parliament; theatrical per-
formances banned (until 1660)   Rule of Cardinal Mazarin in
         France (until 1661)

Torelli brings Italian scenery   1645
to France
Invention of chariot-and-pole
system of scene shifting
permits rapid change of
scenes

	1649	Charles I of England beheaded; the Commonwealth (until 1660)
	1651	*Leviathan*, Thomas Hobbes (1588–1678), England
Italian scene designers (Sabbattini, Torelli, Parigi) famous throughout Europe		
	1659	Peace of the Pyrenees; decline of Spanish power
English theaters reopened; royal patents establish theatrical monopolies	1660	Restoration of the English monarchy; Charles II (r. 1660–1685)
	1661	Louis XIV, the "Sun King," absolute ruler of France (r. 1661–1715)
Thomas Betterton (ca. 1635– 1710), foremost English actor	1662	Royal Society founded in England, dedicated to science
The Misanthrope, Molière (1622–73), France	1666	
	1667	*Paradise Lost*, John Milton (1608–74), England
	1669	*Pensées*, Blaise Pascal (1623–62), France
Drury Lane Theater, England	1674	
The Country Wife, William Wycherly (1640–1715), England	1675	
All for Love, John Dryden (1631–1700), England; *Phèdre*, Jean Racine (1639–99), France	1677	
Comédie Française, first national theater company in France	1680	
	1687	Issac Newton (1642–1727) formulates laws of universal gravitation
	1689	Glorious Revolution in England of William and Mary (r. 1689–1702)
	1690	*Essay Concerning Human Understanding*, John Locke (1632–1704), England

THEATRICAL		SOCIAL/POLITICAL/CULTURAL
Jeremy Collier publishes attack on the immorality of the English stage	1698	
The Way of the World, William Congreve (1670–1729), England	1700	

18TH CENTURY

THEATRICAL		SOCIAL/POLITICAL/CULTURAL
(Bibiena family dominates scene design throughout century— "baroque," lavish, and ornate)	1701	War of the Spanish Succession in France (until 1714)
		Peter the Great (r. 1682–1725) begins Westernization of Russia
(French and Italian influence in the court theaters of Germany, Scandinavia, and Russia)	1702	Queen Anne of England (r. 1702–14)
	1714	George I of England (r. 1714–27), House of Hanover
		Baroque music: Johann Sebastian Bach (1685–1750) and George Fredrick Handel (1685–1759)
	1721	Robert Walpole, first English prime minister (1721–42)
Jeppe of the Hill, Ludwig Holberg (1684–1754), beginning of Danish drama	1722	
(Johann Gottsched (1700–66) and Carolina Neuber (1697–1760) begin reforms of German theater)		
The Conscious Lovers, Richard Steele (1672–1729), rise of sentimental comedy in England		
	1726	*Gulliver's Travels*, Jonathan Swift (1667–1745), England
The Beggar's Opera, John Gay (1685–1732), England	1728	

THEATRICAL		SOCIAL/POLITICAL/CULTURAL
The London Merchant, George Lillo (1693–1732), English bourgeois drama	1731	
Zaire, Voltaire (1694–1788), French neoclassical tragedy	1732	(Italy remains divided through-out century)
Licensing Act imposes severe censorship on theater in England	1737	(French painters Watteau, Boucher, and Fragonard stress rococo sensuality in painting)
(First permanent theaters in Germany)	1740	Fredrick the Great of Prussia (r. 1740–86), "Enlightened Despotism"
David Garrick (1717–79), inno-vations in English acting	1748	*Clarissa*, Samuel Richardson (1689–1761), England
Encyclopedia (1748–72) in France, edited by Denis Diderot (1713–84), advocates more realistic drama and staging		
DeLoutherbourg (1740–1812), realism and "local color" in English scene design	1749	*Tom Jones*, Henry Fielding (1707–54), England
The Mistress of the Inn, Carlo Goldoni (1707–93), Italy	1753	
	1755	*Dictionary*, Samuel Johnson (1709–1784), England
	1756	Seven Years' War (until 1763); loss to France of much of colonial empire
The Father of a Family, Diderot, bourgeois drama, France	1758	
		Joshua Reynolds (1723–92), English painter
("Boulevard" theaters built in Paris; growth of popular drama)	1762	*Social Contract* and *Emile*, Jean-Jacques Rousseau (1712–78), France
		Catherine the Great (r. 1762–96) expands Russian power
	1765	Watt's steam engine, England
Minna von Barnhelm, Gotthold Lessing (1729–81), Germany	1767	
Hamburg Dramaturgy, Lessing; first major German dramatic criticism		
She Stoops to Conquer, Oliver Goldsmith (1730–74), England	1773	Thomas Gainsborough (1734–1802), English painter

THEATRICAL		SOCIAL/POLITICAL/CULTURAL
	1775	American Revolution (until 1785)
("Storm and Stress" playwrights in Germany. Friedrich Schröder (1744–1818), major German actor)		
	1776	*Wealth of Nations,* Adam Smith (1723–90), England
The School for Scandal, Richard Brinsley Sheridan (1751–1816), England	1777	(Rise of English colonial power; Industrial Revolution)
	1781	*Critique of Pure Reason,* Immanuel Kant (1724–1804), Germany
The Marriage of Figaro, Beaumarchais (1732–99), France	1783	
(Impulse toward national theater and drama grows in Europe. Beginnings of German Romanticism)	1787	*Don Giovanni,* Wolfgang Amadeus Mozart (1756–1791), Germany
	1789	French Revolution (until 1797)
(Attempts made at greater realism in costumes and scenery)	1793	Painting, *Death of Marat,* Jacques Louis David (1748–1825), France
	1799	Consulate of Napoleon
Mary Stuart, Friedrich Schiller (1759–1805), Germany	1800	

19TH CENTURY

THEATRICAL		SOCIAL/POLITICAL/CULTURAL
	1803	The Louisiana Purchase
Talma (1763–1823), foremost French actor	1804	Napoleon I becomes Emperor of the French
	1807	*Fifth Symphony* of Ludwig van Beethoven (1770–1827), Germany
Faust, Part I, Johann Wolfgang Goethe (1749–1832), Germany	1808	
Pixérécourt (1773–1844), rise of French melodrama	1810	Mme. de Staël (1766–1817); German Romanticism brought to France

THEATRICAL		SOCIAL/POLITICAL/CULTURAL
The Broken Jug, Heinrich von Kleist (1777–1811), Germany	1811	
	1815	Battle of Waterloo The "Metternich System" imposes strict censorship and impedes growth of liberalism in Germany
The Cenci, Percy Bysshe Shelley (1792–1822), England	1819	
Gas lighting introduced	1822	Eugene Delacroix (1798–1863), painter, France
Charles Kemble's (1775–1854) production of *King John* in England; historical accuracy in costumes and sets	1823	The Monroe Doctrine
Boris Gudonov, Alexander Pushkin (1799–1837), Russia	1825	Decemberist Rising in Russia
	1829	Andrew Jackson, President of United States (until 1837)
Edmund Kean (1787–1833), romantic acting in England		
Hernani, Victor Hugo (1802–85), "Romantic" rebellion against neoclassicism in France	1830	In France, Revolution establishes "July Monarchy" of Louis Philippe (r. 1830–48; *The Red and the Black*, Stendhal (1783–1842); August Comte founds Positivism
Lorenzaccio, Alfred de Musset (1810–57), France	1834	
The Inspector General, Nikolai Gogol (1809–52), Russia; *Woyzeck*, Georg Büchner (1813–37), Germany	1836	
	1837	Victoria of England (r. 1837–1901)
William Charles Macready (1793–1873), reforms in English acting and staging		
	1838	*Oliver Twist*, Charles Dickens (1813–1870), England
	1839	Chartist agitation in England to improve condition of working classes

THEATRICAL		SOCIAL/POLITICAL/CULTURAL
The Glass of Water, Eugene Scribe (1791–1861); well-made plays, France	1840	
Theater Regulation Act abolishes monopoly of patent theaters in London	1843	
Maria Magdalena, Friedrich Hebbel (1813–63), Germany	1844	
	1848	Italian War of Independence in France (until 1849) Revolution in Germany and Austria (until 1849)
A Month in the Country, Ivan Turgenev (1818–83), Russia	1850	
	1851	*Moby Dick*, Herman Melville (1819–91), United States *Rigoletto*, Giuseppe Verdi (1813–1901), Italy
Camille, Alexandre Dumas fils (1824–95); "thesis" plays, France First production of *Uncle Tom's Cabin*, most popular American play of century; use of touring companies	1852	The Second French Empire, Napoleon III (r. 1852–70)
	1853	Crimean War (until 1856)
	1857	*Les Fleurs du Mal*, Charles Baudelaire (1821–1867); *Madame Bovary*, Gustave Flaubert (1821–80), France
The Thunderstorm, Alexander Ostrovsky (1823–86), Russia	1859	*Tristan und Isolde*, Richard Wagner (1813–83), Germany. *Origin of Species*, Charles Darwin (1809–1882); *Idylls of the King* (1st vol.), Alfred Lord Tennyson (1809–92); first oil well
M. Perrichon's Journey, Eugene Labiche (1815–88), France	1860	
	1861	American Civil War (until 1865) Liberation of the serfs in Russia
	1862	Bismarck becomes minister-president of Prussia

THEATRICAL		SOCIAL/POLITICAL/CULTURAL
Edwin Booth (1833–93) plays *Hamlet* for 100 nights in London; long "runs" become common	1864	
Georg II, Duke of Saxe-Meiningen (1826–1914) begins reforms in staging; beginning of modern director, Germany	1866	*Crime and Punishment*, Fyodor Dostoevsky (1821–81), Russia
	1867	*Das Capital,* Karl Marx (1818–83), Germany
	1869	*War and Peace,* Leo Tolstoy (1828–1910), Russia
	1870	Franco-Prussian War (1870–71); Paris Commune; Third Republic established; unification of Italy complete
	1871	German Empire founded
Therese Raquin, Emile Zola (1840–1902); naturalism in drama, France	1873	
Paris Opera built, epitome of 19th-century theater architecture	1874	French Impressionist painters
Wagner's Bayreuth theater, innovations in theater architecture, Germany	1876	*Tom Sawyer*, Mark Twain (1835–1910); telephone patented
H.M.S. Pinafore, W. S. Gilbert (1836–1911) and Arthur Sullivan (1842–1900), England	1877	
A Doll's House, Henrik Ibsen (1828–1906), Norway	1879	Invention of the incandescent lamp
The Vultures, Henry Becque (1837–99), France	1885	
Henry Irving (1838–1905), first English actor to be knighted, established role of the director in commercial theater		
The Power of Darkness, Leo Tolstoy, Russia	1886	
French actress Sarah Bernhardt (1845–1923), most famous of the "stars" of the century		

THEATRICAL		SOCIAL/POLITICAL/CULTURAL
Antoine's "Theatre Libre" founded in Paris; electricity replaces gas in theater lighting	1887	
The Father, August Strindberg (1849–1912), Sweden	1888	William II (r. 1888–1918), Emperor of Germany
Freie Bühne Theater, formed in Germany	1889	
Independent Theater of London	1891	
The Second Mrs. Tanqueray, Arthur Wing Pinero (1855–1934), England	1893	
	1894	Dreyfus Affair in France (until 1906)
The Importance of Being Earnest, Oscar Wilde (1856–1900), England	1895	
The Sea Gull, Anton Chekhov (1860–1904), Russia	1896	
Ubu Roi, Alfred Jarry (1873–1907), precursor of Absurdism, France		
Moscow Art Theater founded	1898	

20TH CENTURY

THEATRICAL		SOCIAL/POLITICAL/CULTURAL
	1900	*Freud's Interpretation of Dreams*, Austria
Riders to the Sea, John Millington Synge (1871–1909), Ireland	1901	Theodore Roosevelt (until 1909), Open Door policy
The Art of the Theater, Gordon Craig (1872–1966); *Major Barbara*, Bernard Shaw (1856–1950), England	1905	Einstein's theory of relativity; insurrection in Russia. Separation of Church and State in France
	1907	*Les Demoiselles d'Avignon*, Pablo Picasso (1881–1973), cubist painting
Adolphe Appia (1862–1928), pioneer in nonillusionistic scene design		Marcel Proust (1871–1922)

THEATRICAL		SOCIAL/POLITICAL/CULTURAL
Justice, by John Galsworthy (1867–1933), England	1910	
Theater du Vieux Columbier (1879–1949), France	1913	*Sacre du Printemps*, Igor Stravinsky (1882–1971), Russia, United States
	1914	First World War (until 1918)
Provincetown Players organized, United States	1915	
	1916	Easter Rebellion in Ireland
	1917	United States enters war; Bolshevik Revolution in Russia
Theatre Guild founded, United States	1918	Spengler's *Decline of the West* predicts fall of Western civilization, Germany
	1919	Eighteenth Amendment begins Prohibition (until 1933), United States
	1920	Nineteenth Amendment extends suffrage to women, United States
Man and the Masses, Ernst Toller (1893–1939), German Expressionism	1921	Irish Free State founded
Six Characters in Search of an Author, Luigi Pirandello (1867–1936), Italy.		
The Circle, Somerset Maugham (1874–1965), England		
	1922	*Ulysses*, James Joyce (1882–1941). Mussolini's Fascists take power in Italy
Vahktangov (1883–1922), Evreinov (1879–53), Tairov (1885–1950), Meyerhold (1874–1942): period of postrevolutionary creativity and innovation in Russia (until 1927)		
	1923	Hitler's "Beer-hall Putsch" in Munich
My Life in Art, Constantin Stanislavski (1863–1938), revolution in acting, Russia	1924	*The Trial*, Franz Kafka (1883–1924); Czechoslovakia; death of Lenin, Russia
First Surrealist Manifesto, André Breton (1896–1966), France		

Desire Under the Elms, Eugene
O'Neill (1888–1953), United
States; *Juno and the Paycock,* Sean
O'Casey (1884–1964), Ireland

	1925	*The Dehumanization of Art,* José Ortega y Gasset (1883–1955), Spain
		The Magic Mountain, Thomas Mann (1875–1955), Germany
Meyerhold's production of *The Inspector General,* "constructivist" staging, Russia	1926	Arnold Schönberg (1874–1951), "twelve-tone" music, Austria
The Three-Penny Opera, Bertolt Brecht (1898–1956) "epic theater," Germany	1928	
	1929	*Look Homeward Angel,* Thomas Wolfe (1900–1938); *The Sound and the Fury,* William Faulkner (1897–1962); Stock Market crash
Max Reinhardt (1873–1943), foremost director in Europe		
Private Lives, Noel Coward (1899–1973), England	1930	
Group Theater (until 1941); brought Stanislavski methods to America	1931	Collapse of Spanish monarchy
	1933	New Deal legislation begins Nazis take power in Germany
Brecht and other writers and artists leave Germany		
"Socialist Realism" declared official Soviet style	1934	
The Infernal Machine, Jean Cocteau (1892–1963), France		
Tiger at the Gates, Jean Giraudoux (1882–1944), France; *House of Bernarda Alba,* Federico Garcia Lorca (1899–1936), Spain	1935	Italy attacks Ethiopia
		Nuremberg laws deprive Jews of German citizenship; purges in Russia
Federal Theater Project (until 1939) *Waiting for Lefty,* Clifford Odets (1906–1963), United States; *Murder in the Cathedral,* T. S. Eliot (1888–1965), England		
	1936	Spanish Civil War (until 1939)
Tyrone Guthrie (1900–1970), director of Old Vic, England	1937	

THEATRICAL		SOCIAL/POLITICAL/CULTURAL
The Theater and Its Double, Antonin Artaud (1896–1948), France	1938	
	1939	Second World War (until 1945)
	1941	*For Whom the Bell Tolls,* Ernest Hemingway (1898–1961)
Antigone, Jean Anouilh (1910–) France	1943	*The Myth of Sisyphus,* Albert Camus (1913–60), France
No Exit, Jean-Paul Sartre (1905–) France	1944	Liberation of France
Compagnie Madeline Renaud-Jean-Louis Barrault, founded in France	1946	
The Maids, Jean Genet (1910–) France	1947	
A Streetcar Named Desire, Tennessee Williams (1911–); Actors' Studio founded, United States		
The Bald Soprano, Eugene Ionesco (1912–), France	1949	Creation of East and West Germany
Brecht opens Berliner Ensemble in East Berlin		*1984,* George Orwell (1903–1950)
Death of a Salesman, Arthur Miller (1916–), United States		
	1950	Korean War (until 1953)
The Queen and the Rebels, Ugo Betti (1892–1953), Italy; Jean Vilar (1912–1971) made director of Théâtre National Populaire	1951	
Waiting for Godot, Samuel Beckett (1906–), France	1953	Death of Stalin
	1954	"McCarthy-Army" Hearings
Separate Tables, Terence Rattigan (1911–), England	1955	
Look Back in Anger, John Osborne (1929–), England	1956	Russia crushes Hungarian revolt; Krushchev denounces Stalin
The Visit, Friedrich Dürrenmatt (1921–), Switzerland		
	1957	Sputnik I, first man-made earth satellite
Biedermann and The Firebugs, Max Frisch (1911–), Switzer-	1958	Fifth Republic of France

THEATRICAL	SOCIAL/POLITICAL/CULTURAL

land; *The Birthday Party*, Harold
Pinter (1930–   ), England

Marat/Sade, Peter Weiss (1916–); Polish Theater Laboratory founded by Jerzy Grotowski (1933–)	1959	
The Zoo Story, (American premiere), Edward Albee (1928–), United States	1960	
	1961	Berlin Wall
Cafe LaMama opened, off-off-Broadway theater	1962	Cuban Missile Crisis
National Theater established (England's first state-subsidized theater)	1963	
	1964	Resignation of Khrushchev
Tango, Slawomir Mrozek (1930–), Poland	1965	
Ceremonies in Dark Old Men, Lonne Elder III (1931–), United States	1969	

The preceding historical survey follows the development of theater in Western civilization but another important theater, The Oriental Theater, was evolving along a path of its own. The following section traces Oriental Theater in India, China and Japan. Theater emerged also in such places as Cambodia and Indonesia.

THE ORIENT

THEATRICAL	SOCIAL/POLITICAL/CULTURAL

INDIA

Natyasastra, principal critical work on Sanscrit drama	ca. 50/ 100	
	ca. 320	Gupta dynasty reunites Northern India after 500 years division; golden age of classical Sanscrit
Sanscrit drama highly developed *The Little Clay Cart*		

THEATRICAL		SOCIAL/POLITICAL/CULTURAL
Shakuntala, Kalidasa, best known Sanscrit playwright	ca. 400	
	ca. 600	Earliest known use of the zero and decimal
Bhavabhuti, highest ranked playwright after Kalidasa	ca. 730	
Decline of Sanscrit drama	ca. 1150	
Indian dance drama, puppet and folk plays	ca. 1192	Beginning of Muslim rule
	1526	Mogul Empire (until 1761)
	1790	British power established in India
King of the Dark Chamber, Rabindrath Tagore (1861–1941)	1914	

CHINA

	618	T'ang dynasty founded (until 907)
Academy of the Pear Orchard, school for dancers and singers established by Ming Huang	712	Emperor Ming Huang (r. 712–56), brief flourishing of arts and literature
	ca. 850	Advent of block printing
Development of "Northern" and "Southern" schools of drama during Sung dynasty	960	Sung dynasty (until 1279), flowering of arts, literature, and scholarship
Scholars and artists move south during Yüan dynasty, but a vigorous popular drama flourishes in the North	1260	Yüan dynasty, China ruled by Mongol Khans until 1368
Southern drama becomes predominant during Ming dynasty and develops highly literary and romantic drama	1368	Ming dynasty, Mongol rulers expelled
	1644	Ch'ing dynasty, Manchurian rulers (until 1912)
Gradual decline of Southern drama; Peking eventually		

replaces Soochow as cultural capital		
	1839	Beginning of "opium" wars
"Peking opera," a less literary and more theatrical form becomes dominant	ca. 1875 1900	Boxer Rebellion

JAPAN

	645	Beginning of great period of cultural infusion and cultural growth (until ca. 800)
Development of traditional dance forms		
	ca. 1020	*The Tale of Genji*, classic Japanese novel, by Murasaki Shikibu
	ca. 1100	Civil strife encourages the rise of military government and feudalism
Zeami Motokiyo (1363–1444), development of the Noh drama	1395	Rule of Yoshimitsu (r. 1395–1408), stable period of artistic and literary creativity, but followed by civil wars
	ca. 1542	First Europeans to visit Japan
	1568	Period of national unification (until 1600)
First appearance of Kabuki, a more popular and theatrical form than Noh	ca. 1600 1640	Friction with foreigners and religious disputes leading to cultural and political isolation
Noh drama becomes associated with the aristocracy and its conventions are rigidly standardized	ca. 1650	
Japanese doll theater established in Osaka (Bunraku)	1685	
Chikamatsu Monzaemon (1653–1724), Japan's most famous playwright, wrote for the Bunraku and the Kabuki	ca. 1800	
Kabuki becomes the most popular form	ca. 1853	Japan open to the West, beginning of continuing occidental influence

SELECT BIBLIOGRAPHY

Aristotle, *Aristotle's Theory of Poetry and Fine Art.* Critical Text and Translation by S. H. Butcher. (4th ed.) New York: Dover Publications, Inc., 1951.

Artaud, Antonin. *The Theater and Its Double.* Tr. by Mary C. Richards. New York: Grove Press, 1958.

Beckerman, Bernard. *Dynamics of Drama: Theory and Method of Analysis.* New York: Alfred A. Knopf, Inc., 1970.

Bentley, Eric. *The Life of the Drama.* New York: Atheneum Press, 1964.

Brecht, Bertolt. *Brecht on Theatre.* Tr. by John Willett. New York: Hill and Wang, 1965.

Brockett, Oscar G. *History of the Theatre.* (2d ed.) Boston: Allyn & Bacon, Inc., 1974.

Brockett, Oscar G. and Findlay, Robert R. *Century of Innovation: A History of European and American Theatre and Drama Since 1870.* Englewood Cliffs, N.J.: Prentice-Hall, Inc., 1973.

Brook, Peter. *The Empty Space.* New York: Atheneum, 1968.

Clark, Barrett H. (ed.). *European Theories of the Drama.* Newly revised by Henry Popkin. New York: Crown Publishers, Inc., 1965.

Corrigan, Robert (ed.). *Comedy: Meaning and Form.* San Francisco: Chandler Publishing Company, 1965.

Corrigan, Robert (ed.). *Tragedy: Vision and Form.* San Francisco: Chandler Publishing Company, 1965.

Esslin, Martin. *The Theatre of the Absurd.* (Rev. ed.) Garden City, N.Y.: Doubleday & Company, Inc., 1969.

Fergusson, Francis. *The Idea of a Theater.* Princeton, N.J.: Princeton University Press, 1949.

Gassner, John. *Masters of the Drama.* (3d ed.) New York: Dover Publications, Inc., 1954.

Gassner, John and Allen, Ralph (eds.). *Theatre and Drama in the Making.* 2 vols. Boston: Houghton Mifflin Company, 1964.

Grotowski, Jerzy. *Towards a Poor Theatre.* New York: Simon and Schuster, 1968.

Jones, Robert E. *The Dramatic Imagination.* New York: Meredith Publishing Company, 1941.

Kerr, Walter. *Tragedy and Comedy.* New York: Simon and Schuster, 1967.

Kirby, Michael. *Happenings.* New York: E. P. Dutton & Co., Inc., 1965.

Mitchell, Loften. *Black Drama.* New York: Hawthorn Books, 1967.

Nagler, Alois M. *Sources of Theatrical History.* New York: Theatre Annual, Inc., 1952.

Novick, Julius. *Beyond Broadway.* New York: Hill and Wang, 1968.

Oenslager, Donald. *Scenery Then and Now.* New York: W. W. Norton & Company, 1936.

Roberts, Vera M. *On Stage: A History of the Theatre.* (2d ed.) New York: Harper & Row, 1974.

Schechner, Richard. *Environmental Theater.* New York: Hawthorn Books, Inc., 1973.

Schevill, James. *Breakout! In Search of New Theatrical Environments.* Chicago: The University of Chicago Press, 1972.

Stanislavski, Constantin. *An Actor Prepares.* Translated by Elizabeth Reynolds Hapgood. New York: Theatre Arts Books, 1936.

NOTES

INTRODUCTION

1 Robert Edmond Jones, *The Dramatic Imagination*, 1967 ed., Theatre Arts Books, New York, 1941, p. 40.

2 Bernard Beckerman, *Dynamics of Drama: Theory and Method of Analysis*, Alfred A. Knopf, Inc., New York, 1970, p. 129.

3 Ernest Hemingway, *A Farewell to Arms*, Charles Scribner's Sons, New York, 1949, p. 119.

CHAPTER ONE

1 Jerzy Grotowski, *Towards a Poor Theatre*, A Clarion Book, Simon and Schuster, New York, 1968, p. 19.

2 Jean-Claude Van Italie, *The Serpent: A Ceremony*, written in collaboration with The Open Theater, Atheneum, New York, 1969, p. ix.

3 Walter Kerr, "We Call It 'Live' Theater, But Is It?", *The New York Times*, January 2, 1972.

4 Gustave Le Bon, *The Crowd: A Study of the Popular Mind*, 20th ed., Ernest Benn Ltd., London, England, 1952, p. 23.

5 Ibid., p. 27

6 B. F. Skinner, *Science and Human Behavior*, The Macmillan Company, New York, 1953, p. 312.

7 Martin Esslin, *The Theatre of the Absurd*, Anchor Books, Doubleday and Company, Inc., Garden City, New York, 1961, pp. xv–xvii.

8 Bernard Beckerman, *Dynamics of Drama: Theory and Method of Analysis*, Alfred A. Knopf, Inc., New York, 1970, p. 9.

CHAPTER TWO

1 J. A. Hadfield, *Dreams and Nightmares*, Penguin Books, Inc., 1954 (new edition 1961), p. 8.

CHAPTER THREE

1 Notes on *King Lear* are from William Shakespeare, *King Lear*. Edited by G. K. Hunter, Penguin Books Ltd., Harmondsworth, Middlesex, England, 1972, pp. 243–244.

CHAPTER FOUR

1 Erving Goffman, *The Presentation of Self in Everyday Life*, Doubleday Anchor Books, Garden City, New York, 1949, p. 72.

2 Robert Ezra Park, *Race and Culture*, The Free Press, Glencoe, Illinois, 1950, p. 249.

3 From *Death of a Salesman* by Arthur Miller, Copyright 1949 by Arthur Miller. Reprinted by permission of The Viking Press, Inc., New York, 1968, pp. 100–103.

4 Theodore Shank, *The Art of Dramatic Art*, Dickenson Publishing Company, Inc., Belmont, California, 1969, p. 36.

CHAPTER FIVE

1 Richard Findlater, *The Player Kings*, Weidenfeld and Nicolson, London, England, 1971, p. 25.

2 Constantin Stanislavski, *An Actor Prepares*, Theatre Arts Books, New York, 1948, p. 73.

3 Constantin Stanislavski, *My Life in Art*, Meridian Books, New York, 1946, p. 465.

4 Harold Pinter, *The Homecoming*, Grove Press, Inc., New York, 1966, pp. 33–35.

5 Stanislavski, *An Actor Prepares*, p. 38.

6 Harold Clurman, *On Directing*, The Macmillan Company, New York, 1972, pp. 261 ff.
7 Walter Kerr, drama review, *The New York Herald Tribune*, January 10, 1961.
8 Jerzy Grotowski, *Towards a Poor Theatre*, A Clarion Book, Simon and Schuster, New York, 1968, p. 133.
9 Ibid, p. 147.

CHAPTER SIX

1 Michael Kirby, "The New Theatre," *TDR*, vol. 10, no. 2, Winter, 1965, New Orleans, La., p. 31.
2 John Gassner, editor, *A Treasury of the Theatre (From Henrik Ibsen to Arthur Miller)*, revised edition, distributed by Henry Holt and Company, published by Simon and Schuster, New York, ninth printing, 1959, p. 1103.
3 T. E. Kalem, *Time Magazine*, November 29, 1971.
4 From the book *Naked Masks: Five Plays* by Luigi Pirandello. Edited by Eric Bentley. Copyright, 1922, by E. P. Dutton & Co. Renewal copyright, 1950, by Stefano, Fausto and Lietta Pirandello. Reprinted by permission of the publishers, E. P. Dutton & Co., Inc., New York, 1957, pp. 266–267.

CHAPTER SEVEN

1 Alvin B. Kernan, *Character and Conflict: An Introduction to Drama*, 2d ed., Harcourt, Brace & World, Inc., New York, 1969, p. 286.
2 Kenneth MacGowan, *A Primer of Playwrighting*, Dolphin Books, Doubleday and Company, Inc., Garden City, New York, 1962, p. 62.

CHAPTER EIGHT

For the discussion on climactic and episodic drama the author is indebted to material from Bernard Beckerman, *Dynamics of Drama: Theory and Method of Analysis*, Alfred A. Knopf, Inc., New York, 1970.
1 Jean Anouilh, *Antigone*, in *Five Plays*, vol. I, Hill and Wang, Farrar, Straus & Giroux, Inc., New York, 1958, p. 23.
2 John Gassner, *A Treasury of the Theatre (From Henrik Ibsen to Arthur Miller)*, distributed by Henry Holt and Company, Inc., published by Simon and Schuster, New York, 1959, p. 457.
3 Albert Camus, *Le Mythe de Sisyphe*, Gallimard, Paris, France, 1942, p. 18.
4 Eugene Ionesco, *The Bald Soprano*, in *Four Plays*, Grove Press, Inc., New York, 1958, p. 39.
5 Samuel Beckett, *Waiting for Godot*, Grove Press, Inc., New York, 1954, p. 28b.
6 Michael Kirby, "The New Theatre," in *TDR* vol. 10, no. 2, p. 27, Tulane Drama Review, New Orleans, La., Winter, 1965.

7 John Cage, "An Interview," in *TDR*, vol. 10, no. 2, p. 55, Tulane Drama Review, New Orleans, La., Winter, 1965.

CHAPTER TEN
1 Friedrich Nietzsche, "The Birth of Tragedy," from *Works in Three Volumes*, Carl Hanser Publishers, Munich, Germany, vol. 1, p. 94.

CHAPTER TWELVE
1 The Performance Group, *Dionysus in 69*, The Noonday Press, Farrar, Straus and Giroux, Inc., New York (no pagination).
2 Arthur Waley, *The Nō Plays of Japan*, Grove Press, Inc., New York (no date), pp. 10–11.
3 Antonin Artaud, *The Theater and Its Double*, Grove Press, Inc., New York, 1958, pp. 96–97.

CHAPTER THIRTEEN
1 Robert Edmond Jones, *The Dramatic Imagination*. Theatre Arts Books, New York, 1941 (eighth printing 1967), p. 25.
2 Ibid., pp. 23–24.
3 Reprinted from *The Dramatic Imagination*. Copyright 1941 by Robert Edmond Jones, with the permission of the publishers, Theatre Arts Books, New York, 1967, pp. 71–72.

INDEX

Abraham and Isaac, 28
Absurdist theater (*see* Theater of the Absurd)
Acting:
  dramatic characters, 87–101, 168
    with dominant trait, 93
    extraordinary, 88–90
    human concerns and, 97–100
    as images of ourselves, 100–101
    juxtaposition of, 95–97
    major, 96, 262
    minor, 96, 262
    nonhuman parts, 93–95
    orchestration of, 96–97
    prototypical, 90–92
    realistic and nonrealistic contrasted,
      154
    stock, 92–94
    variety of, 65
  in everyday life, 56–65
    distinguished from stage acting, 61–65

Acting:
  in everyday life: illustrated in drama,
    58–60
    imitation, 56
    recent studies, 58
    role playing, 57–60
  nature of, 61–65
  techniques and styles of, 67–85
    actor-audience contact, 83–84
    believability, 67–69
    emotional recall, 75–76
    inner truth, 75
    judgment of, 84
    through line of role, 76
    New Theater and, 82–83
    physical movement, 78–82
    realism, 70–76, 154, 157
    special demands of stage, 76–82
    specifics, 72–75
    Stanislavski, 70–76, 151, 173

Acting:
  techniques and styles of:
    vocal projection, 77–78
Actor(s):
  -audience relationship, 13–15, 83–84, 300, 309
  as basic element of theater, 12–13
  casting, 284–285
  direction of, 286–288
  judging, 300
  scene design and, 234, 248
  separation from audience, 19–22
  (*See also* Acting)
Actors Workshop of San Francisco, 25
Adamov, Arthur, 195
Adding Machine, The (Rice), 26, 159, 239, 240, 323
Aeschylus, 116, 124, 172, 217, 280
After the Fall (A. Miller), 285
Age of Enlightenment, 162
Albee, Edward, 91, 115, 133–134, 195, 328
Alchemist, The (Jonson), 93
All My Sons (A. Miller), 89–90
Allegory, 158–159, 321
All's Well That Ends Well (Shakespeare), 192
Amédée (Ionesco), 28
American Dream, The (Albee), 133–134
American Hurrah (van Itallie), 155, 273
Anastasia (Maurette), 287
And They Put Handcuffs on the Flowers (Arrabal), 205
Androcles and the Lion (Shaw), 152
Annals, Michael, 241
Anouilh, Jean, 46–47, 88, 123, 187
Antagonist, 95
Antigone (Anouilh), 46–47, 123, 294, 295
Antigone (Sophocles), 46–47, 95, 97
Antony and Cleopatra (Shakespeare), 86, 87, 124, 273
Apache Indians, 214, 215
Appia, Adolphe, 250–251
Area lights, 252
Arena stage, 212–216, 308
  disadvantages of, 215–216
  economics of, 213–214
  history of, 214–215
  intimacy of, 213
  light sources, 253
  structure of, 212–213
Arena Stage, Washington, D.C., 214, 216
Aristophanes, 25, 28, 93–94, 163, 183–184, 186, 237
Aristophanic comedy, 186, 322
Arms and the Man (Shaw), 186, 327
Armstrong, Will Steven, 211
Aronson, Boris, 239, 241
Arrabal, Fernando, 195, 205
Arsenic and Old Lace (Kesselring), 185
Artaud, Antonin, 222–224, 327–328

Audience:
  director and, 286–287
  imagination of, 25–37
    creation of illusion, 26–29, 63, 65, 246–247
    metaphor, function of, 30
    "reality" of, 31–32
    separation of stage reality from fact, 32–34
    symbols, function of, 29–30
    theater as metaphor, 34, 36
  imperfections in production and, 297–298
  integration of elements and, 298–302
  judgment of actors by, 300
  perspective of, 39–51
    background information on plays or playwrights, 45–46
    background of spectators, 46–47
    link between theater and society, 40–45
    preconceptions, 47–48
    variety in modern theater, 47–50
  role of, 11–23
    as basic element of theater, 11–12
    as group experience, 15–19
    makeup of, 18–19
    participatory theater and, 20–21
    relationship with actors, 13–15, 83–84, 300, 309
    separation from actors, 19–22
    at tryouts, 289–290
Auditions, 285
Avant-garde plays, 79–81, 321–322
Awake and Sing (Odets), 71

Bacchae, The (Euripides), 205
Back lighting, 253
Balcony, The (Genet), 263, 264
Bald Soprano, The (Ionesco), 133, 134, 185, 186
Bankhead, Tallulah, 179
Barrault, Jean-Louis, 328
Beckerman, Bernard, 2, 19–20, 22
Beckett (Anouilh), 88
Beckett, Samuel, 18–19, 80–81, 97, 106–107, 132–133, 135, 136, 140, 194–195, 328, 329
Bedroom farce, 190
Belasco, David, 237
Bel Geddes, Norman, 251, 326
Believability of dramatic characters, 67–69
  (*See also* Realistic theater, acting)
Betterton, Thomas, 281
Bibiena, Carlo, 209
Bibiena, Ferdinando, 209
Bibiena, Giuseppe Galli, 210
Birds, The (Aristophanes), 24, 25, 28, 93, 186
Birth of Tragedy (Nietzsche), 173
Birthday Party, The (Pinter), 134
Black theater movement, 50
Blackouts, 251, 254

Blacks, The (Genet), 1, 20, 272
Blocking, 286
Blood Wedding (Lorca), 236
Body Language (Fast), 58
Bolshoi Theater, St. Petersburg, 208
Border lights, 252
Bourgeois drama, 179–180, 322
Boxes, 208
Boy Friend, The (musical), 190
Boys from Syracuse, The (musical), 188–189
Brand (Ibsen), 116, 128
Brando, Marlon, 104, 105
Brecht, Bertolt, 46, 62, 73, 89, 90, 111–112, 119,
    124–128, 130, 247, 322–323
Broadway theaters, 47, 48, 204–208, 210–211
Brook, Peter, 149, 225, 239, 328
Büchner, Georg, 128
Bullins, Ed, 33
Burg Theater, Vienna, 209
Burlesque, 185, 190–191, 322
Business aspects, 291–292

Cabaret theater, 50
Caesar and Cleopatra (Shaw), 262
Cage, John, 137
Calderón de la Barca, Pedro, 128, 175
Camus, Albert, 132, 194
Candide (musical), 14
Čapek, Josef, 94
Čapek, Karel, 94
Carousel (musical), 27
Casting, 284–285
Cat on a Hot Tin Roof (Williams), 99, 121
Catholic Church, 12–13
Caucasian Chalk Circle, The (Brecht), 62, 118,
    119, 124, 126, 127, 130
Central image:
  directors and, 284
  in lighting, 251
  in scene design, 241–242
Century of Progress, 162
Chagall, Marc, 235
Chairs, The (Ionesco), 134
Chambers Street Theater, New York, 209
Changing Room, The (Storey), 139
Character, comedy of, 187–188
Characters (*see* Dramatic characters)
Charley's Aunt (Thomas), 28, 308
Chekhov, Anton, 70, 76, 96–98, 114–116, 129,
    155, 157, 193–194, 322, 324
Chekhov, Michael, 74
Cherokee Reservation, North Carolina, 18
Cherry Orchard, The (Chekhov), 114, 116, 129,
    155, 193
Chinese theater:
  basic stage of, 221

Chinese theater:
  heroic dramas, 175
  historical outline, 349–350
  makeup, use of, 271
  physical movement, 81–82
  symbolic scenery in, 238–239
Chorus:
  in Greek theater, 12
  in musical theater, 81
Cid, The (Corneille), 88, 175
Circle theater (*see* Arena stage)
City Center Repertory Company, New York,
    188
City Dionysia, 112
Claptrap, 68–69
Climactic plot, 119–124
  characteristics of, 120–124
  combined with episodic plot, 129
  compared with episodic plot, 128–129
Clouds, The (Aristophanes), 28, 186
Clurman, Harold, 31, 76
Coleridge, Samuel Taylor, 34
Color:
  in costume design, 268, 270
  in lighting design, 253–254
Comedies of Menace, 195
Comedy, 159–160, 163–164, 183–191, 322
  Aristophanic, 186, 322
  burlesque, 185, 190–191, 322
  of character, 187–188
  comic premises, 186
  commedia dell'arte, 92–94, 188, 322
  contrast between social order and individual,
    184–185
  costumes and, 274, 300
  farce, 28, 163, 189–190, 235–236, 323
  Greek theater, 40, 112
  of ideas, 191
  integration of elements in, 300
  lighting and, 256, 300
  of manners, 187, 191, 322
  plot complications, 188–190
  Restoration, 187, 263, 280–281, 283, 322,
    327
  satire, 191, 236, 327
  scene design and, 235–236, 256
  slapstick, 185
  suspension of natural laws, 185
  tragicomedy, 191–196, 322, 328–329
  verbal humor, 187
Comedy of Errors, The (Shakespeare), 188–189
Comic point of view (*see* Comedy)
Comic premise, 186
Commedia dell'arte, 92–94, 188, 322
Commune (Performance Group), 223
Company (musical), 239
Computerized lighting cues, 254–255
Concept of director, 234, 239, 282–284

Conflict, plot and, 106–110, 113–115, 131–132
  (*See also* Serious drama)
Congreve, William, 93, 97, 187, 191, 281
Conklin, John, 291
Constant Prince, The (Polish Laboratory Theater), 224
Contemporary theater (*see* Modern theater)
Continuity in roles, 76
Contractor, The (Storey), 139
Cool lighting, 254
Corneille, Pierre, 88, 124, 125
Corrales, 219
Costume designer (*see* Costumes)
Costumes, 1, 259–270
  comedy and, 274, 300
  consistent viewpoint, 264–266
  in everyday life, 260–261
  exaggerated, 263, 264
  information provided by, 261–263
  integration with other elements, 272–273
  practical requirements, 266
  producer or manager and, 292
  realistic and nonrealistic contrasted, 155
  resources of designer, 268–270
  role of designer, 266–270
  sketches, 265–268
  symbolic, 260–261, 263
Counterpoint, 130
Country Wife, The (Wycherly), 187
Covent Garden Theatre, London, 208
Coward, Noel, 191
Craig, Gordon, 251, 326
Created or found space, 221–228, 308
  adaptation of space to fit production, 224–225
  Artaud and, 222–224
  historical precedents, 227–228
  multifocus environments, 226–227, 243, 308
  nontheater buildings, 224
  outdoor settings, 225, 227–228
  scene designer and, 242–243
  street theater, 49, 225–226, 228, 327
Creative dramatics, 20
Credibility of characters, 67–69
  (*See also* Realistic theater, acting)
Crew, 289
Cross fades, 251, 254
Crucible, The (A.Miller), 106, 159, 321
Cues, lighting, 254–255
Culture, link between theater and, 40–45
Cutouts, 247
Cycle plays, 112, 141–142, 215, 324–325
Cyrano de Bergerac (Rostand), 116, 129, 176

Dali, Salvador, 235
Dance, 99–100
  actor training in, 81

David (Michelangelo), 2, 3
Days of Absence (Ward), 271–272
Death of a Salesman (A. Miller), 58–60, 92, 129, 159, 172, 241–242
Deputy, The (Hochhuth), 328
Designers, 288–289, 292
  (*See also* Costumes; Lighting; Scene design)
Desperate Hours, The (Hayes), 177, 178
Details, importance in acting, 72–76
Dewhurst, Colleen, 54, 55
Dexter, John, 305, 306
Dialectic, 130
Dialogue, 108
Dimmer, 250
Dinner theater, 50
Dionysus in 69, 139, 205–206, 222
Director, 168, 197, 279–290
  audience's point of view and, 286–287
  casting by, 284–285
  central image or metaphor and, 284
  concept of production and, 234, 239, 282–284
  designers and, 239, 243, 288–289
  historical perspective, 280–281
  pace of play and, 287–288
  playwright and, 282, 296
  power of, 290
  in rehearsals, 286–287, 289
  responsibility of, 290
  rhythm of play and, 251, 287–288
  tryouts and, 289–290
Dithyrambs, 12
Doctor Faustus (Marlowe), 77, 89
Doctor in Spite of Himself, The (Molière), 187
Doll's House, A (Ibsen), 90–91, 112, 154
Domestic drama, 179–180, 322
Doubling, 61–62, 64
Down lighting, 253
Downstage, 245, 246
Dramatic characters, 87–101, 168
  with dominant trait, 93
  extraordinary, 88–90
  human concerns and, 97–100
  as images of ourselves, 100–101
  juxtaposition of, 95–97
  major, 96, 262
  minor, 96, 262
  nonhuman parts, 93–95
  orchestration of, 96–97
  permanence of, 100
  prototypical, 90–92
  realistic and nonrealistic contrasted, 154
  stock, 92–94
  variety of, 65
Dramatic script (*see* Script)
Dramatic structure, 104–105
  conventions, 106–110
    equal contest, 114–115

Dramatic structure:
  conventions: part of total experience, 300
    prize or goal, 115–116
    space limit, 111–112
    strongly opposing forces, 113–114
    time limit, 112
  lighting and, 255–256
  nonsense and nonsequitur, 132–138
    in New Theater, 136–138
    in Theater of the Absurd, 132–136
  patterns, 140
  plot: aspects of, 106–110
    climactic, 119–124, 128–129
    combination of forms, 129
    comparison of forms, 128–129
    development, 116–117
    distinguished from story, 107–108
    dramatic devices used with, 130–132
    episodic, 119, 124–129
    obstacles and complications, 109–110
    opening scene, importance of, 108–109
  problems of, 143–144
  realistic and nonrealistic contrasted, 154
  ritual, 138–139
  scene design and, 255–256
  series of events, 140–142
  significance of, 142–144
Dream Play, A (Strindberg), 154, 254–255
Drottningholm Theater, Stockholm, 208
Drury Lane Theatre, London, 208
Duchess of Malfi, The (Webster), 89, 177
Dürrenmatt, Friedrich, 196, 329
Dutchman (Jones), 5

Egmont (Goethe), 176
Egyptian theater, 331
Eldridge, Florence, 174
Electra (Euripides), 116
Electra (Sophocles), 95, 116–117, 155, 175, 239, 241
Eliot, T. S., 88
Elizabethan theater, 324
  culture and, 41–42
  nonrealism in, 151, 153
  vocal demands, 77
Emotional recall, 75–76
Emperor Jones (O'Neill), 89
English theater:
  acting styles, 69
  comedy of manners, 187, 191, 322
  directors, 280–281
  heroic drama, 175
  historical outline, 335–348
  Jacobean drama, 177
  melodrama, 177

English theater:
  Restoration drama, 187, 263, 280–281, 283, 322, 326–327
  stock characters, 93
  thrust stages, 219–220
  (See also Elizabethan theater)
Environment *(see* Stage spaces)
Environmental theater, 322
Epic theater, 323
Episodic plot, 119, 124–129
  characteristics of, 124–128
  combined with climactic plot, 129
  compared with climactic plot, 128–129
Equus (P. Shaffer), 304–306
Esslin, Martin, 132, 134, 328
Euripides, 116, 124, 163, 167, 172, 178, 205
Every Man in His Humour (Jonson), 93
Every Man out of His Humour (Jonson), 93
Everyman, 94, 97, 159, 325
Everyman Players, 271
Exaggeration:
  in acting, 68–69
  in costume design, 263, 264
  in melodrama, 176–179
  in scene design, 235–236
  (See also Comedy)
Existentialism, 135–136, 323
Exit the King (Ionesco), 253
Exposition, 120
Expressionism, 158, 159, 239, 240, 323
Extraordinary characters, 88–90

Fabric, costume, 270
Fact, separation of stage reality from, 32–34
Familial relationships, plot and, 114–115
Fantasticks, The (musical), 228
Fantasy, 25
  distinguished from reality, 32–34
  realistic acting and, 75
  (See also Nonrealistic theater)
Farce, 28, 163, 189–190, 235–236, 323
Farewell to Arms, A (Hemingway), 3–4
Faust (Goethe), 89
Feydeau, George, 189, 190
Films:
  distinguished from theater, 13–16, 55, 99
  point of view in, 150
Firth, Peter, 306, 307
Flashbacks, 27–28, 248
Flats, 246–247
Flea in Her Ear, A (Feydeau), 190
Floodlights, 252
Fly, 209, 247
Fly loft, 209, 247
Focus in lighting, 252
Folk plays, 325

Follow spot, 252
Footlights, 252–253
Fortune Theatre, London, 219, 220
Found space (*see* Created or found space)
Fourposter, The (De Hartog), 270
Fourth wall (*see* Proscenium stage)
French theater, 48, 78, 111, 119, 121, 176, 187, 337–341, 343–347
Freud, Sigmund, 31
Frogs, The (Aristophanes), 93–94, 237
Front of the house, 292
Funny Girl (musical), 13

Games People Play (Berne), 58
Garrick, David, 69, 281
Gassner, John, 97, 125, 128
Gel, 250
Genet, Jean, 1, 62, 128, 195, 263, 264
Genre:
   defined, 168
   problem of, 163–164
   significance of, 196–197
   (*See also* Comedy; Serious drama)
Ghosts (Ibsen), 120, 122, 128, 155
Gillette, A. S., 237
Giraudoux, Jean, 186, 187
Glass Menagerie, The (Williams), 66, 67, 72–73, 75, 155, 159
Globe Theatre, London, 219, 220
Godspell (musical), 13, 254
Goethe, Johann Wolfgang, 89, 124, 127, 128, 176
Goetz von Berlichingen (Goethe), 124, 127, 176
Goffman, Erving, 56
Goldsmith, Oliver, 187, 191
Good Woman of Setzuan, The (Brecht), 247
Gorki, Maxim, 180
Grass, Gunter, 195
Great God Brown, The (O'Neill), 273
Great White Hope, The (Sackler), 216
Greek theater:
   arena stages, 214–215, 227–228
   beginnings of, 12
   comedies, 40, 112
   culture and, 40–41
   directors, 280
   doubling of characters, 61–62
   heroic drama, 175
   historical outline, 332
   human concerns in, 98
   juxtaposition of characters, 95
   juxtaposition of chorus to main action, 130
   masks, use of, 63, 272
   nonhuman parts, 93–94
   nonrealistic techniques, 158
   thrust stages, 217–218

Greek theater:
   tragedies, 40–41, 112, 116–117, 160–161, 169–172
   vocal demands, 77
   (*See also* Aeschylus; Euripides; Sophocles)
Grotowski, Jerzy, 11–12, 20, 42, 83, 221–222, 224–225, 310, 325, 328
Ground plan, 243, 245
Group behavior, 16–19
Group improvisations, 20
Guerilla theater, 225
Guthrie, Tyrone, 283
Guys and Dolls (musical), 26, 27
Gypsy (musical), 266

Hadfield, J. A., 33–34
Hair (musical), 38, 39
Hamlet (Shakespeare), 68, 69, 96, 108–111, 127, 154, 161, 163, 167, 169–171, 191, 254
Hansberry, Lorraine, 180
Happenings, 137, 143, 324
Happy Days (Beckett), 80–81
Harris, Julie, 62, 63
Hart, Lorenz, 189
Harvey (Chase), 28
Hauptmann, Gerhart, 180
Haymarket Theatre, London, 209
Hedda Gabler (Ibsen), 95–96, 108, 128, 172
Heightened realism, 158
Hellman, Lillian, 89, 154, 177–179, 302
Hemingway, Ernest, 3–4
Henry IV, Part 1 (Shakespeare), 176, 191
Henry IV, Part 2 (Shakespeare), 176
Henry V (Shakespeare), 176
Heroic drama, 163, 175–176, 324
Hilberry Theatre Repertory Company, 190
History play, defined, 324
Hodges, C. Walter, 220
Homecoming, The (Pinter), 73–74, 134
Hotel de Bourgogne Theater, Paris, 208
House, defined, 208
House of Bernarda Alba, The (Lorca), 236
Humor (*see* Comedy)
Hunt, Peter, 291
Hunter College, New York, 21

I Do, I Do (musical), 270
Ibsen, Henrik, 70, 90–91, 95–96, 108, 111, 112, 115, 116, 120, 122, 124, 128, 154, 155, 157, 172, 174, 244, 263
Iceman Cometh, The (O'Neill), 172
Illusion, creation of, 26–29, 63, 65, 246–247
Imaginary Invalid, The (Molière), 93
Imagination, 25–37
   creation of illusion, 26–29, 63, 65, 246–247

Imagination:
  metaphor, function of, 30
  realistic acting and, 75
  "reality" of, 31–32
  separation of stage reality from fact, 32–34
  symbols, function of, 29–30
  theater as metaphor, 34, 36
Imitation in everyday life, 56
Importance of Being Earnest, The (Wilde), 327
Impressionism, 324
Impromptu of Versailles, The (Molière), 68–69, 280
In the Matter of J. Robert Oppenheimer (Kipphardt), 32, 33
Incentive, plot and, 115–116
Inner truth in acting, 75
Insect Comedy, The (Capek and Capek), 94, 97, 98
Intellectual conflict, plot and, 131–132
Investigation, The (Weiss), 328
Ionesco, Eugene, 28, 79, 94, 133, 134, 154, 184, 195, 236, 253, 322, 328
Irving, Henry, 281

Jacobean theater, 177
Jacobs, Sally, 239
Japanese theater:
  basic stage of, 221, 222
  heroic drama forms, 175
  historical outline, 350–354
  Kabuki, 221, 222, 271, 324, 350, 351
  Noh, 216, 221, 326, 350
  physical movement, 81–82
Jesus Christ, Superstar (musical), 211
Johnson, Samuel, 162
Jones, James Earl, 170
Jones, LeRoi (Imamu Amiri Baraka), 5
Jones, Robert Edmond, 1–2, 233–235, 326
Jones Beach musical theater, 18
Jonson, Ben, 93, 322
Julius Caesar (Shakespeare), 170, 261
Juno and the Paycock (O'Casey), 187, 194, 195
Juxtaposition:
  of ιracters, 95–96
  of chorus or narrator to main action, 130
  in episodic drama, 126–127

Kabuki theater, 221, 222, 271, 324, 350, 351
Kalem, T. E., 99
Kaplan, Herb, 291
Kazan, Elia, 285
Kemble, Charles, 281
Kernan, Alvin B., 106
Kerr, Walter, 14–15, 79–80

Kesselring, Joseph, 185
Kierkegaard, Soren, 193
King Lear (Shakespeare), 34, 35, 45, 46, 126–127, 161, 162, 169–171, 249, 297, 300–302
King Oedipus (Sophocles), 108, 120, 121, 309
Kirby, Michael, 95, 137
Kopit, Arthur, 160
Kordian (Polish Laboratory Theater), 224–225
Kyoto, Japan, arena theater at, 215, 216

Langer, Suzanne, 1
Language, 168
  of modern tragedy, 173
  realistic and nonrealistic contrasted, 155
  of traditional tragedy, 171
Lark, The (Anouilh), 62
Le Bon, Gustav, 16–17
Lee, Eugene, 203
Lemmon, Jack, 195
Lessing, Gotthold Ephraim, 128, 180
Lesson, The (Ionesco), 134, 195
Lies Like Truth (Clurman), 31
Life Is a Dream (Calderón de la Barca), 175
Lighting, 1, 231, 232, 249–256
  aesthetic function of, 250–251
  comedy and, 256, 300
  controls, 254–255
  dramatic structure and, 255–256
  functions of, 252
  point of view and, 256
  realistic and nonrealistic contrasted, 155
  technical rehearsal for, 289
  types of lights, 252–254
Lighting technicians, 289
Lilliom (Molnár), 27
Lillo, George, 180
Lindfors, Viveca, 90
Line in costume design, 268, 269
Little Foxes, The (Hellman), 89, 90, 154, 178, 179, 302
Liturgical drama, 324
Living Newspaper Drama, 328
Living Theater, 19, 43
Loden, Barbara, 285
Logic, comedic treatment of, 185
London Merchant, The (Lillo), 180
Long Day's Journey into Night (O'Neill), 97, 115, 154, 174–175, 309
Long Wharf Theater, New Haven, 220
Look Back in Anger (Osborne), 92
Lorca, Federico García, 174, 236
Lower Depths, The (Gorki), 180
Lyric theater, defined, 325
Lysistrata (Aristophanes), 186

Macbeth (Shakespeare), 26, 72, 127, 162, 169–171, 191, 263
Macbird (Garson), 191, 327
MacGowan, Kenneth, 113
Macready, William Charles, 281
Madwoman of Chaillot, The (Giraudoux), 186
Maeterlinck, Maurice, 327
Majestic Theater, New York, 47
Major characters, 96, 262
Makeup, 270–274
  masks, 1, 62, 155–157, 264, 265, 272–274
  realistic and nonrealistic contrasted, 155
Malcontent, The (Marston), 177
Malden, Karl, 178
Man For All Seasons, A (Bolt), 202, 203
Manager, 291–292
Marat/Sade (Weiss), 125
Marceau, Marcel, 153
March, Fredric, 174
Mark Taper Forum, Los Angeles, 220
Marlowe, Christopher, 42, 77, 89, 128
Marston, John, 177
Masks, 1, 62, 155–157, 264, 265, 272–274
Masque, 324
Matthau, Walter, 195
Meaning of play, 302–308
Measure for Measure (Shakespeare), 191–192
Medea (Euripides), 171, 173
Medieval theater, 308, 325
  comic scenes, 191–192
  cycle plays, 112, 141–142, 215, 324–325
  historical outline, 333–334
  miracle plays, 228, 308, 325
  morality plays, 28, 158–159, 308, 325
  stage spaces, 228
Melodrama, 164, 176–179, 309, 325
Menaechmi, The (Plautus), 188
Merchant of Venice, The (Shakespeare), 114, 250
Metaphor:
  directors and, 284
  function of, 30
  "reality" of, 31
  theater as, 34, 36
Michelangelo, 2, 3, 161
Microphones, 78
Middle Ages (*see* Medieval theater)
Midsummer Night's Dream, A (Shakespeare), 148, 149, 239
Mielziner, Jo, 241–242
Miller, Arthur, 58–60, 89–90, 92, 106, 115, 124, 129, 159, 172, 174, 285, 321
Milner, Ron, 46
Mime, 325
Ming Cho Lee, 239–241, 244, 249
Minor characters, 96, 262
Miracle plays, 228, 308, 325

Misanthrope, The (Molière), 93
Miser, The (Molière), 93
Miss Julie (Strindberg), 61, 89, 109, 113, 114
Miss Sara Sampson (Lessing), 180
Modern theater:
  extraordinary characters, 89–90
  familial relationships in plots, 115
  physical movement, 78–81
  prototypical characters, 90–92
  ritual, 139
  tragedy, 172–175
  tragicomedy, 193–196
  variety of experiences, 47–50
  (*See also* New Theater)
Molière, 68–69, 93, 124, 163, 183, 184, 187–188, 191, 197, 280, 285, 322, 327
Monson, Lex, 64
Moon for the Misbegotten, A (O'Neill), 55
Morality plays, 28, 158–159, 308, 325
Mostel, Zero, 79–80
Motel (van Itallie), 273
Mother Courage (Brecht), 73, 89, 90, 112
Motivation, plot and, 115–116
Mourning Becomes Electra (O'Neill), 115, 268, 270
Movement on stage, 78–82
Much Ado about Nothing (Shakespeare), 240
Multifocus theater, 226–227, 243, 308
Multimedia presentations, 227
Murder in the Cathedral (Eliot), 88
Music, transitory nature of, 2
Musical theater, 81, 82, 141, 246, 325
My Fair Lady (musical), 210–211, 262
Mystery plays (*see* Cycle plays)
Myth of Sisyphus, The (Camus), 132

Narrator, juxtaposition to main action, 130
Natural laws, suspension of, 185–186
Naturalism, 70, 157–158, 326
  (*See also* Realistic theater)
Neighborhood theater, 225
New stagecraft, 326
New Theater, 42, 49, 205–206, 322, 326
  acting requirements, 82–83
  nonhuman parts, 95
  nonsequitur, 136–138
  ritual, 139
  stage space (*see* Created or found space)
New York Shakespeare Festival, 10, 11, 18, 64, 221, 240, 244
Newman, Paul, 178
Nietzsche, Friedrich, 173
No Exit (Sartre), 111, 122
Noh theater, 216, 221, 326, 350
Nonhuman parts, 93–95
Nonrealistic theater, 151–154, 156

Nonrealistic theater:
advantages of, 158
contrasted with realistic, 154–155
forms of, 158–159
scenery, 238–240
Nonsense and nonsequitur, 132–138
in New Theater, 136–138
in Theater of the Absurd, 132–136
Nontheater buildings, use of, 224
Nova Jerusalem, 225, 226

Observed theater, distinguished from participatory theater, 19–22
Obstacles, plot, 109–110
O'Casey, Sean, 187, 194, 195
Odd Couple, The (Simon), 309
Odets, Clifford, 71
Off-Broadway theater, 49
Off-off-Broadway theater, 49
Offstage, 246
Oh, Dad, Poor Dad, Mama's Hung You in the Closet, and I'm Feelin' So Sad (Kopit), 160
Old Comedy, 322
One-act plays, 141–142
O'Neill, Eugene, 55, 89, 97, 115, 124, 154, 174–175, 268, 273, 323
Open Theater, 139
Opening scene, importance of, 108–109
Opera, 99–100
Opposing forces, plot and, 113–114
Orchestra, 208, 217
Orchestration of characters, 96–97
Orghast, 225
Oriental theater, 175
arena stages, 215, 216
basic stage of, 221, 222
historical outline, 348–351
makeup, 271
physical movement, 81–82
(See also Chinese theater; Japanese theater)
Osborne, John, 92
Othello (Shakespeare), 33, 95, 168–171, 235, 303
Our Town (Wilder), 27, 75–76, 97, 112, 130, 131, 154
Outdoor theater, 225, 227–228

Pace of play, 287–288
Painting, distinguished from scene design, 234–236
Pantomime, 81, 82, 153, 326
Parallel plot, 126
Park, Robert Ezra, 58
Park Theater, New York, 209
Parthenon, 41

Participatory theater, 19–22
Patterns as dramatic structure, 140
Peer Gynt (Ibsen), 116, 124, 128, 244, 263
Performance Group, The, 139, 205–206, 222, 223
Performers (see Acting; Actors)
Pericles, 40
Pericles (Shakespeare), 64
Phaedra (Racine), 123
Philadelphia, Here I Come (Fried), 28
Physical movement on stage, 78–82
Picasso, Pablo, 235
Pinter, Harold, 73–74, 134, 195
Pippin (musical), 258, 259, 264–265, 267, 311
Pirandello, Luigi, 100, 132, 322
Platform stage, 219
Platforms, 246
Plautus, 124, 188
Play of ideas, 131, 326
Playwright:
background information on, 45–46
develops meaning, 303
devises plot, 107–108, 116
director and, 282, 296
point of view of, 163, 280
tragicomedy and, 193
(See also Comedy; Dramatic structure; Serious drama)
Plot:
aspects of, 106–110
distinguished from story, 107–108
obstacles and complications, 109–110
opening scene, importance of, 108–109
climactic, 119–124, 128–129
combination of forms, 129
comparison of forms, 128–129
development of, 116–117
dramatic conventions, 110–116
equal contest, 114–115
prize or goal, 115–116
space limit, 111–112
strongly opposing forces, 113–114
time limit, 112
dramatic devices used with, 130–132
episodic, 119, 124–129
realistic and nonrealistic contrasted, 154
Plot complications (comedic), 188–190
Point of view, 149–199
of artists, 160, 163, 168
categories, problems of, 163–164
genre, significance of, 196–197
scene design and, 197, 233–234, 256
of society, 160–162
(See also Comedy; Nonrealistic theater; Realistic theater; Serious drama)
Polish Laboratory Theater, 11–12
Polsky, Milton, 21

Poor Theater, 326
Preconceptions, audience, 47–48
Presentation of Self in Everyday Life, The (Goffman), 56
Presentational theater (*see* Nonrealistic theater)
Previews, 289–290
Primal scream, 83
Probability, comedic treatment of, 185
Producer, 291–292
Projection, voice, 77–78
Prometheus Bound (Aeschylus), 172
Props, 289
Proscenium stage, 206–212
  advantages of, 210–212
  Broadway theaters, 204–208, 210–211
  disadvantages of, 212
  European theaters, 208–210
  light sources, 253
  scene design and, 209–211
  structure of, 207–208
Protagonist, 95
Protagoras, 161
Prototypical characters, 90–92
Psacharopoulos, Nikos, 278, 279
Psychodrama, 20, 21
Psychological gesture, 74
Publicity, 292

Quem Quaeritis, 13
Quick changes, 266

Race and Culture (Park), 58
Racine, Jean Baptiste, 111, 121–124, 163, 172
Radical theater, 42
Raisin (musical), 216
Raisin in the Sun, A (Hansberry), 180
Raked stage, 208, 245
Ramps, 246
Realistic theater, 151–154, 326–327
  acting, 70–76, 154, 157
    emotional recall, 75–76
    inner truth, 75
    specifics, 72–75
    Stanislavski and, 70–76
  advantages of, 157
  contrasted with nonrealistic, 154–155
  costumes, 155
  forms of, 157–158
  lighting, 251
  scene design, 155, 211, 236–238
Reality, distinguished from fantasy, 32–34
Rehearsals, 286–289
Renaissance theater, 160–162, 324, 334–338
Representational theater (*see* Realistic theater)

Restoration drama, 187, 263, 280–281, 283, 322, 327
Revenger's Tragedy, The (Tourneur), 177
Revues, 141
Rhinoceros (Ionesco), 28, 79, 94, 98, 154
Rhythm:
  lighting design and, 251
  in production, 251, 287–288
Rice, Elmer, 26, 159, 323
Richard II (Shakespeare), 176
Ring Round The Moon (Anouilh), 211
Ritual as dramatic structure, 138–139
Ritualistic theater, 43
Rivals, The (Sheridan), 187
River Niger, The (Walker), 115, 155
Robards, Jason, 54, 55, 174, 285
Rodgers, Richard, 189
Role playing:
  in everyday life, 57–60
  on stage (*see* Acting)
Roman New Comedy, 322
Roman theater, 218, 322–323
Romanticism, 176, 327
Romeo and Juliet (Shakespeare), 61, 108, 127, 155, 219, 250, 262–263
Ronde, La (Schnitzler), 143
Rostand, Edmond, 94, 116, 129, 176
Rowe, William, 190
Royal Hunt of the Sun, The (P. Shaffer), 231, 241
Royal Shakespeare Company, 273
Royal Theater, Turin, 208
Run-through, 289
R.U.R. (Capek), 94

St. Joan (Shaw), 176, 262
Salle des Machines, 209
San Quentin prison, 18–19
Sardou, Victorien, 124
Sartre, Jean-Paul, 111, 122, 323
Satire, 191, 236, 327
Scene design, 231–248
  aesthetics of, 233–243
    central image or metaphor in, 241–242
    distinguished from painting, 234–236
    nonrealistic, 155, 238–240
    realistic, 155, 211, 236–238
    total theater environment, 242–243
  dramatic structure and, 255–256
  in everyday life, 232–233
  lighting and, 252
  objectives of, 248–249
  point of view and, 197, 233–234, 256
  practical aspects of, 243–248
    materials, 245–248
    physical layout requirements, 243–245

Scene design:
  practical aspects of:
    proscenium stages, 209–211
    technical rehearsals and, 289
Schechner, Richard, 322
Schiller, Johann Christoph Friedrich von, 128
Schnitzler, Arthur, 143
School for Scandal, The (Sheridan), 188, 189
School for Wives ((Molière), 182, 183
Screen projection, 247, 248
Screens, The (Genet), 62
Scribe, Augustin Eugène, 124
Scrims, 247–248
Script:
  background information, 45
  blueprint for production, 4
  director works on, 282, 283
  meaning in, 302–308
  point of view in, 151, 280
  scene design consistent with, 233
  (*See also* Dramatic structure; Playwright)
Second City, 50
Secondary characters, 95–96
Series of acts or episodes, 140–142
Serious drama, 159–164
  bourgeois or domestic drama, 179–180
  heroic drama, 163, 175–176
  lighting and, 256
  melodrama, 164, 176–179, 309, 325
  scene design and, 236, 256
  tragedy, 159–164, 167–175, 328
    costumes, 263
    Greek theater, 40–41, 112, 116–117, 160–161, 169–172
    modern, 172–175
    society's point of view and, 160–162
    traditional, 169–172
  tragicomedy, 191–196, 322, 328–329
Serpent, The (van Itallie), 139, 140
Set design (*see* Scene design)
Shaffer, Peter, 304–306
Shakespeare, William, 4, 26, 42, 45–46, 68, 72, 78, 87, 109, 114, 124, 126, 128, 149, 153, 155, 161–163, 167, 169–170, 172, 178, 188–189, 191, 192, 219, 235, 239, 249, 250, 254, 261, 282–283, 285, 303, 324
Shakespeare Theater, Stratford, Ontario, 220
Shank, Theodore, 63
Shaw, George Bernard, 176, 184, 186, 187, 191, 262, 322, 327
She Stoops to Conquer (Goldsmith), 187
Sheep Well, The (Vega), 124, 180
Sheridan, Richard Brinsley, 187–189
Short plays, 141–142
Shot in the Dark, A (Achard), 62, 63
Simonson, Lee, 239, 240, 326
Six Characters in Search of an Author
  (Pirandello), 100, 132

Skene, 217–218
Sketches, costume, 265–268
Skinner, B. F., 17
Slapstick comedy, 185
Sleuth (A. Shaffer), 13
Slice-of-life drama, 158
Society:
  link between theater and, 40–45, 308
  point of view of, 160–162, 184–185
Sociodrama, 20
Sophocles, 46–47, 95, 97, 116, 120, 121, 124, 155, 161, 172, 175, 239, 241
Sound amplification, 78
Sound of Music (musical), 13
Spanish theater, 48, 78, 209, 219, 334–337
Spatial relationships, 286–287
Specifics, importance in acting, 72–75
Spectacle, proscenium stage and, 210–211
Spectators (*see* Audience)
Spill, 252
Spine of characters, 76
Spotlights, 252
Stage floor, 245–246
Stage fright, 71
Stage left, 245, 246
Stage right, 245, 246
Stage spaces, 203–209
  arena stage, 212–216, 308
    disadvantages of, 215–216
    economics of, 213–214
    history of, 214–215
    intimacy of, 213
    light sources, 253
    structure of, 212–213
  created or found space, 221–228
    adaptation of space to fit production, 224–225
    Artaud and, 222–224
    historical precedents, 227–228
    multifocus environments, 226–227, 243, 308
    nontheater buildings, 224
    outdoor settings, 225, 227–228
    scene designer and, 242–243
    street theater, 49, 225–226, 228, 327
  creating environments, 204–206
  proscenium stage, 206–212
    advantages of, 210–212
    Broadway theaters, 204–208, 210–211
    disadvantages of, 212
    European theaters, 208–210
    light sources, 253
    scene design and, 209–211
    structure of, 207–208
  scene design and, 209–211, 243–245
  thrust stage, 216–221, 308
    advantages of, 221

Stage spaces:
  thrust stage: history of, 217–221
    structure of, 216–217
  variety in environments, 228
Stagehands, 289, 296
Stanislavski, Constantin, 70–76, 151, 173, 193
Stein, Gertrude, 303
Stereotypes, 92–93
Stock characters, 92–94
Storey, David, 139
Story, plot distinguished from, 107–108
Street Sounds (Bullins), 33
Street theater, 49, 225–226, 228, 327
Streetcar Named Desire, A (Williams), 13, 87, 104, 105, 109, 113–114, 136, 154, 172
Strindberg, August, 61, 70, 89, 108–109, 111, 113, 115, 124, 154, 157, 174, 176, 254, 324
Strip lights, 252
Stroll in the Air, A (Ionesco), 28
Structure of play (*see* Dramatic structure)
Studio Arena Theatre, Buffalo, 294, 295
Style:
  costumes and, 263–266, 274
  lighting and, 251
  scene design and, 236–240, 248
  (*See also* Acting, techniques and styles of)
Subject matter (*see* Point of view)
Subplot, 126
Subtext, 173
Sullivan Street Theater, New York, 228
Surrealism, 327
Suzman, Janet, 86, 87
Sword fights, 78
Symbolism, 34, 327–328
  in costume design, 260–261, 263
  function of, 29–30
  in *King Lear*, 301
  in lighting, 232, 251
  "reality" of, 31
  in scene design, 232–239

Tandy, Jessica, 104, 105
Tartuffe (Molière), 184, 191, 197, 327
Tate, Nahum, 162
Taylor, Robert U., 231, 242
Tear-away seams, 266
Teatro alla Scala, Milan, 209
Teatro Espagnol, Madrid, 209
Technical rehearsal, 289
Technique (*see* Acting, techniques and styles of)
Television, distinguished from theater, 14–16, 55
Tempest, The (Shakespeare), 155
Tension, plot and, 106–110, 113–115
  (*See also* Serious drama)

Terence, 124
That Championship Season (J. Miller), 78–79, 152
Thayer, David L., 237
Theater:
  basic confrontation in, 100–101
  basic elements, defined, 5–7
  distinguished from other performing arts, 13–16, 99
  future of, 310
  as group experience, 1–2, 15–19
  human concerns as subject matter of, 97–100
  integration of elements, 272–273, 298–302
  link between society and, 40–45, 308
  meaning in, 302–308
  as metaphor, 34, 36
  risks in, 296–297
  transitory nature of, 3–4
  variety of experiences in, 47–50, 308–310
Theater of the Absurd, 19, 132–136, 308, 328
  comedies, 184–185
  dramatic structure, 133–134
  existential characters, 135–136
  scene design, 236
  tragicomedy, 194–195
  verbal nonsense, 134–135
Theater of Cruelty, 328
Theater of Fact, 328
Theater games, 20
Theater of Protest, 44
Theater-in-the-round (*see* Arena stage)
Theatricalism, defined, 328
Theme:
  in *Equus*, 304–305
  in *King Lear*, 301–302
  in *The Little Foxes*, 303
  (*See also* Comedy; Heroic drama; Meaning of play; Point of view; Tragedy; Tragicomedy)
Thespis, 12
Three Sisters, The (Chekhov), 98, 114, 116
Threepenny Opera (Brecht), 291
Through line of roles, 76
Thrust stage, 216–221, 308
  advantages of, 221
  history of, 217–221
  structure of, 216–217
Time limit of plays, 112
Torelli, Giacomo, 209
Tourneur, Cyril, 177
Towards a Poor Theatre (Grotowski), 12, 325
Traditional theater:
  extraordinary characters, 88–89
  physical movement, 78
  ritual, 139
  tragedy, 169–172
  vocal demands, 77, 78

Tragedy, 159–164, 167–175, 328–329
  costumes, 263
  Greek theater, 40–41, 112, 116–117, 160–161,
    169–172
  modern, 172–175
  society's point of view and, 160–162
  traditional, 169–172
Tragicomedy, 191–196, 322, 329
Trapdoors, 245
Trestle stage, 219
Trial of the Catonsville Nine, The (Berrigan),
  32
Trilogy, defined, 112
Trinity Square Repertory Company, Provi-
  dence, 203
Troilus and Cressida (Shakespeare), 192, 282–
  283
Trojan Women, The (Euripides), 166, 167
Tropes, 13
Tryouts, 289–290
Turntable, 245
Tyrone Guthrie Theater, Minneapolis, 220, 228

Uncle Vanya (Chekhov), 76, 96–97, 193–194
Unto These Hills, 18
Upstage, 245, 246

van Itallie, Jean-Claude, 14, 155, 273
Vega, Lope de, 124, 128, 180, 219
Venus and Adonis (Shakespeare), 4
Verbal humor, 187
Verbal nonsense, 134–135
Virginia Museum Theater, Richmond, 242
Visit, The (Dürrenmatt), 196, 329

Vocal projection, 77–78

Wagon stage, 219
Wagons, 211, 245–246
Waiting for Godot (Beckett), 18–19, 97, 106–107,
    132–133, 135, 136, 140, 194–195, 329
Walker, Joseph, 115, 155
Walpole, Horace, 159–160
Ward, Douglas Turner, 271–272
Warm lighting, 254
Way of the World, The (Congreve), 93, 183
Weavers, The (Hauptmann), 180
Webster, John, 177
Well-made play, 329
West Side Story (musical), 13, 113, 153, 155,
    263
What the Wine Sellers Buy (Milner), 46
Where's Charley? (musical), 28
White, Ruth, 81
White Devil, The (Webster), 177
Who's Afraid of Virginia Wolf? (Albee), 91
Wilde, Oscar, 187, 191, 327
Wilder, Thornton, 27, 75–76, 97, 112, 130, 131,
    154
Williams, Tennessee, 67, 72–73, 87, 99, 105,
    113–115, 121, 124, 154, 155, 159, 172, 174
Williamstown Theater Festival, 211, 279, 291
Wings, 209
Wit, verbal, 187, 191
Would-be Gentlemen, The (Molière), 93, 187–
  188
Wycherly, William, 187, 191, 281

Zipprodt, Patricia, 1, 259, 264–265, 267